ORIENTAL ENDEAVOUR

ORIENTAL ENDEAVOUR

David Creamer

Whittles Publishing

Published by
Whittles Publishing Ltd.,
Dunbeath,
Caithness, KW6 6EG,
Scotland, UK

www.whittlespublishing.com

ISBN 978-184995-034-3

Printed by www.printondemand-worldwide.com

CONTENTS

TO ALL THOSE SAILING THE HIGH SEAS,
EXCLUDING PIRATES

ABOUT THE AUTHOR

Born in Beckenham, Kent, in 1947, David Creamer joined HMS *Worcester* as a cadet in 1961 and began his seagoing career with the Bibby Line of Liverpool in 1964. Specialising in the gas tanker trade, he spent twenty-two years at sea working his way up though the ranks before leaving the sea after nine years as Master in 1986 to manage his own tool hire business ashore. The call of the sea proved too strong and in 1996 he appointed a manager to run his business and returned to the Merchant Navy. Since 1999 he has worked for a Dutch shipping company, now called Redwise, delivering vessels of all shapes and sizes around the world. His spare time is spent between Spain, where he has a second home, keeping a watchful eye on his successful business in North Wales, and writing about his experiences at sea. This story is a sequel to his first book, *Rats, Rust & Two Old Ladies*, also published by Whittles Publishing, which recounts a voyage he made sailing two Mississippi-style tugboats from Bahrain to Trinidad. Writing is obviously in the family: he is now editing his great-uncle's autobiography about life at sea in the 1920s, which he hopes will be published some time in the not too distant future.

AUTHOR'S NOTE

In 2003, when the voyage about which this book is written occurred, piracy and the hijacking of merchant ships was prevalent off many of the Indonesian islands, but was relatively unknown in the Gulf of Aden and the Indian Ocean. This is no longer the case. Somali pirates have become experts in boarding unarmed commercial vessels, forcing their crews to sail to the Somali coast and then holding them captive until a ransom, often amounting to millions of dollars, is negotiated for their release.

The navies from many seafaring nations have been deployed in the area to protect the international merchant fleets. In the eyes of many mariners, they have been spectacularly unsuccessful. While international law has, in many instances, prevented the armed forces from reacting in the robust manner they might desire, merchant seamen find it particularly galling and disheartening to learn that many of the photographs exhibited in the world's press showing pirates in the act of boarding merchant vessels have been taken from warships in the close vicinity. We occasionally read of Somalis being disarmed and their boats being sunk, only to learn in subsequent reports that they have been taken back to Somalia and released ashore. It would be far too cynical of me to suggest that they might just re-arm themselves, jump into a replacement boat funded from foreign aid, and hope to be more successful in their next attempt at some good old-fashioned buccaneering.

In February 2010 a private security firm, employed by a shipping company to protect one of its cargo vessels, was heavily criticised for engaging Somali pirates in an exchange of gunfire that resulted in the death of one of the attackers; it was suggested that the lives of seamen being held to ransom would be put at risk. The critics failed to recognise that piracy exists purely for financial gain; the killing of hostages would be counterproductive in achieving their extortionate demands.

The picture in the book, 'Dad's Army Recalled', is jocular and lighthearted, and taken in 2003, but it highlights the helplessness and frustration that seafarers feel today when sailing in piracy waters. My ultimate wish is to welcome a politician into my crew so that he or she might see the situation at first hand; it is only then that seafarers will receive the protection they need and the pirates the response they so richly deserve.

During the course of 2010, 4185 seafarers were attacked with firearms and rocket-propelled grenades, 1090 seafarers were taken hostage, 516 seafarers were used as human shields and as many as 488 seafarers were subject to abuse or torture by pirates.

In February 2011, 33 ships and 712 seamen were being held hostage by Somali pirates. My thoughts are with those seafarers – may you arrive home safely to your loved ones soon.

On August 19th 2011, the UK media reported that the joint European naval operation in the Indian Ocean is advertising for a 'pirate cultural adviser' to cope with very special needs of up to 400 prisoners captured in action. Commander Harry Harrison of EU Navfor said: 'The intention is to seek advice on the pirates' methodology and modus operandi'.

ACKNOWLEDGEMENTS

As with my first book, *Rats, Rust & Two Old Ladies,* I have to begin by thanking three tugboat crews; my British and Thai colleagues who sailed the *Eden* on her delivery voyage in 1999 from Avonmouth in the UK to Buchanan in Liberia, and the two Dutch and Myanmar crews aboard the *Oriental* tugs during our seemingly never-ending delivery voyage in 2003 from Abidjan in Côte d'Ivoire to Singapore. I also have to thank my Dutch managerial colleagues and superintendents, the ship's agents and chandlers, and everyone else who participated in the venture. Without all concerned, there would have been no story to tell and no book to write.

The team at Whittles Publishing in Dunbeath, Scotland deserve my heartfelt thanks and gratitude for having the confidence to take on my second book, knowing the endless hassle they had with publishing my first.

I have to thank my brother, Geoff, for editing and punctuating my work, and my wife, Hilary, who had to undergo many hours of living in solitude during my periods at home between voyages, when I would selfishly escape to my computer to further my unrealistic dream of literary recognition.

My thanks to Remy Weggemans & Pieter Van Noord for allowing me to use some of their images.

Last, but not least, thank you, dear reader, for helping to keep my impossible dream alive!

Ship's Particulars

Edengarth, renamed *Eden*, renamed *Oriental Tug No. 2*,
   current trading name unknown

Classed: Lloyds 100 A1

Builder: Richards, Lowestoft in 1976

Gross tonnage: 367 tons

Net tonnage: 110 tons

Length overall: 37.23 metres

Breadth: 10.31 metres

Draught (aft): 4.9 metres

Main engine: Ruston 16RK3CM

BHP: 3520 at 900 rpm

Propeller: Lips Controllable Pitch

Rudder: Steerable Kort Nozzle

Free speed: 14 knots

Bollard pull: 50 tons continuous, 54 tons maximum

Towing winch: Donkin twin drum

Auxiliaries: 3 × Gardner 6LXB marine generators

Fuel oil capacity: 94 tons

FW capacity: 21.8 tons

Dispersant capacity: 32.2 tons (oil pollution dispersant)

Foam capacity: 39.4 tons (firefighting)

Accommodation: 10 persons

1

IN THE BEGINNING

A taste of Eden

Tuesday, 31 August 1999 was an unusually hot and airless summer's day with just a trace of cloud in the sky, a day for lazing on the beach rather than one for travelling by rail to the south-west of the country to join a tugboat.

The Miles Arms Hotel was homely without being luxurious. My room on the first floor was clean and tidy with wallpaper a little tired and a pocket-sized en suite shower that had been added into one corner of the room many years after the hotel had been built. The dining room and adjacent lounge bar were comfortably furnished for the wining and dining of their travel-weary guests. Colin proved to be a congenial and generous host. From what I can recall, the never-ending supply of Hardy's Australian Shiraz Cabernet Sauvignon that accompanied our informal dinner was entirely effective in erasing the discomforts of our respective train and car journeys, as was that famous utterance from the battle of Trafalgar, 'Kiss me, Hardy', in sending my tired but overactive brain into the depths of a restless sleep.

Casting the effects of our self-inflicted excesses to one side, we enjoyed an impossibly large cooked breakfast in the hotel before driving the short distance down to the docks to board the tugboat *Edengarth*, which was in the process of being sold. We had been contracted by the new owners to carry out the delivery voyage from Avonmouth to Buchanan in Liberia, a country torn apart by a bitter civil war that had ended in 1996, but appeared to be flaring up yet again.

The *Edengarth*, owned by Cory Towage Ltd, was one of a class of tugs built by Richards of Lowestoft in the 1970s. A traditional-looking tugboat with a three-deck-high tapering superstructure, she had a mast with a fire-monitor platform, a raised deck with a large towing winch sandwiched between twin funnels, and a long, raking, rounded stern. Powered by a single Ruston engine of 3,520 horsepower, she was capable of making fourteen knots in a strong following wind.

The first members of the crew to arrive later in the morning were Lockluang Sophon and Chaikoon Thamrong from Thailand. A captain and chief engineer, they had been employed by the new Singaporean owner to familiarise themselves with the boat on the voyage to Buchanan, and they would then become responsible for her operation in Liberia once our delivery contract had been completed. Realising that I would never be able to remember their given names had I heard them repeated a hundred times, I decided, rather unkindly, to nickname them 'Dickie Thai' and 'Bow Thai'. They accepted their new identities with beaming and friendly smiles and the traditional Far Eastern bows of their heads. Their total lack of conversational English prevented them from voicing their eternal gratitude, or perhaps even understanding that a change in their names had just occurred.

Shortly after midday, Steve, John, another Colin, and Peter had completed the seagoing complement. Having one crew member too many for the number of cabins available, we were left with little choice but to offer our riding guests, Dickie and Bow, the opportunity for experiencing that friendly years-old naval practice of 'hot-bedding' it together in the chief engineer's cabin. They voiced no complaints about sleeping in the same bunk, although I made sure that their seagoing work rotas would keep their off-duty sleeping hours apart to avoid any embarrassing or awkward complications.

Storing the boat with all the essential items for our fifteen-day voyage to Liberia took most of the afternoon and several trips in Colin's estate car. By early evening hunger, physical tiredness and the need for liquid refreshment dictated that we should retire to the Miles Arms Hotel, where much to the surprised delight of Dickie and Bow, the hotel chef managed to rustle up an eastern speciality that looked suspiciously like a pre-packed Thai curry and rice straight from a supermarket freezer. It bore little resemblance to the tasty and spicy food that can be purchased from a Bangkok street stall, but they both appeared to enjoy their meal and the pints of beer that inevitably followed. When the bar finally closed we went back to the docks for our first night of sleeping aboard, leaving Colin, our manager, the pleasure of staying a second night in the hotel and footing the costly bill for our evening of introduction and crew bonding. With their seagoing work-rota not yet in force, we left the unfortunate Dickie and Bow to sort out their own 'hot-bed' arrangements.

The sale of the tugboat from Cory Towage to the new owners became drawn out and complicated thanks to the loss of the electronic money transaction somewhere between Singapore, New York and London. It took Captain Mok, the owner's marine superintendent, who was visiting Avonmouth to ensure the transfer of both boat and funds went smoothly, nearly two days to resolve the issue before the exchange could finally be made. With a flourish of paint brushes and black paint, the *Edengarth* was renamed the *Eden* and re-registered under the St Vincent and Grenadines flag.

The two Lloyd's surveyors employed by the new owner boarded shortly afterwards to carry out the statutory surveys of the tugboat's safety equipment, load-line and radio equipment. While the safety and loadline surveyor found only some minor defects, the same couldn't be said for the radio surveyor from South Wales, who was an overly conscientious and thorough person. Finding an aerial fault on the main radio receiver, he insisted upon climbing the vertical ladder onto the monkey island above the wheelhouse to see the problem for himself. I waited with bated breath, knowing full well I wouldn't have to wait too long before the excrement hit the fan.

The loud and extremely foul profanity was not the language to be expected from a Welsh surveyor who had, in all probability, been raised within the strict traditions of a Nonconformist chapel upbringing. To say that he disapproved of my mounting arrangements for the antenna of our portable satellite communications unit would have been putting it mildly. In order to confirm the equipment was working correctly, I had, only temporarily, secured the small multi-directional dome aerial to a wooden broomstick which, in turn, had been taped to the vertical handle of a manually operated fire monitor. It took Colin and me some considerable effort and endless degrees of patience, not to mention blatant lying, to explain the situation, but at least it had conveniently distracted him from the main radio aerials, which had been the reason for his climbing onto the monkey island in the first place.

He reluctantly issued the *Eden* with her safety radio certificate, knowing full well he would probably never set eyes on the boat again. The multi-directional dome antenna, minus the broomstick, had to be hurriedly repositioned away from the fire monitor before the vital documents were signed. He left a few minutes later, still scratching his head in puzzlement as to why he had accepted our tongue-in-cheek assurances that the voyage from Avonmouth to Buchanan in Liberia would be made as a 'coastal' passage. Shortly after lunch, I was the proud caretaker of a new and complete set of trading certificates that permitted the *Eden* to sail on an international voyage to foreign lands. The name change had been successfully completed.

During the afternoon, we manhandled over 4,000 litres of lubricating oil in drums onto the aft deck. As we had no crane or lifting device, every 200-litre drum had to be carefully lowered on a rope from the quayside onto the deck before it could be rolled into position, stood up and then lashed to the towing frame. Captain Mok had informed us that lubricating oil would be a rare, if not totally unavailable, product in war-torn Liberia. The drums would ensure the boat had an adequate supply until replacement stocks could be obtained.

After four days of preparation we were ready to sail. Colin, our manager, took the short ride with us to the lock that separates the Avonmouth docks from the River Severn. As we let go the ropes, he said his farewells, solemnly shook our hands and jumped ashore. It was only after acknowledging his final parting wave that I belatedly remembered he had never satisfactorily explained how he was proposing to get us home safely from Liberia. He had managed to sound almost convincing in his evasive assurances that something would be sorted out once we had got there.

We were destined for a country that had only recently been devastated by seven years of civil war, a war that had seen Samuel Doe, the ex-President, appearing on videotape to be gruesomely tortured and summarily executed. The victor, Charles Taylor, leader of the National Patriotic Front of Liberia and one of the three principal warlords from the civil war, had been elected President in 1997, but was already losing control of his desperately impoverished country to a new rebel group in the north that was backed by the Guinea government. Another civil war and further tribal conflict appeared imminent. Like my shipmates, I had no desire whatsoever to find myself trapped in Liberia and unable to escape the warring factions seemingly intent on further destroying themselves and their country for the second time within a few years. I only hoped, for all our sakes, that Colin's eternal enthusiasm and optimism for our home-going travel arrangements would prove to be well founded.

Brass, braid and brazen

Three thousand one hundred and sixty-six miles later, after fifteen relatively trouble-free and monotonous days at sea, we tied up alongside the only remaining jetty at Buchanan in Liberia, just a few metres behind the *Eden*'s sister vessel, the *Moin*. She had arrived two days ahead of us from Lisbon in Portugal.

The port area was a scrap merchant's dream, with rusted hulks of fishing boats and larger stern-trawlers lying half-sinking and scuppered around the harbour. On the opposite side of the basin in which we had moored, the remains of a large loading gantry and the twisted steel supports for a conveyor system that disappeared out of sight over the hill beyond the port leaned precariously at different angles, blown up and destroyed in the civil war. Buildings and godowns set back from the jetties and quaysides stood gutted and roofless, holes in the walls bearing testament to the shell and rocket fire. It appeared to be wanton destruction on an unbelievable scale, with the town, or what was left of it, lying devastated in the distance.

The local population had turned out in full strength to give us an inquisitive reception. Obviously the arrival of a second tugboat was confirmation that plans were afoot for their idle and ruined deep-water port. They milled shiftlessly around the dilapidated and filthy quayside, ever alert to the slightest opportunity to jump onto the main deck and acquire whatever came to hand. Although their smiles and greetings appeared outwardly friendly and sincere, it was difficult not to sense the underlying current of oppression, fear and intimidation that hung over us, and the harbour, like a dark and threatening storm cloud.

About a dozen port officials, in the guise of customs, immigration, and port health authorities, came on board to clear the boat inwards. Both female and male, they were all kitted out in a dazzling array of different coloured uniforms and insignia, some shabby and some not so shabby. Rank was difficult to ascertain: from the amount of gold braid being proudly displayed either on epaulettes or on sleeves, it appeared that only the Heads of Departments had honoured us with their presence. The number of gold stripes, or the faded colours between them, seemed to bear little indication of the wearer's function or seniority. Everyone, without exception, was either armed with a holstered pistol or carried a Kalashnikov rifle. I had no idea, and absolutely no intention of asking, whether or not their weapons were loaded.

The ship's certificates and port-entry papers I had prepared prior to our arrival were passed along the messroom table from one official to the next. Every paper was carefully studied with little or no understanding before eventually being stamped or scribbled upon with an illegible signature by the person seated at the end of the table. In the meantime their colleagues were systematically pilfering the cupboards and storeroom of anything that appeared remotely edible or useful. Black plastic bin-liners that had been purchased in vast numbers in Avonmouth for the collection and disposal of the boat's garbage while she was working in Buchanan became a much sought after commodity for the carriage and handling of stolen foodstuffs and whatever else took the officials' fancy. The relentless progress in emptying the shelves was directly related to the speed at which the paperwork was being completed. I felt immensely sorry for both Dickie and Bow, who had to stand back helplessly with crestfallen eyes to witness the procedural chaos and the virtual plundering of what remained of their precious stores. The food stocks left over from the voyage had all but completely disappeared within a few hours of their arrival in the country in which they were contracted to spend a minimum of twelve months. Two hours later and all was quiet. The officials departed with their ill-gotten gains, and we were left to our own devices with little or no food and still none the wiser as to how we were going to get home.

A white face, in the form of our ship's agent, appeared on the quayside. He had left the capital, Monrovia, with his local driver some six hours earlier to drive to Buchanan through the jungle with its countless roadblocks and endless obstructions. A Frenchman, he appeared as happy to see us as we were to see him. Our happiness lay in the five handwritten flight tickets he had brought with him for a flight in the morning from Roberts International Airport to Abidjan in Côte d'Ivoire, and then on to Europe. He stayed with us for less than an hour answering our many questions before bidding us au revoir. He had the unenviable pleasure of having a six-hour return journey back to Monrovia.

Peter, our seaman-cum-cook, had not been wasting his time. He had made the acquaintance of Alfred, a local entrepreneur who claimed to be an out-of-work Liberian seaman and who, for the price of a couple of beers, would be willing to assist us in any way possible. Succumbing to the thirst of a dry and parched throat, Peter had despatched Alfred with twenty US dollars in his sweaty hand to buy bread and beer. The debate became quite heated as to whether we would ever see him again. I shared everyone else's opinion, except Peter's, that our Alfred would now be taking his wife to the local Savoy Hotel for afternoon tea before secretly hiding the change in the bank under his mattress. Honesty can never be measured by appearances.

One hour later, Alfred was spotted staggering down the quayside laden with loaves of bread and a plastic crate filled with one-litre bottles of beer. Our seafaring friend from Liberia had proved the doubters, and myself, all wrong. The twenty US dollars had gone a long way, for even the beer was chilled. After taking our late lunch of bread and local ale, we set off towards the town with Alfred as our guide. As we trooped through the security area, the armed guards stationed at the remains of the dock gates instructed us to stay within port limits. We were warned not to venture, under any circumstances whatsoever, outside Buchanan and into the nearby jungle, although the town itself we would find quite safe.

Our first port of call was a semi-derelict building posing as the 'Beach Bar and Night Club', but a temporary shortage of customers had created a cash-flow problem that prevented the stocking of beer or any other refreshments. Perhaps it became alive at night-time. We stayed for a few minutes to ponder the litter-strewn beach before traipsing across some waste ground to enter what was left of the town. Buchanan was a collection of buildings without roofs, doors or windows, a town littered with rusted and derelict vehicles abandoned on tarmacked and dirt roads cratered with shell-holes, a desperately poor community without running water, sewerage or electricity, and one that was buried deep in mountains of festering garbage covered in flies and alive with skeletal cats. Buchanan had paid a heavy price in the civil war, and an even heavier price in the three years of peace; not a pothole had been filled, or a building repaired.

Alfred told us that the Nigerian peacekeeping force had not only stripped the town of anything of any value, but had also done most of the damage in retribution for centuries-old tribal disputes and never-forgiven grudges. He led us to a semi-derelict building on the corner of a street with a covered terrace area fitted out with a collection of home-made rustic wooden tables and seating. Incredibly, a few minutes later, some cold beers arrived that tasted surprisingly good and were unbelievably cheap. The enterprising owner had set himself up with a rusty old chest freezer and a portable generator. We were on our second round of beers and quietly minding our own business when a jeep pulled up noisily outside. The small crowd of onlookers, who had been leaning on the broken balustrade of the terrace watching our every move with the fascination of not having seen a white person before, melted quietly away. The two young soldiers dressed in their military fatigues and clutching their Kalashnikov rifles, dismounted from their dented and battered vehicle and made their purposeful approach. My bowels had a sudden and incredible urge to open.

We were advised we had strayed outside port limits. Some parts of the town were inside those limits but other parts, including the bar, were not. A totally innocent Alfred had unwittingly led us across an imaginary boundary into a restricted area. I was convinced the area changed with either the persons seen to be walking around within it, or perhaps with the time of day. The soldiers seemed in no hurry and, although not overly friendly, appeared to be reasonably civil. After scrounging a few cigarettes and a couple of beers, they led the way back to the docks in their jeep with us walking closely behind. After we had given him a few dollars for his troubles, Alfred wisely decided to flee in the opposite direction.

We filed in a single line through the security area just inside the broken gates of the docks. A large, imposing, heavily built person in a dark green uniform and with the leather flap of his holstered pistol already unclipped, approached me. The instruction to me to follow him was quite clearly a command and not a request.

I entered a room. There was no door and half the roof was missing so I could see the blue afternoon sky. There was not a cloud in sight. Across one corner of the room was a wooden desk that had seen better times. Behind the desk sat another large person, also dressed in a dark green uniform, but this one was lavishly decorated with gold braid, insignia and a row of shining medals. A business card was handed to me as a way of introduction. I was, apparently, privileged to be in the company of the Pier Superintendent, a Mr George H. Too Wesley Senior. He certainly looked every inch the part. Glancing over my shoulder, I could see another uniformed person or assistant, complete with his mandatory Kalashnikov rifle, standing not too far behind me. To say I felt concerned and lonely would have been the understatement of the year. George H. Too Wesley Senior fiddled with a pencil and then glanced up at me with dark staring eyes, before advising me that the fine for the offence of taking my crew into a restricted area outside port limits was 1,000 US dollars.

The menace in his voice was extremely worrying. I glared at him with all the contempt I felt. I did a quick mental count of the US dollars I and the ship's cash account could muster, guessed at what everyone else might have to contribute, and came to the conclusion that his demand was way beyond the amount I could raise. I fidgeted uncomfortably, sensing that the assistant behind me with the Kalashnikov rifle was also fidgeting. I was about to start arguing when a young female, all breasts and buttocks that were impossibly squeezed into a dark uniform similar to that of George H. Too Wesley Senior, but without the medals, walked into the room. She brushed past me, smiled lovingly at George, as if to say 'Aren't I a clever girl?', and tipped out a black plastic bin-liner full of ship's stores onto the desk. Little did she realise, but my prayers had just been answered. I coughed to clear my throat before saying, in a surprisingly strong voice, that the value of the ship's stolen stores that had just been dropped onto his desk was also about 1,000 US dollars.

I didn't wait for a reply, but turned and walked out of the room. I didn't dare pause for breath, or even glance at the assistant with the Kalashnikov rifle. Had I done so, I would probably have started running. It was, and still remains, the most foolhardy and stupid act of defiance I think I have ever made. I continued walking, nothing too hasty, back out into the late afternoon sunshine and across the dusty and rubbish-strewn quayside before climbing onto the *Eden*. The ice-cold beer the others had saved for me did little to soothe my nerves or to stop my involuntary shaking. Surprisingly, I never had the dubious pleasure of meeting George H. Too Wesley Senior again, but I still have his business card as a chilling memento.

Dickie and Bow had been visiting the other tugboat, the *Moin*, to meet her full Thai crew who had joined the previous day. At least their safe arrival was a good omen for our travelling in the opposite direction the following morning. We were invited on board for an evening meal. I never did discover whether her delivery crew had been more successful in hiding their stores, or whether the Thais had already been able to make some local purchases. It made no difference, the food was excellent and the last of our beer was soon consumed.

With the arrangements having been made for us to leave the *Eden* early in the morning, we said our fond farewells to Dickie and Bow before turning in for the night. They had been our shipmates for just a short voyage, but despite the language difficulties, there had already been a typical seafaring bonding. In many ways, I felt extremely sorry for them. They had accepted, albeit willingly, their dubious one-year contract of employment in Singapore without having the remotest idea of what their job entailed, or what dangers would confront them. I was sure they would be paid a mere pittance for their efforts, trials and tribulations. From the little I had seen of Buchanan and the people within, I was more than glad to have a ticket to leave.

A fun farewell

Thinking it better to be safe than sorry, I slept behind a locked cabin door for the night. I wasn't too sure if George H. Too Wesley Senior and his heavily armed sidekicks might come looking for me, not that a locked flimsy cabin door would have made the slightest difference to my safety had they done so.

Dawn was just breaking as we struggled down our makeshift wooden plank gangway with our baggage and the specialist ship's delivery equipment that was to accompany us on our flights back to the UK. The large minibus that had pulled up alongside the *Eden* already appeared half-full of people. Three armed guards, a driver and the agent's assistant, a local man attired in a safari suit that had seen better days, flip-flops, and a proper canvas-covered pith helmet reminiscent of the Doctor Livingstone era, were to accompany us on our journey through the jungle to the airport. Just before climbing into the minibus, I turned to take one last look at the *Eden*, not realising then that I would be seeing her again just four years later. I'm uncertain whether my look was one of affection or sorrow.

With the minibus engine badly misfiring we left the quayside and negotiated our way without stopping through the gap in the broken dock gates. Passing noisily through the deserted and rubble-strewn streets of the devastated and silent town, we drove onto a dirt-track road leading into the heavily foliaged jungle. The road was in an appalling state, with huge craters and felled trees partially blocking the single dirt carriageway, and deep, barely negotiable fords that bypassed the blown-up bridges that had once crossed the shallow rivers and gorges. Scattered on either side of the road lay ramshackle wooden dwellings with oil-lamps still burning as daylight fast approached. Scraggy chickens could be seen scratching around inside makeshift pens, while packs of flea-ridden dogs roamed freely, desperately searching for the odd morsels of food. Occasional passers-by stopped to stare at us as we went past: quite obviously a minibus overloaded with baggage, five white passengers cowering timidly in their seats, three gun-toting military guards, a driver and another local person wearing a Livingstone-lookalike pith helmet, was not a regular sight.

The roadblock obstructed the track as we rounded a corner. The agent tensed and our guards nervously gripped their Kalashnikov rifles more tightly. Three armed men in tatty and long-worn camouflage fatigues appeared from behind a wooden barrier of felled timber and sauntered casually towards our vehicle. We remained silent with our heads either ramrod straight or partially bowed so as to avoid eye-contact with them. Although the language of Liberia is English, it was difficult to understand the dialect and what was being said. The agent reached into a plastic bag he had been carrying and passed a wad of banknotes to one of the outstretched hands. The financial donation was obviously considered insufficient and, after a brief and nerve-racking delay, a carton of two hundred cigarettes was added to the banknotes. A short but heated discussion followed before the barrier was reluctantly lifted. We carried on our way and our guards relaxed once again. The agent smiled and assured us we would arrive safely.

Two more roadblocks and three very long hours later, we arrived at Roberts International Airport. The single-storey terminal building was of crude block-work construction supporting a corrugated iron roof. The large windows at the front of the building were surprisingly intact and were being cleaned by a team of women armed with rags and buckets. The main passenger entrance door was still closed, the airport not yet open for business. We parked alongside one or two other minibuses and taxis in a sandy area adjacent to the terminal and unloaded our vehicle. Conspicuous by our foreign features, we soon attracted some young helpers who, for a small fee, assisted us in lugging our baggage towards the building. The entrance doors opened about twenty minutes after our arrival, more than sufficient time for our ever-resourceful Peter not only to locate, but also to negotiate the purchase of five one-litre bottles of chilled local beer. Breakfast had never tasted so refreshingly wonderful.

The agent led us to the wooden check-in desk, which had a huge set of scales at one side for the weighing of baggage. The weight of every item of luggage was painstakingly handwritten on our tickets. We were then led to another desk to pay our thirty US dollars departure tax to the Ministry of Finance before presenting ourselves, strongly smelling of beer, to the Ministry of Health. The white-coated middle-aged medical clerk and his young assistant reminded me of my old head-master and teacher standing behind the lectern at school assembly, ticking off the roll call. He scrutinised all our vaccination certificates and copied the details into a huge leather-bound ledger, slowly and meticulously scribing every entry in beautiful copperplate writing, using a traditional quill pen, ink-well and blotter. The ledger was a true work of art and a genuine example of medical record-keeping that could tell a thousand therapeutic tales. I just hoped it would be kept for posterity.

With the formalities over, we were instructed to be seated in the waiting area, a relatively small space open to the roof and equipped with wooden bench seats placed in neat rows. It gave the appearance of being a traditional waiting-room at a railway station in almost every detail, except for the black and white photograph of an unsmiling President Charles Taylor on the end wall and a complete lack of graffiti. The agent, highly conspicuous in the small crowd in his flamboyant attire, sat with us for a few minutes before making his excuses and leaving. He had done his job by delivering us safely to Roberts International Airport.

We were on our own, quietly subdued, everyone deep in his own thoughts. The unmistakable sound of an aircraft with turboprop engines echoed around the building as it taxied towards the tarmacked boarding area. The plane that was to fly us out of Liberia had arrived, and not a moment too soon as far as I was concerned. The recurring and awful nightmare of seeing George H. Too Wesley Senior, accompanied by his brassiere-bursting companion, charging in through the airport doors in a final effort to claim his dodgy fine money, was unnerving me. We sat and waited while the two dozen or so disembarking passengers noisily thronged the entrance hall for a few minutes before moving on outside.

The electronic-sounding voice surprised everyone. Startled, we all looked up. With no mains electricity in the terminal, or in the country as a whole as far as I could gather, a male member of the airport staff was endeavouring to make the flight's boarding announcement by shouting into a battery-operated megaphone. His features were completely obscured by the metal trumpet. With the mouthpiece held too close to his face, the words were distorted and barely understandable: 'Weasua Air Transport announces the departure of its international flight, WTC 005 to Abidjan. All passengers should proceed to Gate Number Three for passport control and immediate boarding.'

Gates One and Two were mere figments of the imagination and nowhere to be seen. There was only one gate, a broken door hanging loosely at an angle from a solitary hinge. On the other side of the opening, a long table was manned by a couple of uniformed staff who gave our tickets and passports a final, very cursory inspection before we were waved on. A couple of heavily armed soldiers ensured we didn't stray into any prohibited areas as we walked towards the aircraft.

The Russian flight crew of the Tupolev Tu-330 had kept its engines running, clearly with the intention of keeping the turnaround time to a minimum. The agent had assured us that the airport was considered relatively safe, although the word 'safe' could be interpreted in many ways with a rebel army already controlling the northern parts of the country. As we moved towards the plane, the control tower came into view. There was virtually nothing left of the observation platform at the top of the concrete tower, and the tower itself was full of gaping holes from shell and rocket fire. The damage from the first civil war did little in convincing me that taking the flight was the most sensible decision I had ever made, but my travel options were severely limited. We boarded the aircraft using its own small and very rickety gangway. Our baggage and the few items being carried by the thirty or so other passengers had been stacked on the floor between the cockpit and the first rows of passenger seats. A rope cargo net had been thrown over the pile to keep everything in place during the flight.

The stained and tired-looking red patterned floral wallpaper that had been used to line the inside of the passenger cabin was peeling at the edges and at the joins. We sat down in the seats at the front of the plane, just behind our baggage, reasoning that with the exception of the flight crew, we would be the first to take off and the first to land. Steve, our chief engineer, who had occupied a window seat, quietly advised us that there were quite a few rivets missing on the wing. As we stood up together to take a closer look, the co-pilot hastily closed the cabin door and motioned to us to take our seats and to fasten our seatbelts. We were going to fly whether we liked it or not.

Within seconds the propeller pitch had been adjusted, the brakes released and we were rolling forward and turning towards the end of the runway. The craters down its length were clear for us all to see. The noise and vibration increased dramatically with the plane's sharp acceleration. It appeared to me as if the pilot was actually steering his aircraft around the bomb-craters as we swayed slightly from side to side gathering speed. We had travelled only a very short distance before a final thud from the wheels confirmed we were airborne and climbing steeply, very steeply. The West Country voice announcing that the pilot was now flying fifty feet higher than those at the back of the aircraft broke the ice and made us all laugh, perhaps a trifle more loudly than usual, but that was to hide our nervousness and obvious unease. We relaxed a little and sat back deeper into the uncomfortable seats. The plane levelled off above the carpet of jungle and set a course for Abidjan in Côte d'Ivoire.

Our general manager's assurances that he would sort something out once we had got there were still fresh in my mind, as if it had been only the day before when we had been sailing from Avonmouth bound for Buchanan.

We had made our escape from Liberia, unscathed, but just a little bit shaken.

2

FOUR YEARS ON – JUNE 2003

A flight to Abidjan

After an epic and very special voyage delivering the *Justine*, a Mississippi river tugboat, from Bahrain to Trinidad, I was to spend several enjoyable weeks on leave relaxing at home before the telephone call came from Holland. The personnel manager for the Dutch crewing agency for whom I have worked for many years was enquiring whether I would be interested in commanding a tugboat for a delivery voyage from Abidjan to Singapore.

My initial response was hesitant and slightly less than enthusiastic: like most, if not all, seafarers blessed with the freedom of choice, I become extremely concerned the moment West Africa is mentioned. Nigeria and some other countries within the region haven't earned their unenviable reputations for piracy, murder and hostage taking without very good cause, although some parts are more safe than others. I could recall having flown out of Abidjan before on a couple of previous occasions and not being overly worried about my well-being. I didn't think Côte d'Ivoire, although not entirely without its troubles, was one of those countries to which the Foreign Office advised against travelling, or even visiting.

Despite my concerns, there must have been sufficient interest in my reply for me to be told that there were two tugboats, named *Oriental Tug No. 1* and *Oriental Tug No. 2*, which would be sailing together in convoy to Singapore. The owner's crews would shortly be moving the two boats from a port in the south of Liberia to Abidjan, where we would be expected to join them in about two weeks' time. Liberia: the very mention of the country brought back profound and not so fond memories of my fraught couple of days aboard the *Eden* in Buchanan some four years earlier. I wondered how Mr George H. Too Wesley Senior and his big-busted, light-fingered, but not so clever, female colleague were faring and why it should be that I had instantly been able to recall his name, while others, far more important in both social and business matters, can slip the mind completely. George H. Too Wesley Senior is a name I am unlikely ever to forget. My persistent questioning on the telephone revealed that the UK branch of the company had indeed delivered the two boats to Liberia some time ago and that the names *Eden* and *Moin* did sound familiar, although the Dutch office hadn't been involved in the original contract.

I needed no further confirmation. I had already heard more than enough to be convinced that the two boats were the *Eden* and the *Moin*. I couldn't even begin to speculate on how they might have fared after four years in war-torn Liberia without the benefits of repair yards, maintenance facilities or spare parts. They had been twenty-three years old when we had delivered them from Lisbon and Avonmouth to Buchanan, but now – four years later? Admittedly, twenty-seven is not that old in tugboat years, but some extensive repairs and maintenance would probably be required unless they had been properly looked after. For some unknown reason, I agreed to travel to Abidjan so I could find out for myself.

Why did I accept the appointment if I had really been so concerned about the condition of the boats? I have repeatedly asked myself that question, and can arrive at no logical or remotely sensible answer. Perhaps I relish the challenge of attempting to achieve something strange or a little out of the ordinary, or perhaps it was just the typical seafarer's longing to return to sea after a few weeks spent ashore. Seafaring, paradoxically is a very insular profession. As sailors we like to be on our own, secure in our own self-governing environment and away from all the issues, nonsense and stresses of today's society, and yet, when we're away, we become desperate for news of that very same society from which we were so keen to escape only a few days or weeks before. The likelihood of my giving a similar response in the future is very real: it is the seafarer's way.

Leaving home at four o'clock in the morning for the two-hour taxi ride over the Welsh mountains to Manchester airport has become one of my regular journeys and is a small price to pay for residing in a beautifully scenic and rural area of North Wales. My travel plans were to fly from Manchester to Paris, where I would meet up with my Dutch colleagues for the ongoing flight from Charles de Gaulle Airport to Abidjan. I will always remember that short European inter-city flight to Paris. As the plane taxied towards the terminal building after landing, we came to a halt to allow an Air France Concorde to cross ahead of us. Small tricolour pennants in red, white and blue had been draped from her distinctive drooped nose cockpit and large crowds of spectators had lined both the airport perimeter fence and the public viewing areas patriotically waving their French flags. The cabin staff on our flight explained that she had just made her final landing before being decommissioned. That day, 27 June 2003, was a sad and emotional one indeed for aviation history.

Meeting old friends is always a special event; meeting my old friend and chief engineer, Remy Weggemans, was very special. We had only recently sailed together delivering the *Justine* from Bahrain to Trinidad, which had been a trip that neither of us would forget for as long as we lived. Our reunion in the middle of the airport terminal consisted of the usual noisy two-way verbal greetings followed by the almost statutory over-zealous bear hugs, and the prolonged and violent shaking of each other's hand as if we had become permanently attached at the wrists. I only hoped that our personnel department hadn't decided that, if we had recently accepted a voyage involving much drama and primitive conditions on the *Justine* without too much complaint, then perhaps we would manage another challenge on the *Oriental* tugs. I suspected all would be revealed within a few days.

Remy hadn't changed one bit, not that he should have changed in the three months we had both been at home. He was still the same Remy with his long grey hair worn at shoulder length over the collar of his traditional denim shirt, and with the waist of his jeans concealed under the bulge of his ample stomach. His silver-grey beard and moustache remained neatly trimmed and tidy and complemented the permanent smile that creased his rounded and friendly face.

With the exception of Jaap Smit, the general manager of the company, who would be overseeing and assisting us in preparing the two boats for their voyage, and whom I had met on several previous occasions, I recognised only Mieke Wiechmann-van Oversteeg. She would be sailing with me on the *Oriental Tug No. 2* as cook-cum-seaman, or is it 'seawoman' in these mixed up days of sexual equality and politically correct job descriptions? I had met Mieke before in the Arabian Gulf when we had been preparing three tugboats together for their respective delivery voyages. She is married to Erik, a long-serving Master in the company, and they have been sailing as a captain and cook team for many years. On this occasion, Mieke was hitching a working lift to Singapore where she hoped to join Erik, who had last been heard of somewhere deep in the backwaters of Papua New Guinea training some locals in the finer arts of handling crewboats and tugboats.

I hadn't previously met Marco Wehrmann, who would be sailing with me as chief officer. Thirty years old and unmarried, he has a sincere, self-confident and professional air about him. He is a tall man, clean-shaven with a serious, but friendly face and fair hair. His frame is in perfect proportion to his height, neither slim nor overweight. Standing next to one another with the top of my head barely level with his broad shoulders, we must have appeared as an extremely unlikely captain and chief officer team to be joining a tugboat in West Africa.

Introductions were made to the other members of the group. There was Pieter, the captain of the *Oriental Tug No. 1*, Willem, his chief engineer, André, his chief officer, and Mark, the cook. We all shook hands and subconsciously tried to match the face to the name and if not to the name, then at least to their position on board. I have found that discussing matters of route planning and navigation with the cook instead of the captain is never a good start to a working relationship.

Pieter is a similar age to me and of average height with a slim, but not quite athletic, build. His ruddy, narrow face is partially hidden under a full beard that has become discoloured by a combination of grey hair and the light brown nicotine staining that comes from having a hand-rolled cigarette almost permanently between his lips. He carries a well-weathered complexion from his years of sailing the seas and of being a Port of Rotterdam pilot, and from living with his wife and family on board his yacht moored on the south coast of Portugal when he's not at sea. Pieter, quite literally, spends his entire life afloat.

As the two captains, we had a difficult task ahead of us. We had the responsibility not only of looking after our own tugboats, but also of being able to assist and understand one another in times of need or difficulty. From my limited experiences of sailing in convoy with another boat, I instinctively knew that both Pieter and I would have to swallow our personal pride on occasions, grit our teeth, smile, and arrive somehow at those awkward compromise decisions that would not necessarily be ideal for the individual or his crew, but would be the most appropriate for the venture as a whole. Time would only tell if we could work together as the team our voyage would require.

Flight AF702 to Abidjan was like most international flights: the usual dreary and monotonous affair where the cabin staff make every reasonable effort to ensure that you are as comfortable as the cramped conditions permit; that you have been served your choice from the 'in-flight' menu of 'healthy eating' food, and that you have been watered from a drinks trolley that always starts in the aisle at the furthest point possible from your seat allocation, so that when it finally arrives thirty minutes later your choice has become limited by the consumption of your fellow passengers. Airlines could make a fortune by auctioning the seat row number from which the trolley will commence its service!

The six and a half hour flight ended in the early evening, when we were herded together in the Arrivals area at Abidjan airport so that we could pass through Immigration and Customs Control as a group and allow the ship's agent to claim a discount on the authorities' 'formality' charges. It is the way of West Africa! We were assured that the four items of baggage that had been lost in transit would be located and brought to us as soon as possible.

The Novotel was perfectly comfortable and acceptable for the short stopover we would be making, no different from any other international multi-storey type hotel that can be found in every major city in the world, all with their identical shaped rooms, familiar linen and faded decorative co-ordination, and the usual exorbitantly priced mini-bar, the satellite television and the tray with its complimentary tea and coffee making facilities.

The evening meal, a buffet-style dinner, and the couple of beers we had to accompany our food, rounded off what had been a long day. Tired from our travels, we retired early for the night. The two tugboats would be awaiting us in the morning.

The *Oriental* tugs

The minibuses collected us and our baggage from the hotel shortly after breakfast and took us to an area just off the docks from where we could board a launch to take us out to the two tugboats. The narrow and steep gravel path leading down to the water's edge where the boat was secured to the loose planking of a rickety causeway made it extremely awkward for manhandling our suitcases and the ship's equipment. By the time the boat was loaded and we were all on board, there was very little freeboard remaining. I made sure I was seated in the middle, where I had the best possible chance of remaining dry on the trip out to the mooring buoys.

The two tugs were secured together and moored to a single buoy. As we drew closer, I instantly remembered the distinctive superstructures, twin funnels and long raking sterns as belonging to the *Eden* and the *Moin*. Being the only person in the

Oriental Tugs Nos. 1 & 2 *moored to a buoy in Abidjan. Our first glimpse of the tugs*

group to have seen them before, my casual nod in the affirmative confirmed to the others that we had come to the right boats.

There was no one around on deck to greet us, or to help with our baggage and equipment as we clambered aboard, a difficult task in itself when trying to leap from a small and bobbing boat onto the rubbing strake of the tug. Unknowingly we had boarded my command for the voyage to Singapore, the *Eden*, now known as the *Oriental Tug No. 2* after being renamed during her lengthy stay in Buchanan. I thought the choice of name to be particularly unimaginative and one that would probably cause a great deal of confusion with her sister when entering ports or dealing with awkward or intransigent authorities.

Standing on her aft deck and looking towards the instantly recognisable twin funnels, towing winch and the high, tapering wheelhouse, I had the very strange feeling of coming home again after an incredibly long time away. Everything appeared so surprisingly familiar, even after a four-year absence. I half expected to see my old acquaintances, 'Dickie Thai' and 'Bow Thai', waving to me as a welcoming party, but later remembered that they had signed twelve-month contracts and would have been relieved many moons ago and before my unexpected return.

We left our baggage on the stern and climbed over the raised watertight doorsill from the main deck and into the accommodation. Entering the darkened housing from the glaringly bright sunlight outside made it almost impossible to see where we were going. The paintwork was dingy and the deck filthy, the only light being that which filtered in through the open doors. I led the group along the cross-alleyway, past the galley and into the mess. Very little appeared to have changed.

Seated at the end of the long table that ran athwartships across the room were two oriental persons who didn't look at all like Thais to me. Our manager, Jaap Smit, made the introductions and asked their names. 'Shwe Myint', the captain, and 'Tin Nyunt', the chief engineer, were the replies. They were quite clearly Burmese, or whatever one calls a person today from Myanmar, the country's new name. I sailed many years ago with Burmese people when the company from Liverpool in which I served my apprenticeship had operated a cargo and passenger service between Europe and Rangoon in Burma, as it was known in those days. I had always found the Burmese people to be a genuinely sincere and warm-hearted, friendly race.

After a few minutes talking, for both Shwe and Tin spoke understandable English, it became apparent that they had no inkling of the agreement between their employers and our company that they should remain on board as members of our crew for the delivery voyage. They had been advised that neither tugboat would be returning to Buchanan, and that Singapore was the intended destination, but the notion that they should accompany us on the voyage had come completely out of the blue.

The Myanmar captain and chief engineer of No. 1 tug emphatically agreed with their colleagues. They had sailed the two boats to Abidjan and, as far as they were concerned, that was as far as they were going, and no further. Singapore was completely out of the question. Besides, Captain Shwe and the chief engineer from No. 1 tug had already been on board their respective boats continuously for two years and eight months without being given the leave they had earned and was due to them. I thought that to be separated from their homes and families for that length of time was not only inhuman, but also stretching the boundaries of employing cheap labour just a little too far. They had no particular desire to extend their contracts any further, a decision none of us could argue with, given the circumstances. Our manager was faced with the first of many problems that would occur in the next few days. Either the Singaporean owners would have to persuade their long-serving, but unhappy captains and chief engineers to remain on board, or replacement crew members from Holland would have to be employed by our company.

During the course of our conversation, the two captains and chief engineers were to reveal yet another and potentially far more serious personnel problem. The Liberian crews serving on both the boats had neither been paid for weeks nor received their entitlement of travel vouchers or tickets for their journey back to Liberia. They were being supported by the Côte d'Ivoire Seamen's Union, who had instructed them to exercise a lien on the two boats by remaining on board until the employers had paid them in full.

It soon became obvious that we would be spending a second night in the Novotel hotel. With the indefinite possession of the accommodation by the Liberian crews, we would be unable to proceed with any preparations for the long voyage ahead. From our initial and very cursory inspection, the boats quite clearly required a huge amount of work before they would even start to look habitable, although the Liberians apparently found them sufficiently comfortable to be able to continue with their committed occupation in the hopes of receiving their wages.

Later in the day Captain Shwe produced the key for a cabin we had found on the lower deck that had been partially stripped to provide furniture spares for the other cabins. We now had somewhere reasonably secure to stow our seagoing baggage and the high-value ship's equipment, charts and books that we have to move around with us from one delivery voyage to the next.

The engine room gave every appearance of being a complete and unmitigated disaster area. The lack of any proper maintenance facilities and the shortage of spare parts had, as anticipated, taken its terrible toll. One generator was totally inoperative and judged to be beyond economic repair, while the other two were in such poor condition that it had been deemed necessary to connect us by electrical cable to No. 1 tug so that she could provide a limited power supply for both the boats. Tin Nyunt advised a disconsolate Remy that the main engine was running with high crankcase pressure and that various pumps and other auxiliary items were barely usable, or had been stripped for vital spares to keep other essential services running. The situation on board No. 1 tug was not much different.

We went back to the hotel in the early evening somewhat traumatised by what we had found. The couple of beers before our evening meal did little to raise our low morale, or to lift the tone of conversation beyond the mood of hopelessness and depression to which we had succumbed. An early night was had by one and all.

An inoperative generator

Things only marginally improved the following day. We started cleaning the galley, but it was futile without suitable cleaning materials or hot water. With Shwe, Tin and the Liberian crew still cooking and living on board, our half-hearted efforts to help Mieke were little more than a complete and total waste of time.

We retired to the mess where I decided to investigate what, on the previous day, had appeared to be quite large cracks in the dirty and stained Formica wall panels. A closer scrutiny of the cracks revealed vertical movements. The 'cracks' were, in fact, columns of very small ants making either a vertical ascent up the wall panel to the join of the deckhead, where they disappeared from sight, or a vertical descent from the same location, but down to three large earth-filled tins in which some tropical plants were in the final stages of death by dehydration. The columns never once faltered or wavered. The ascending ants kept to the left and the descending ants to the right, the two traffic flows forming one perfectly straight and narrow column. The discipline and traffic control were beyond belief.

We had no intention, or desire, of upsetting Shwe or Tin and their deeply held religious doctrines. Buddhism strongly believes in the sanctity of all life, including insects. The four of us, Mieke, Marco, Remy and I, were, however, unanimous in our determination to have not only the mess, but also the whole boat, ant and vermin free. We waited patiently until no one was around. The dying plants were taken from the mess and out onto the main deck where they were given the water they so desperately needed. The fading foliage, the tins, and quite probably a very large number of little ants, were quietly dropped over the side into the river. The weight of the soil in the tins ensured they sank quickly and without trace. The current made it unlikely that there would be any survivors.

Back in the messroom, the plants' timely removal caused a great deal of confusion and bewilderment within the ant colony, so much so that the two-way traffic up and down the bulkhead panel instantly became omni-directional as they all scarpered hurriedly and haphazardly towards the safety of the Formica deckhead above. Any stragglers losing their way paid the ultimate price by being squirted with insect spray from an aerosol that had, according to its price label, been purchased in Avonmouth four years before and had been stowed in a cupboard drawer ever since. The squirting continued intermittently for the best part of the afternoon as the odd one or two targets committed suicide by showing their faces. The launch came alongside in the early evening to take us back to the hotel, leaving the Liberians on board to keep ship and to await their wages and travel tickets.

We celebrated our ant-culling skills with a couple of extra beers before tucking into our buffet dinner. Our third night in the hotel saw us firmly into the habit of retiring early to bed. It had, after all, been a successful and hard day's work.

The Carena shipyard, Abidjan

We made an early start from the hotel so that we could be on board the tugboat for eight o'clock, when some shoreside electricians were due to arrive to assist Remy in trying to coax some life from the generators. According to Tin, the problems had always occurred with the electrical generating part of the machines rather than with the Gardner engines. While the engines were just as old, they had proved to be more reliable and were more easily maintained. Jaap, our manager, stayed ashore to try and resolve some of the more pressing personnel problems with the Singaporean tugboat owners, and to organise further shore assistance with carrying out some of the essential work required before we could even contemplate starting the voyage.

With the generator repairs progressing, the much-needed clean-up in the mess commenced in earnest with some cleaning materials the ship's chandler had brought out to the boats. Although we had considered our ant cull the previous day to have been particularly successful, large numbers of little ants were still to be seen. After watching their activities for a few minutes, it became clear that parties of 'scout' ants were being despatched from their hiding places in the deckhead above, obviously with instructions to report back to their troop leader with news of the situation in the room below. For many unfortunate scouts, their leader would never receive their reports. Their final 'kamikaze' mission down the bulkhead panels ended with a squirt of lethal Deltamethrin until the contents of the aerosol had been exhausted. Others who escaped became more daring, scurrying at will around the mess and taking advantage of our temporary loss of firepower. Replacement sprays would have to be ordered with the chandler.

Later in the morning, the decision was made that we should proceed to the local ship repair yard to carry out further repairs and maintenance. Conveying tools, personnel and spare parts to and fro between the shore and the mooring buoy was proving uneconomical in both cost and time. We could ill afford the many hours spent waiting for the launch to arrive at one end or the other. A berth alongside in a shipyard would make life so much easier with its direct access to skilled labour, workshops, and instant communications.

A local pilot boarded to guide us the four miles or so upriver to the repair yard. Remy and Tin were successful in starting our main engine, but for the boys on No. 1 tug a problem with the cooling water system meant that their faithful old Ruston remained still and quiet. Since the two boats were already secured to one another, it was only a matter of putting out additional ropes between us and letting go from the mooring buoy. Off we set with one engine, the two tugboats lashed together. With less than half the distance to the yard remaining, the thick cloud of black smoke that suddenly and chokingly billowed from No. 1's funnels confirmed her reluctant engine had finally been persuaded to start. Obviously Willem's immense loss of pride at having to be towed to the yard had spurred him and his Myanmar colleague to greater efforts. We let go the ropes between us and proceeded on our individual ways.

The stern-first mooring onto the quayside was one of those painstakingly slow and awkward approaches, backing our way down carefully between other ships that had been moored in a similar manner. The yard had been extremely helpful in accommodating us with only a few hours' prior warning and had managed to create the space on their jetty. It was late in the afternoon before we had finally secured. No. 1 tug made a similar manoeuvre and tied up safely alongside us.

Shwe and Tin came to see me after we had moored. Faces creased with large and beaming smiles, they seemed hugely pleased with themselves. They happily announced that they would be doing the voyage to Singapore with us after all. Maung, the Myanmar ex-captain of No. 1 tug, had also agreed to remain, but his chief engineer, quite rightly, had had more than enough. After two years and eight months away, he was finally going home to see his family and his young son, who had been born seven months after his joining the boat in Buchanan and of whom his only sighting had been from a couple of well-handled and creased photographs he had been passing to everyone to admire. How he came to receive the pictures in Liberia was a question without an answer: perhaps one of the visiting ships had acted as a mail-boat. No wonder there were tears in his eyes when he came to say his fond farewells. He had already been deprived of sharing the first two years of his young son's life.

I never did discover what financial inducement had been offered, or indeed the demands that had been made by the three who were to sail on the voyage. I suspect they had played 'hard to get' with the owner's local representative until he had eventually buckled under the combined assault of their persuasive and determined arguments. The Myanmars were exceedingly happy with the final outcome, unlike our manager, Jaap, who now had the task of finding a Dutch second engineer to fly out to Abidjan at extremely short notice to replace the home-going chief engineer. The Liberian crews were still totally deadlocked in their negotiations with the owners for their wages and travel tickets and refused point-blank, quite rightly in my opinion, to leave the sanctuary of the two tugboats, and with it the loss of their bargaining power. Looking at the situation from the outside, I would have thought it would have been in the owner's best financial interests to resolve the issue quickly. Our hotel bill for accommodating eight persons, along with the inevitable extras such as meals and additional agent's expenses, were all being charged to the Singaporean owner's account and would probably far exceed the perfectly legitimate demands being made by the seamen. While it was frustrating not being able to even inspect the cabins, let alone to sort out and clean them, we had absolutely no objection to the sit-in continuing. As far as we were concerned, the Liberians could remain on board until all the repairs had been completed and we were within twenty-four hours of being ready to sail. No one in their right mind would willingly exchange the undeniable luxuries of a modern international hotel for the very basic and squalid conditions aboard the two boats.

We retired to our comforts for another night. The resident trio playing in the hotel lounge was on good form and joined in with our party celebrations. Jaap, our manager, had tried to keep the matter of his birthday quiet, but a telephone call from his office colleagues in Holland had soon put paid to that idea. To be fair, he quite willingly maintained the right and proper traditions of all nautical birthdays by paying for the few beers we consumed before and after our meal, the bottles of wine we had with our meal, and the Irish Coffees he insisted upon us having at the end of our meal. He only became a little uncomfortable when the Liberian female singer with the shapely hourglass figure and a husky voice insisted upon holding his sweaty hand and dragging him, very reluctantly, onto the dance floor so that she could stare seductively into his eyes while singing 'Happy Birthday'. The other hotel guests and some local non-resident visitors loved it. Despite his protests and attempts to leave the floor there was to be no escape for the blushing and deeply embarrassed Jaap, who was passed the microphone for a couple of well-known numbers. The lounge area emptied quite rapidly after that. Some people have much better voices than others for karaoke.

The next morning we heard that the Liberian crews had, at long last, reached a settlement and had agreed to leave the boats at midday. Finally we could get into the cabins and the two bathrooms to confirm with our very own eyes the conditions we already knew existed. Only then would we be able to start cleaning them and sorting out what would be needed for the voyage in the way of mattresses, bedding and all the other domestic bits and pieces.

Later in the morning I watched the Liberians lining up on deck to report, one by one, to an oriental gentleman seated at a makeshift table. They were each given a thick wad of well-used banknotes that was slowly and meticulously counted out in front of them, followed by a flight ticket from Abidjan to Roberts International Airport in Liberia. Each and every crew member then placed either his mark or signature on the ship's articles to complete the 'signing off' formalities and to confirm that he had been paid his wages in full and final settlement of his contract of employment.

The whole rigmarole was closely observed and silently scrutinised by one of the largest black persons I have ever seen. He was, quite simply, immense from the top of his enormous and clean-shaven head, down through his bull-like and shapeless neck, to the soles of his over-sized feet that were housed in home-made flip-flops that had been roughly shaped from pieces of tread-bare car tyres. The presence of this huge and formidable figure standing close to the table and the bundles of money was intimidating, which was probably the reason behind his attendance in the first place. I never did discover whether he was the security guard for the owner's agent, a Côte d'Ivoire union official, or merely an uninvited spectator too large to be told he shouldn't have been there. In one respect I felt very sorry for the crew: I wondered if they knew what was in store for them for their flight home to Liberia, and whether any of them had ever seen the inside of an aircraft before, let alone one with floral wallpaper and rivets missing from its wings. I suppose there was a remote possibility that after four long years, the interior had been redecorated and the wings repaired.

Now that the accommodation was finally free of the Liberians, we could make a thorough and critical inspection of the lower deck cabins and the two bathrooms. I think we had all feared the worst and our fears were confirmed. The whole lower deck was filthy and would have to be cleaned many times over from top to bottom to eradicate the years of neglect. The cabins were no different, smelling musty and strongly of body odours, and with the bare mattresses on the bunks sweat-stained and yellow and no longer fit to sleep upon. The pillows were in a similar dirty and soiled condition, hard and lumpy, and had been used without pillowcases. Every item of furniture, every deckhead, bulkhead and deck would have to be scrubbed clean and disinfected before we could even think about taking up occupancy. Even the ants had worked their way down from the deck above and were busily scurrying around in the alleyway looking for pastures green.

Shwe and Tin seemed not the slightest bit bothered with the dreadful squalor that confronted them when they moved down from the captain and chief engineer's accommodation into two of the lower deck cabins. Either their bonus for sailing with us to Singapore had been more than generous, or they had become so accustomed to the conditions during the time they had been on board that they had grown to accept them as being normal. I quickly realised why Shwe had shown no concern with his move. Not only had he displayed a willingness to accept the disgusting surroundings, he had left the captain's cabin, my home for the voyage ahead, in a similar state to those down below. Remy's cabin had been left in only a marginally better condition.

It was only later that the horrible truth dawned upon me. We had achieved the cleaning of the mess and the galley utilising cleaning materials purchased through the ship's chandler in Abidjan. The boat had been working in Buchanan for four long years where even simple and basic items such as cleaning cloths, surface cleaners, liquid soaps, disinfectants and all the other domestic paraphernalia we casually take for granted would have been either unavailable, or simply unaffordable. I suddenly felt so desperately sorry for Shwe and Tin, and incredibly guilty and humiliated for thinking that they might have contributed to, or even condoned, the awful squalor we had found on board. Their living conditions in Liberia must have been quite appalling.

The bathroom and sanitary facilities were absolutely revolting and would have been instantly condemned as totally unhygienic in any other part of the world. Remy and I shared a bathroom located on the opposite side of the alleyway to our cabins and adjacent to the foot of the stairwell leading up to the wheelhouse. It was no longer functional as a bathroom. The toilet bowl was cracked through at the front and the waste outlet at the back deposited whatever was being flushed straight onto the painted deck. The flexible rubber sealing attachment that joined the porcelain to the waste pipe was missing, no doubt purloined to keep the bathroom toilet on the main deck operational. The plastic hinge lugs for the lavatory seat were still bolted to the bowl, but the seat itself had long disappeared. Inside the shower cubicle stood a used and dented 200-litre oil drum filled with water and, floating on the surface, a battered saucepan clearly intended for use as a scoop. The shower fittings had been removed and the hot and cold inlet pipes blanked off. Somewhat surprisingly, the washbasin appeared intact, but without either a plug or functional taps.

In the main deck bathroom, things were only marginally better, with the toilet, although cracked and minus the seat, still working. The shower cubicle, a filthy and dark area in one corner, had the appropriate hot and cold taps that, between them, produced a supply of cold water to the old and corroded showerhead. This couldn't be said for the two side-by-side washbasins, which gave every impression of being in reasonable order apart from an absence of water from the taps. As in the bathroom one deck above, the 200-litre oil drum, filled with water and complete with a small saucepan, was obviously intended as a reservoir and a supply for the basins.

Mieke was understandably depressed with our lack of sanitary facilities. All women, whether at sea or ashore, see a spotless and well-equipped bathroom as being a requisite for clean and comfortable living. Both Marco and Remy shared not only my discomfort, but also my embarrassment, at seeing what she was going to have to put up with, not that we could be held in any way to blame. The *Oriental* tugs didn't even come close to providing the most basic of standards. The lack of facilities and available time in Abidjan meant we would have to postpone our plumbing repairs until Las Palmas. We had to face up to the stark reality that our voyage to the Canary Islands was going to be exceedingly disagreeable, and one that would involve a very taxing and unpleasant ten or eleven days of nautical camping. To be fair to Mieke, her complaints to Jaap about the appalling living conditions were no louder, or more vociferous, than anyone else's;

Main deck bathroom. Oriental Tug No. 2 *in Abidjan*

her strident and assertive female voice simply made them just a little more noticeable and clearly heard. Having said that, we were all in the same boat, we were all members of the same crew and Mieke, like us all, had accepted her contract quite willingly and without coercion.

To say that Remy and I were even slightly disillusioned would have been the understatement of the year: we had both pledged, quite independently, that we would never again sail in conditions similar to our previous voyage on the Mississippi river tugboat, the *Justine*, and yet here we were, being confronted once more with squalor equal to, or possibly even worse than before.

No one argued with Jaap's managerial decision that we should stay in the hotel for another night. He too was clearly embarrassed by what he had seen during the course of the day. We would start again in the morning.

Shwe Myint and Tin Nyunt

During the afternoon, shortly after the Liberian crews had left the boat, I had the opportunity to sit quietly in the mess to talk with Shwe and Tin. I wanted to learn what life had been like for them living aboard the *Oriental Tug No. 2* in Buchanan.

My visit four years previously, when the boat had been named *Eden*, had given me the briefest of insights into what might have been expected. I was very curious to know if my initial fears had been overly pessimistic, or whether conditions had improved with the passing of time.

Shwe, the captain, had been in Liberia for an incredible two years and eight months. He is a short man with a wiry and typically slim oriental build, and a thin, weather-seasoned face etched with deep lines across his brow and cheeks that give him a friendly and permanently warm expression. When we first came on board his hair was uncharacteristically long and curly, hiding his ears and sweeping down over his shirt collar in the traditional hippy style of the seventies. It gave him an almost distinguished, but unconventional, appearance, which added a certain mystique to his features that made you want to look twice, or more closely at him. He exudes peace and sincerity. Quietly spoken, I never once heard him raise his voice during

Left: Watchkeeping Officer Shwe Myint; Right: Second Engineer Tin Nyunt. Oriental Tug No. 2

the three months I sailed with him. He was born in 1958 in Yangon, or Rangoon, as it was known then, and still is today in most traditional circles.

The mention of his birthplace brought back countless happy memories of my many visits to Rangoon in the middle and late 1960s, when I had been sailing aboard a cargo liner initially as a deck cadet, and then later as third officer. I watched his eyes moisten momentarily as I talked of visiting the magnificent Shwe Dagon temple, and how I had been totally overawed by the 100-metre-high pagoda covered in gold leaf that glistens glaringly in the bright Asian sunshine. I recalled seeing the Buddhist monks with their shaven heads and dressed in their shapeless saffron-coloured robes, and hearing, but not understanding, their worshipful chanting and the deep, strident notes emitting from the huge gongs that were being struck every so often without apparent rhyme or reason. We laughed when I remembered how I had been told by the old toothless ship's carpenter from Liverpool never to look back at the Shwe Dagon as we sailed down the river estuary towards the open sea. Even the most surreptitious of glances back, the carpenter had assured me, would mean I would be destined to return at a later date, and Rangoon was really not the sort of place I should think about visiting too often. In the same breath, he had told me that despite never once looking back at the temple when his ship was proceeding out to sea, he had revisited Rangoon on every single voyage he had made in the previous twenty years. I had come to the conclusion, and both Shwe and Tin agreed, that giving the Shwe Dagon a backward glance was probably one of those magical myths that had originated in some ancient seafarer's fantasy or maritime legend.

I remembered the loading of the huge teak logs, one of Myanmar's principal exports. They were floated downriver, lashed together in enormous and virtually unmanageable rafts, to be moored alongside the ship. The logs were then hoisted on board one by one, swinging precariously on a length of chain that had been passed under the log and secured by merely wrapping the end of the chain around itself a few times. I can, even now, recall hearing the hatch foreman excitedly shouting his orders and frantically waving his hand signals to the winchmen who controlled the hoisting wires of the two derricks rigged in union-purchase fashion over the hatch square and the ship's side. Manoeuvring and lowering the over-long and swinging tree trunks down through the hatch opening to the men waiting patiently below inside the ship's holds was a skilled and dangerous job. I can still picture the sarong-clad stevedores, either in bare feet or in flip-flops, releasing the chain, and then accurately flipping the logs into position so that they ended up as one solid and immovable mass, safe and secure for the long sea passage ahead.

I made Shwe and Tin laugh with my story of the Chinese carpenters, who were employed by the captain every time we visited Rangoon to assist the ship's carpenter in making new wooden hatchboards for the voyage ahead. On the particular voyage in question, when not so many hatchboards had been required, he had utilised their cabinet-making skills to make him a complete teak bedroom suite comprising bed ends, two bedside tables, a dressing table and a chest of drawers, and a large wardrobe that had to be carefully dismantled before it could be stored in the pilot's cabin for the homeward voyage. It had been an extremely fascinating and unforgettable experience watching the gang of local carpenters outside the chippy's workshop inside the fo'c'sle head, squatting for hour upon hour on their haunches holding pieces of cut timber between their gnarled toes as if they were vices, while the wood was carefully planed to size and cleverly jointed ready for later assembly.

The finished furniture had looked absolutely beautiful, a tribute to the patience and expertise of the carpenters, and our commodore captain had been very pleased. He was slightly less than pleased upon arriving at Birkenhead at the end of the voyage some ten weeks later to discover that the air conditioning in the pilot's cabin had been left running continuously for the whole of the passage. The cool and dehumidified air had dried the freshly cut wood so aggressively that it had split on almost every surface and become warped and misshapen out of all recognition. He took his twisted and useless teak bedroom suite home in pieces in the back of his car to cut up as firewood, the most expensive hatchboards the company had ever unknowingly purchased in all the years of sailing their ships on the Ceylon and Burma service.

We talked about the Shan state in the south of the country located along the border with Thailand, where the peasants make handwoven 'Shan bags', a small type of intricately and colourfully decorated cloth shoulder bag. In my visits to Rangoon I must have purchased from one of the stevedore foremen more than a hundred bags, which I then sold on to a local shopkeeper back home in North Wales for a threefold profit to supplement my meagre wages as a permanently poor and cash-strapped deck cadet. Flower power and hippies ensured that demand outstripped supply. The money I earned from the bags gave me the finances to purchase second-hand suit jackets in the Birkenhead Sunday market prior to sailing for Burma. These were then sold for a generous mark-up to the stevedores in Rangoon to permit me to buy more Shan bags. And so the world goes round.

Tin Nyunt, the chief engineer, had been on board for only eight months. I say 'only', not because an absence from home of eight months should be considered as of being of no real significance, but by comparison to Shwe's interminable two years and eight months away. Taller than Shwe, and with a slightly heavier build, Tin still appeared undernourished, without an ounce of spare fat. He has a rounded face, large and sparkling dark eyes, and a pale oriental complexion. On one side of his chin he proudly sports a small mole from which a few nurtured strands of long facial hair escape the cutting edges of both razors and scissors, as is the Asian custom. Like Shwe, Tin possesses a friendly and agreeable nature, a wonderfully warm and happy smile and a soft, almost melodic voice that I never heard raised. Born in 1961, he had every intention of marrying his devoted girlfriend as soon as he arrived back in Yangon. From the way Tin talked, there was never any doubt in my mind that she would still be waiting for him, had he spent many years away from his home.

We started discussing Buchanan and how life had been aboard the tugboat. They told me their stories, slowly and without exaggeration or embellishment, since that would have been against their nature. I found their fortitude and ability to make do and mend against all the odds not only incredible, but also almost unbelievable.

Most basic commodities had been either completely unavailable, in short supply, or so expensive as to be beyond their limited budget. In the thirty-two months he had been on board, the only fresh meat Shwe had ever eaten had been chicken wings. They laughed and shrugged their shoulders when I asked if the local chickens had lived sufficiently long to develop either breasts or legs. They had been able occasion-ally to scrounge some tins of cooked meat from a visiting ship, but only if the local officials hadn't stolen them first. No wonder they both gave the appearance of being anorexic. Rice could be purchased along with an intermittent supply of locally grown vegetables, but the likes of sugar, coffee, spices, milk, tinned goods, and such basics as toilet paper and soap were unheard of luxuries. The local authorities with their inconsiderate habit of pilfering the storerooms of the visiting ships as soon as they had berthed, made the scrounging of essential items all the more difficult for those on the tugboats. Joining the ranks of officials and being given a uniform, even as one of the lowest of the low, was probably the most sought after local dream. It meant gaining access to prized commodities that would otherwise never be seen, as we had had the misfortune to discover when we had arrived on the *Eden* four years previously. The Myanmars had managed to supplement their meagre diet by occasionally catching fish but, with several poisonous varieties living within the polluted harbour, they had to be careful. Even acquiring a fishing line and a simple hook had proved not so easy.

Shwe and Tin shook their heads when I enquired about 'Dickie' and 'Bow'. I realised they would never have introduced themselves by nicknames given to them by the master of a delivery crew, but I was surprised to learn that there had been no Thais aboard when Shwe had arrived on the scene. Perhaps they had been thoroughly sensible and had made an early escape from Liberia back to their homes in Thailand.

The shortage of fresh water presented a huge and continuous problem. Water supplies inside the dock area were non-existent, but there was a standpipe of sorts in the centre of town from which the local population filled their buckets or containers. During the rainy season, the ever-resourceful Myanmars had to improvise by rigging up large water catchments made from plastic sheeting that could funnel the rainwater into both the tugs' tanks. The collected rainwater then had to last them throughout the year until the next rainy season some seven months later. The 22 tons of fresh water had to be shared by half a dozen men for the washing of hot and sweaty bodies, cleaning clothes, and cooking and drinking. Surviving on 18 litres of water per person per day requires draconian measures and the strictest of controls. Shwe and Tin's very practical solution of placing oil drums filled with water inside the two bathrooms had suddenly become an immensely sensible idea that not only effectively reduced consumption, but also removed the risk of finding a tap left running or having a water pipe leak.

The supply of fuel was another area of great difficulty. The Oriental Timber Corporation, which probably owned the two tugboats through subsidiary or parent companies, had also been granted the logging and exporting timber rights in the south-east of the country, along with the full management control of the port of Buchanan. The company's diesel fuel, which was held in tanks ashore, was a strictly rationed commodity intended mainly to supply the dozens of trucks and machines involved in the logging operation. Shwe and Tin told me that the two tugboats received only minimal quantities at any one time: barely sufficient to ensure the company's exporting operation didn't come to a complete standstill. When lying idle, which was for a large part of the year since they were assisting only two ships a month in and out of the port, they had to berth alongside one another and connect a power cable between them so that one boat's generator could provide the electrical requirements of both boats together. Faced with the harsh economics of frugality, it was an extremely effective method of conserving their precious fuel.

Spare parts and assisted shoreside maintenance were out of the question. The two chief engineers worked as a team, helping each other whenever possible to plan and carry out essential maintenance. Breakdowns and failures were of real concern, with sacrifices invariably having to be made if an essential piece of machinery failed. Spare parts were robbed from Peter in order to pay Paul, until Peter became a dying breed when there was virtually nothing left to be purloined. The boats had slowly, but surely, ground to a virtual halt. Without spares there was very little the engineers could do; miracles had already been achieved by their ingenuity and their improvisational skills.

Their social life had been what they made of it, although there was a bit of the 'dark horse' in Shwe. He revealed he had got married in Buchanan. I suspect that at this point his English became somewhat confused. It had not been a wedding as we know it, with the usual bouquets of flowers and singing and expensively dressed relatives congregating together in a church or temple, but a civil affair without ceremony, witnesses or any official in attendance. It may have been a marriage of convenience perhaps, but one without vows or the issuing of a marriage certificate. I thought a meeting of opposite sexes would have been a more accurate description; Shwe and a young local lady had met, they had talked, and later they had agreed to cohabit. Shwe had claimed his conjugal rights, and in return his 'wife' had claimed some financial assistance towards the housekeeping and the upkeep of her home. The result of the union was the birth of their daughter – a little girl of mixed Afro-Asian blood, who would grow up not only never knowing her father, but also wondering why her features appeared so different from those of the other local children. She was just under one year old when her daddy left town. Shwe had not the slightest intention of ever returning to Liberia, of that I was quite convinced. Perhaps a little later in life her mother would explain how, once upon a time, a Burmese captain had arrived in the port and visited home.

The second civil war to be waged in Liberia within a few short years had arrived in Buchanan. Sailing the two boats from their home port to Abidjan had been navigation by trees. The radars and GPS systems on both boats had fallen victim a couple of years before to the high temperatures and unbearable humidity of the African summer. The only navigational aids available to Shwe and Maung were two out-of-date charts and the magnetic compasses on each boat. They had steered their way by recognition and instinct. Having made the trip on one prior occasion to bunker essential fuel when none had been available to them in Buchanan, there were some landmarks they remembered that could be identified on the chart. They had no sextants or navigational books with which to calculate their position, only the knowledge that, by sailing east and following the coastline, they would eventually arrive at the lagoon entrance marking the channel into the port of Abidjan. Shwe and Maung had each spent nearly fifty-five hours continuously on their bridges, hand steering the two boats along the West African coast, assisted only occasionally by the two chief engineers. The local Liberian crews had, apparently, taken no interest in the proceedings, only sailing to make up the numbers and to ensure that they eventually received their wages. Four hundred and thirty very long miles later they arrived safely in Abidjan, tired and exhausted, but physically safe.

It was little wonder they had been so relieved to see us two or three days later. Whether they went home or decided to sail with us to Singapore, an immense burden of responsibility was being lifted from their shoulders. They more than deserved the break after the length of time they had been on board.

The sting

As the ship's chandler was unable to provide any new bedding until the following day, Jaap's decision that we should all spend another night in the hotel was not totally unexpected. It would require many more hours than those remaining in the late afternoon and early evening to make the lower deck habitable and the bathrooms even remotely hygienic. Shwe and Tin, along with Captain Maung on No. 1 tug, seemed perfectly happy to stay aboard their respective boats and showed no apparent concern at having to sleep on their old and filthy mattresses for another night. They declined our invitation to eat with us back at the hotel, clearly preferring to prepare their own meal from some basic stores that had been delivered earlier in the day. I suspected they were looking forward to a few hours on their own, and the opportunity to sort themselves out without either the Liberians or us to distract them.

Sitting in the minibus travelling back to the hotel I realised we were probably about to enjoy our last night of creature comforts for quite some time, possibly until the end of the voyage a few weeks away. The questionable pleasures of taking a cold shower standing in a rusty steel cubicle and rinsing our faces with water from a 200-litre oil drum in the middle of a dingy and dirty bathroom were likely to be no more than just a few hours away. I had seen Jaap's reaction to the state of the two boats and knew that deep down he had some very real concerns about the appalling conditions we all faced. By extending the number of nights we stayed in the hotel he was doing his level best to keep us as comfortable as possible for as long as possible. He had an ulterior motive: it was not beyond the realms of probability that, if the two crews were to spend a long time living aboard the boats in Abidjan before we sailed, someone would declare that enough was enough and go home before the voyage had even started. The ripple effect would begin and before long there would be no one left on board to honour the company's contract.

We were enjoying our evening meal in the hotel when the new second engineer entered the dining room to introduce himself. He had just flown out from Holland to replace the Myanmar chief engineer, who had been repatriated to Rangoon a couple of days earlier. The complement of No. 1 tug was back to full strength again. We held back the serving of our main course until he had left his luggage in his room and joined us for the remainder of the meal. Like the previous nights, there was very little inclination to stay up late, and after a nightcap at the bar we retired to our rooms for what was likely to be our last night's sleep for at least a few weeks in a large and comfortable air-conditioned room.

Breakfast was a quiet and subdued affair before we handed in our keys for the final time at reception. We met up outside to load the few items of missing baggage, which had been located in France, into the back of the minibuses before boarding for our one-way trip from the city centre back to the boats and the Carena shipyard. The mood was one of sombre and silent resignation as we waited patiently to set off.

No one could recall seeing Arno, the new second engineer, at breakfast, and he was nowhere to be found outside. Jaap checked with reception only to discover that he had left the hotel without checking out after receiving a wake-up call at 6.30 in the morning. He had been accompanied by a couple of well-dressed local gentlemen, and had been seen in the back seat of a car being driven away with them. A member of the hotel staff took Jaap up to Arno's room. A quick search revealed his passport and wallet were not with his other documents in his flight bag, although his suitcase and hand luggage were still lying undisturbed on the baggage stand.

Jaap stayed behind at the hotel to make further enquiries while we travelled down to the boats to carry on with the repairs and cleaning. Our cellphones never stopped ringing as Jaap kept us posted on his progress in his search for our young colleague. Both hospitals and the police had been called, but to no effect. Arno was neither receiving medical attention, nor being held in one of the local jails under arrest. The tape from the security cameras covering the hotel reception and lobby were examined and showed him leaving the main entrance, apparently quite willingly and not under duress. The two local guys escorting him had obviously been aware of the security measures and had succeeded in keeping their faces hidden. The strip of film would be of little or no use in identifying them. Arno had quite simply disappeared into the depths of beyond.

As the morning dragged on, we became all the more anxious, knowing full well that West Africa is not one of the most desirable of places to go missing. He was already a member of our team despite only joining us the previous evening. It made absolutely no difference that he was barely known to most of his new shipmates. Mieke's shout of relief a couple of hours later signalled that Arno had managed to call Jaap on his cellphone to explain that he was without any money and sitting safely in the lounge of a hotel on the opposite side of the city. A short while later, after returning to the Novotel to collect his luggage, he was climbing the gangway with Jaap. I'm quite sure there would have been a celebration party had we had some beer on board.

The story was told in Dutch, and then repeated in English. Arno had been the unwary victim of a quite clever scam. After leaving the bar the night before, he had received a telephone call in his room instructing him to be in the hotel lobby at 6.45 in the morning, where the ship's agents would collect him to take him to the immigration authorities. Quite innocently he had followed the instructions and two local men, purporting to be the ship's agents, had met him at reception. They had shown him their business cards as proof of identity and to confirm they were from the right agency. After ensuring he had his passport and wallet, they set off in a car to another hotel, where they would be meeting the immigration officer who would be authorising a 'temporary entry visa'. Cups of coffee were arranged in the second hotel while they patiently waited for the 'officer', who had been unexpectedly delayed.

Shortly after nine o'clock in the morning and just after the banks had opened, the 'agents' suggested that some time might be saved if they visited the nearby bank, where Arno should withdraw local currency to the value of 500 American dollars, which was the fee for the appropriate visa. His suspicions that the procedure appeared to be somewhat irregular were put at rest by the convincing reassurances of the 'agents' that he would be reimbursed in the agency office later upon presentation of the immigration department receipt. He reluctantly agreed to walk over the road to the bank, where he withdrew the money using his credit card.

They returned to the hotel and were served yet more coffee while they waited. Another telephone call was made to the 'immigration officer', who advised that, due to the unavoidable delays, the arrangements and meeting place had been changed. Arno, rather naively with the benefit of hindsight, relinquished control of his money to the 'agents', who assured him that they would return in fifteen minutes with the visa. As far as I'm aware, he's still waiting to this day.

The crime was reported to the police, who readily admitted it was unlikely that the perpetrators would ever be apprehended. Our genuine agents told Jaap that it was not the first time such a sting had occurred. The crooks were well informed, not only having prior knowledge of the particular shipping agency to which their intended victim had been assigned, but also of his full name, the name and room number of the hotel and the number of nights he would be staying, and the name and details of the ship he would be joining. It was a simple but exceedingly clever scam, which was more than likely to succeed with the young, gullible, and more inexperienced seafarer. It was thought the con men had 'friends' in the immigration department at the airport, who would be able to glean most of the information required for the sting from the details on the entry card that every passenger must complete upon arrival in the country. The missing link to the equation was establishing in which hotel their victim would be staying: an underpaid hotel receptionist, an agent's runner with expensive tastes, the taxi drivers, or simply a telephoned line of enquiry to the few international hotels in the city would soon reveal the information they needed.

A rather chagrined, but slightly relieved, Arno was back among his friends and shipmates. Although his bank account was 500 dollars poorer, he was safe and unharmed, and richer in the knowledge of having an unforgettable, albeit undesirable, experience he could pass on to his grandchildren later in life.

Final preparations

Despite the distraction of temporarily losing Arno, the emergency repairs on both boats were progressing surprisingly well. Remy pronounced himself reasonably satisfied with the quality of work being carried out by the shipyard, with one generator already back in use and providing electrical power. Repairs were continuing with the second generator, and both the main-engine and generator-engine cooling water systems, which had previously seen many sections of corroded pipework patched and welded, and patched again, were having some lengths of pipe renewed and the valves repaired.

Our stay in the Carena shipyard was not intended to be a lengthy or protracted affair: we were only there to carry out those repairs we considered to be essential for safely making the sea passage north along the West African coast to Las Palmas in the Canary Islands. The seasonal weather, the requirements of the boats' insurers, and the need to take sensible precautions had already determined our voyage plan: we would be sailing the long way round to the Far East via the Mediterranean, Suez Canal and the Red Sea, and across the Indian Ocean.

The middle of winter in the southern hemisphere and the age and neglected condition of the two boats had all been influential in rejecting the shortest route to Singapore, via South Africa and the Cape of Good Hope. After rounding the Cape we could well have been faced with the steep and huge mountainous seas that can be encountered off Durban, 'abnormal waves' as they are so appropriately named in the pilot books. The 20-metre-high walls of seawater and the seemingly bottomless holes that can suddenly appear in the ocean without any warning make no allowance for the size or type of ship. Extensive structural damage and, more critically, personal injuries can sometimes occur. I was certainly happy not to be facing the dangers of abnormal waves and the unpredictable South African winter, where a tugboat could be overwhelmed, swamped, or even possibly sunk. Steaming north to the sultrier climate of the Canary Islands would be a far kinder voyage for the two old and worn-out boats and their crews. The downside would be the hassle and bureaucratic nightmare of the Suez Canal, every seafarer's most intensely disliked waterway, and the unbearable and suffocating heat of the Red Sea in the height of the summer.

While the repairs continued unabated in the engine room, Marco and I kept ourselves busy in the wheelhouse, unpacking the cases of standard ship delivery equipment that had been carried out from Holland, and installing the GPS position-finding receiver and the portable satellite communications unit that would keep us linked to the outside world for the duration of our trip. I remembered the unfortunate positioning of the antenna with its broomstick taped to the handle of the fire monitor four years previously in Avonmouth. I managed this time to find a more suitable location on the monkey island that would ensure uninterrupted reception, and be less likely to attract the attention of any visiting, or over-inquisitive, radio surveyor.

Pieter and I discussed and agreed a voyage plan to our first port of call, Las Palmas, which detailed our intended route and identified suitable ports of refuge where further emergency repairs could be carried out. Sailing in convoy and having to keep the boats together at all times would mean consultation and joint agreement, at least in principle, on our route for every inch of the thousands of miles to Singapore. Pilot books, tide tables, light lists and all the other assorted nautical publications for the voyage were sorted out, checked off and tidied away into the chart-table drawers. Navigational waypoints were plotted, courses and distances listed, and pencilled lines representing our intended track laid off on the charts. In the wheelhouse we were ready to start our fifteen-day voyage towards Las Palmas.

On deck we turned our attention to safety matters. We prepared emergency muster lists and boat lists and made an inventory of the limited safety and life-saving equipment on board. As there were no testing facilities available in Abidjan, the classification society and insurers had already stipulated that all the equipment would have to be landed ashore in Las Palmas for careful examination by authorised specialist companies before the statutory safety certificates required to make the ongoing voyage would be issued. Four years of make-do-and-mend, even with the very best of intentions, could never be considered a substitute for proper maintenance and regular surveys. I had absolutely no quarrel with the authorities' requirements: they were, after all, acting in our, and every other seafarer's, best interests.

The accommodation cleaning was never going to be easy, the situation being made all the more difficult by having insufficient time available to do the work and by its position at the lower end of our priority list. There always seemed to be a more important task to hand than making our living quarters and cabins clean and even remotely habitable.

My cabin, like everyone's, was a disaster area. Not only was it filthy dirty, but it had also been modified during the four years in Buchanan. I could understand and cope with the grime: when fresh water is at a premium and cleaning materials are completely non-existent, it is inevitable that bulkheads and furniture will become stained and mucky. The dirt was not the real problem: my concerns lay with the nipple-pink and lime-green linoleum floor covering that had been poorly fitted and was cracked in various places from being compressed and trodden down onto the slightly uneven floor tiles underneath. As it was clearly from the same roll that had been laid in the wheelhouse, I couldn't face the awful prospect of both living and working for the next few weeks of the voyage with the garish pink and lime squares. They offended my eyes and were simply far too psychedelic for my old-fashioned and conservative tastes. Mercifully, Shwe hadn't stuck the linoleum down, probably because the adhesive wouldn't have been available in Buchanan, and it lifted without any real difficulty. Brittle with compression and age, it came away in small and easily handled pieces. Fortunately, the vinyl floor tiles underneath, although dirty and marked, were undamaged. A couple of hours later, after a relentless scrubbing with wire wool and Brillo pads, and with a cocktail of soaps and bleach far more effective than paint stripper, I judged my own cabin to be clean and reasonably fit for habitation.

I also took the plunge and removed the two pictures of a smiling Buddha that had been taped to the bulkhead above the bunk light. I didn't wish to offend Shwe in any way, but I reasoned that had he wanted to keep the pictures when moving cabins, he would have taken them down himself. I didn't particularly like the idea of having Buddha, whether smiling or just downright miserable, peering down at me every time I opened my eyes after being asleep. I felt it might have been just a little too scary and intrusive, not that I have anything against Buddha personally.

Heaven knows how the Myanmars had managed to acquire the four window-type air-conditioning units that had been installed, presumably as a privilege of rank, in the captain's and chief engineer's cabins on both the tugboats; perhaps some kindly manager in Singapore had taken pity on them and had arranged for the units to be shipped out on one of the visiting ships. Electricity supplies were still unavailable in Buchanan, and so it was highly unlikely that they would have been stocked in the local shops. The side-facing porthole in the two upper cabins on each boat had been removed, and the circular hole in the steel plate on the side of the superstructure crudely enlarged and reshaped to accept the rectangular unit. I suspected their untidy installation probably rendered our loadline certificates invalid, but, seeing that they were only one of the many trading documents to have already expired, it made little or no difference for the passage to Las Palmas. No doubt the Spanish surveyors would insist upon the units' removal and the reinstatement of the portholes, but for the time being there was very little that could be done with the extremely rough-and-ready modifications to the steelwork. We would just have to grin and bear it and accept the reasonably comfortable and cool atmosphere in our cabins gratefully and without too many complaints, and not dwell upon the sweaty, stale and airless conditions our shipmates were facing in their cabins two decks down and below the waterline.

In the afternoon the ship's chandler delivered the new mattresses, bedlinen and pillows. We threw the old and festering mattresses out into a heap on the aft deck, never expecting to see them all disappear within a few minutes. A short while later, on the approach road to the dockyard, a line of stained and filthy old mattresses could be seen as if walking on air towards the outskirts of the city. They would be given a new lease of life, no doubt either to be sold in the local market, or lovingly presented to the young wife or unsuspecting girlfriend as a very special hut-warming present. At least they weren't being wasted.

The two cooks, Mieke and Mark, had been busy all afternoon stowing the stores and trying, whenever the opportunity occurred, to clean their galleys to achieve something resembling a hygienic condition. It was a thankless and seemingly endless task that had absolutely no hope of being completed in time for the preparation of our evening meal. Neither galley came anywhere close to European standards for catering and cleanliness, although our Asian colleagues clearly thought differently by willingly accepting the accumulated grime and filth of fours years in Buchanan.

Remy, Mieke, myself, and a couple of others from No. 1 tug accepted Jaap's invitation to return to the hotel for our evening meal, while the remainder decided to go native and investigate the local shanty village just outside the shipyard gates. They were assured there would be no problems with their personal safety provided they stayed close together in a group, but whether the same would apply to their digestive systems after dining in the village remained to be seen. Seafarers are known for their adventurous eating habits and forgiving stomachs.

The first night aboard any ship, whether it be tugboat, tanker or container vessel, is always a little disturbed. Both body and brain need time to adjust to the new and strange surroundings, the unfamiliar smells, and the all too familiar noises that hadn't been heard for several weeks. I had completely forgotten that Remy snores, a loud, rasping, and snorting rattle that reverberates noisily and irregularly from deep within his oesophagus, with the strength to penetrate the back and beyond of even the deafest of salty seadog's eardrums. The single layer Formica wall panel that constituted the flimsy bulkhead separating our two cabins and bunks did absolutely nothing to reduce its volume. To all intents and purposes it was as if we were sharing the same bed, but not the same bedding. It was a restless night without much sleep. To make matters worse, the new mattress felt as hard and lumpy as a boulder-strewn pebble beach, and the new pillows as if they had been stuffed with anything other than foam, duck-down or feathers. The chances of having a proper rest appeared to be stacked heavily against me.

Apart from feeling dog-tired, the new day started well. There seemed little to prevent us from sailing in the afternoon. Most of the shipyard repairs were on their way to being completed, and most of our stores were on board. A new toilet seat, pink in colour especially for Mieke, had been supplied by the ship's chandler and lashed down with thin rope in a seaman-like manner to the top of the toilet bowl in the main deck bathroom. As the once-white porcelain at the back of the bowl was cracked and missing, the securing studs and wing nuts supplied with the seat were of little use. If buttocks and boat stayed steady and still, the rope lashing would ensure the seat remained in position and usable; a more difficult scenario would be hard to imagine with a small tugboat at sea at the mercy of the wind and the waves. There was little more we could do to improve the bathrooms until we arrived in Las Palmas.

The galley cleaning continued while we started making our final inspections in preparation for sailing. We didn't get far before Marco, who had been sealing the deck vents with heavy-duty plastic garbage bags to prevent the ingress of seawater in any bad weather, found large holes in a heavily corroded tank vent pipe just above the level of the main deck. Carefully checking the other vent pipes, we found three more to be in a similarly wasted and potentially dangerous condition. Using brute force and ignorance, we managed to break the rotten steel pipes off at deck level. The open holes leading into the fuel and ballast tanks below were then closed with wooden plugs and covered with hand-mixed cement held in place by rough-and-ready wooden shuttering salvaged from some broken pallets. The crude repair would be sufficiently effective in keeping seawater out until we arrived in Las Palmas, although we knew that we would have to carefully avoid pressurising or drawing a vacuum on the tanks to which the air-pipes had been sealed. We carried on with our inspections.

Jaap wore the contented and happy smile of a well-practised and confident magician having successfully confounded his disbelieving audience and critics with a new and impossibly difficult act. He had somehow managed, against all the odds, to plan and organise the preparations for the voyage without too much time being lost and, more importantly, without a single crew member from either tug having called it a day and gone home. We were as ready as we would ever be, with sufficient fuel, fresh water and food on board for the passage to Las Palmas. The local harbour pilots were ordered for two o'clock in the afternoon and a delighted Jaap confirmed his booking with the agents for an evening flight back home to Holland. For him, Abidjan and West Africa were soon to become distant memories.

Just after lunch the lights went out on No. 1 tug. A major electrical fault had occurred, causing the generator to trip off the main switchboard. No amount of gentle inducement would persuade it, or the spare generator, to go back on line. The shore power cable that Tin had been using in Buchanan to link the two boats together electrically was put back into service so that we could supply power to No. 1 tug until the problem was resolved. The pilots were cancelled and the shoreside electricians asked to attend. Africa was going to remain on our horizon for yet another night.

We convinced a very disheartened Jaap that there was little to be gained by his remaining behind, and that he should catch his flight home as planned. He reluctantly departed after seeking reassurances that we would keep him updated with our fault-finding progress. Some three hours later, the problem was traced to a short circuit in No. 1 tug's galley stove. Their chief engineer, Willem, promised to have the stove working again, minus the short circuit, by midday the following day.

As no one was prepared to commit themselves to a second culinary delight in the nearby shanty town, Mieke managed to work a catering miracle and rustled up an enjoyable evening meal to feed both the crews before some of us went ashore to stretch our legs and to sample the local beer. Mustering up the courage to take a cold shower in the revolting rusty cubicle, I joined Remy, Marco and a couple of the others from No. 1 tug in a quiet wander through the dusty and compacted-earth surfaced streets. The buildings and tumbledown shacks were, without exception, all of wood and corrugated iron construction, some a lot more decrepit than others. There was the usual confusion of electrical cables often seen in such villages, accompanied by the frequent and overpowering wafts of raw and untreated sewage. Horrific smells and the loud sound of music seemed to accompany us wherever we walked. We peered into a couple of semi-darkened and uninviting bars before finding one with an outside terrace and a seating area that overlooked the river close to the yard.

It wasn't long before we were besieged by a bevy of prostitutes dressed either in seam-splitting jeans, or impossibly tight and revealing miniskirts. There were some tall ones and some short ones, some with teeth and some without, some boasting huge and gravity-defying matronly bosoms, and some slightly less well-endowed. Despite their physical differences, they all had one thing in common, the ability to flutter their eyelids and false lashes while asking for drinks, and to offer eternal and undying love had we been so foolish, or gullible, as to buy them one. There was absolutely no sexual attraction to the human wares on offer and, with the potential risks of catching all sorts of nasty diseases or Aids, neither encouragement nor drinks were given. We had an enjoyable evening, watched over closely by our enthusiastic audience of ever-optimistic and persistent young ladies, supped one or two local beers which were surprisingly good and quite cheap, and made our way back through the repair yard gates before they were closed and locked at midnight.

The second night on board was yet another noisy affair. I must have dozed off once or twice, but the new mattresses and pillows were unbelievably hard and lumpy. From the loud complaints I heard in the mess at breakfast time, I wasn't the only one to be suffering from the inferior quality of the local bedding.

Willem was as good as his word: by mid-morning and with the assistance of the local electricians, he had managed to persuade the offending cooker to work without causing the generators to trip off the board. While his repairs could only be considered to be of a temporary nature, they would be sufficient in keeping No. 1 tug in hot food to Las Palmas, where either a new cooker, or further electrical assistance, would be available. The harbour pilots were ordered for a second time.

We spent over an hour searching the boat from top to bottom and from side to side checking for stowaways, until we were confident there were no unwanted guests residing on board. Abidjan has the unenviable reputation for being one of the most popular ports in West Africa from which persons escaping their countries will make the attempt. Stowaways provide every shipmaster with his worst possible nightmare. There becomes an enormously complicated diplomatic and bureaucratic problem if the vessel should enter international waters before the stowaway has either been found or has given himself up. It is often the case that the intrepid escapee will either have no identification papers or have hidden them somewhere on board never to be found. In this modern age of multinational societies and illegal immigration, it is virtually impossible to locate a country willing to accept a stateless person.

Hopefully with no stowaways to cause us such problems, our final checklists for departure were completed in readiness for sailing. The pilots boarded shortly before one o'clock. Two uneventful hours later we had steamed across the lagoon, disembarked the pilots at its entrance, and were on our way into the Atlantic Ocean and a distant Las Palmas. The voyage to Singapore had finally begun.

3

A TRIP TO LAS PALMAS

Fire down below

With the disembarking of the pilots into the pilot cutter stationed just outside the entrance to the lagoon, we were away and truly on our own for the first time since flying out to Côte d'Ivoire eight days earlier. Every ship's Master will confirm the conflicting senses of both elation and apprehension that are experienced when taking his ship back out to the wind and the waves. After being in port for several days there is an almost overwhelming feeling of liberation and total freedom to be at sea once again. 'A ship in harbour is safe, but that is not what ships are built for,' as William Shedd is supposed to have once said. Unlike many of her close African neighbours, Abidjan and Côte d'Ivoire hadn't caused us too many problems. While we had suffered neither from an excess of petty officialdom nor bureaucratic interference, it was still a port from which I was glad to make my escape.

We headed in convoy slowly out into the Atlantic Ocean and turned onto our westerly course that would keep us steaming parallel to the West African coastline. Despite the questionable pleasure of working the first of many bridge watches, with its incredibly monotonous duty of hand steering the boat, I found it surprisingly relaxing to be listening to and feeling the steady and rhythmic beat and vibration of the main engine as the low and featureless shoreline gradually receded into the distance. My mood was one of almost complete contentment, seeing, feeling, hearing, and simply being with the sea once again, although the heartstrings of home and family life were never too far from my thoughts and emotions.

No. 1 tug steamed ahead of us, a position she was likely to keep for most of the voyage after the successful testing of her automatic pilot, the existence of which Captain Maung had, quite incredibly, known nothing about. He was more than a little peeved to learn that his not inconsiderable feat of hand steering for more than two continuous days on the passage from Buchanan to Abidjan had been totally unnecessary, and that he could have sat back and relaxed for the whole trip and watched the device do his work for him. Following No. 1 tug and laboriously hand steering all the way to Singapore was necessitated by our boat not being equipped with an autopilot. Steering in the wake of our sister would be far less difficult than peering up into the flaking silvered mirrors of the periscope positioned above the electronic tiller and straining to see the poorly reflected and swinging compass card of the magnetic compass located in its binnacle on the monkey island one deck above. I had a vague recollection that hand steering the *Eden* four years before hadn't provided too many difficulties and that, once the bows had been pointed in the right direction, she would maintain her course for quite some distance without wandering off. Only time would tell if my memories were correct.

Both boats would be responsible for their own navigation and position fixing. While following No. 1 tug would make our steering considerably less stressful than would otherwise have been the case, following her into danger would be an acute embarrassment, and any official inquiry would inevitably suggest we had taken companionship and trust just a little too far. For this reason alone, virtually every action planned on either boat had to be with the knowledge and approval of the other. The requirements of convoy sailing would keep us joined together in almost every move we made, although hopefully not in the literal sense.

I settled into the bridge watch-keeping routine and waited for Marco, who was checking that all was secure on deck, to come and relieve me. No sooner had the coastline slipped beyond the horizon than the VHF radio crackled into life to disturb the peace and quiet in the wheelhouse.

Pieter's voice sounded remarkably untroubled and calm.

The author Dave Creamer in the wheelhouse. Oriental Tug No. 2

'No. 2 tug, this is No. 1 tug calling.'

I reached for the radio handset and depressed the speech button to reply.

'Go ahead Pieter, receiving you loud and clear.'

'Dave, we're slowing down, we have a fire in the engine room.'

The hesitation in my reply while I collected my thoughts must have seemed like an interminable age to Pieter.

'A fire in the engine room? Okay, we'll come up alongside you, our port side to your starboard side. We'll get our fire hoses ready to help you.'

'Okay, our ship's head is two-six-five degrees.'

'Two-six-five, we're increasing speed now.'

The alarm bells were rung, and with our crew mustered at their emergency stations, everyone was told of the problem aboard our sister tugboat. A dense and choking cloud of dark smoke could be seen billowing from her funnels as the gap between us quickly closed. Within just a few minutes we were running parallel to each other and matching our speeds. A slight adjustment of our course, followed shortly afterwards by a loud squeal of protesting rubber from the tyre fenders, announced we were safely alongside. Mooring ropes were hastily secured between the two boats at the bow so as to keep us together while we both continued steaming at slow speed. On the stern Marco and the others had already gathered our fire hoses, nozzles, and a couple of out-of-date extinguishers ready to pass them across to No. 1 tug in the event that more equipment was needed in their firefighting efforts.

Mark, No. 1's cook, had gone on deck for a leisurely smoke before preparing the evening meal. Innocently drawing long and hard on the stub of his hand-rolled cigarette, he stood nonchalantly leaning against the side of the accommodation housing, obviously quite unaware of the commotion in the engine room beneath his feet. A slightly bewildered expression could be seen creasing his face as he watched our hurried berthing manoeuvre, but he waited until the two boats were secured together before his curiosity got the better of him. Blissful ignorance and puzzled bemusement turned to horrified disbelief as Marco advised him of the fire under the very deck upon which he was standing. He abruptly stubbed out the remains of his cigarette and bolted through the door into the cross-alleyway. We half expected to see him reappear on deck a few seconds later lacing up his life jacket ready for the final act of abandoning ship, but no doubt more pressing needs in the galley, or sheer embarrassment, kept him from showing his face again. We were to laugh about his contribution to the whole affair for many days afterwards.

Fortunately the fire was not as serious as first thought, although all shipboard fires are extremely serious. After disembarking the pilot and clearing the port, the engine power on both boats had been gradually increased to our planned economic speed for the voyage. Although nowhere near approaching full speed, the revolutions were obviously somewhat higher than the engines had run for many a long day. The subsequent increase in the exhaust gas temperature had been sufficient to ignite some heavily oil-soaked lagging around the main engine exhaust pipes inside No. 1's funnels. Both Willem and Arno were extremely concerned that another conflagration of far greater consequences would be started by the burning particles of lagging material that were dropping off and falling in all directions into the engine room. Happily, the fire died out on its own once the oily residues had burned off, and no lasting damage, or further fires, occurred. Within a few minutes, and without resort to the use of any of our standby firefighting equipment, we slipped the mooring ropes that had been keeping us together and slowly steamed apart before adopting our position behind our sister tug. Our course was set again for Las Palmas.

The problems didn't belong exclusively to No. 1 tug. We had been following our shipmates for only a few minutes when Remy had to stop our main engine. One of the cooling water pipes that had missed being renewed in the Carena shipyard had sprung a leak. Some rubber jointing wound tightly around the offending pipe and secured by three or four jubilee clips temporarily stopped the weeping until more permanent repairs could be made. We were underway again within a short while, although at slightly less speed than before.

The stainless steel expansion bellows on the main engine exhaust trunkings on both the boats were leaking, allowing lethal carbon monoxide fumes to escape into the engine rooms before reaching the funnels and the fresh air outside. Unfortunately our engineers were being asphyxiated in the process. In order to keep the gas levels at an acceptable level and to ensure our engineering shipmates remained alive, the engines would have to be run at lower revolutions until the exhaust systems could be renewed or repaired in the next port.

The repair list for Las Palmas was already lengthening, and we had been at sea for only four hours.

Stowaway

We settled into our watch-keeping routine of four hours on and eight hours off. Having Captains Shwe and Maung as members of our crews permitted us to take advantage of the additional certificated manpower by working a traditional deep-sea three-man watch system, with Shwe and Maung working the four-to-eight watch, Marco and André the twelve-to-four, and Pieter and myself the eight-to-twelve. The two four-hour watches a day were a joy to work when compared with the drudgery of the usual six hours on and six hours off, the dreaded two-man watch system we normally practise that slowly, but inexorably, wearies one's very existence into a totally mindless and lifeless state through lack of a decent sleep. Admittedly my eight hours' work a day, as for both Shwe and Marco, involved hand steering continuously for four hours at a stretch, but this was more than compen-

Left: Chief Officer Andre Van Rooijen, No. 1 tug;
Right: Chief Officer Marco Wehrmann, No. 2 tug

sated for me by the luxury of a whole night in bed from midnight until 8 a.m., seven nights a week.

My first morning watch at sea passed quite quickly, despite feeling tired and irritable from not having slept well the night before. The acute discomforts of the boulder-strewn mattress and the unyielding pillow supplied in Abidjan were proving extremely difficult to overcome and sleep had been, at best, a succession of short and restless catnaps. My memory of the voyage to Buchanan had been correct in that the boat steered reasonably well in calm sea conditions and would remain on course for quite a few minutes without the need to adjust the helm. It meant that we didn't have to stay glued in the one position in front of the bridge console for four hours at a stretch, and could take an occasional break from the chair we had lashed down adjacent to the steering tiller, to stretch our legs and to check the boat's position on the chart. It also allowed me a little freedom to participate in the first of what were to become our regular meetings on the bridge every morning when we could pass the time of day, resolve any problems, and enjoy the freshly percolated coffee that Mieke brought to the wheelhouse in a large thermos flask.

Shortly after Marco had relieved me of the steering duties and bridge watch at midday, I set about preparing the daily position report that had to be sent to Holland every day. Since the satellite communications unit had been installed on our boat, I had been given the role of fleet radio officer. A second set would be provided in Las Palmas so that each boat could have an independent means of communication for the onward voyage to Singapore. As it was Saturday, the office was closed, so there was no real urgency in transmitting the report that included not only our noon position, but also our speed, fuel consumption for each boat, and our estimated arrival date in Las Palmas. I waited patiently for Pieter or André to call me on the VHF radio to advise me of No. 1's fuel figures since sailing. I didn't have to wait long.

'Tug No. 2. Come in No. 2 tug, No. 1 calling.'

'Good afternoon, André, go ahead. I've got a pencil and paper ready.'

'Dave, we've found a stowaway in the engine room.'

The totally unexpected disclosure from André, No. 1 tug's chief officer, stunned me into temporary silence. Unsure whether I had heard André correctly, I turned to Marco, who frowned before giving me one of those raised eyebrow 'it can't be true' looks that confirmed I hadn't been mistaken. My mind raced with the options we had available to us. Although it wasn't the time for recriminations, it immediately crossed my mind to wonder whether our shipmates had carried out a proper stowaway search before leaving the shipyard. While a deep-sea cargo ship or tanker, with its physical size and complexity of design, possesses a multitude of hiding places, a simple harbour tugboat with its compact size and uncomplicated layout is far less demanding to search comprehensively. After checking and eliminating the wheelhouse, monkey island, half a dozen cabins and the mess, an engine room and maybe a fire-monitor platform, there are very few places remaining on a tugboat in which an uninvited guest can remain concealed. Someone had managed to defy all the odds and had beaten the system. I tried to gather my thoughts before replying into the VHF handset.

'Understood, you've got a stowaway on board. Is there only one person?'

'We've only found one so far, but he's staying silent. He doesn't seem to understand any English. I think Pieter is speaking in French to him.'

'Has he got any papers or identification on him?'

'No, we found nothing. He's only wearing shorts and flip-flops.'

'Okay, tell Pieter I'm emailing Jaap straight away.'

'Okey dokes, we'll call again in a few minutes.'

The discovery of the stowaway on board No. 1 tug was a huge inconvenience, and one that had the potential for having far-reaching and costly consequences if we made either a hasty judgement or took the wrong action. Fortunately our unwanted intruder had unwittingly assisted us by mistakenly revealing his presence too early, or by allowing himself to be found before we had progressed even further up the African coast. Marco had been carefully studying the charts and pilot books while I had been questioning André on the VHF radio. It seemed as if we had the choices of either continuing on our voyage to Las Palmas, returning to Abidjan, or heading for the port of San Pédro in Côte d'Ivoire some forty miles distant on our starboard beam. After a brief discussion to consider the options, we altered course towards the coast, knowing we had less than four hours to establish the stowaway's nationality and to try and locate any identification papers he might have brought with him. Jaap replied to my message within a few minutes. The ship's agents in Abidjan had been notified and were contacting the immigration and police departments. We continued steaming towards San Pédro while I spoke to Pieter on the VHF radio.

'Pieter, Dave calling. Come in.'

'Yes, Dave. Pieter is here. I think this guy is from the Ivory Coast. He is only speaking French but is saying he's from Ghana. I think he will speak English if he's living in Ghana but he doesn't know any word of English.'

'Pieter, Jaap is saying we must find his papers. The agents are telling Jaap we cannot land this guy until we have some identification papers. They seem to think he will have brought some documents with him.'

'Okay, I will ask him again, but I don't think he is going to tell me where he has put them.'

A continuous stream of emails flew to and fro between Holland, Abidjan and myself – the wonders of modern instant satellite communications – but after a while the contents and thoughts became repetitive. The message being received was unequivocal: we would not be permitted to land a stowaway in San Pédro without any papers, even though the authorities recognised that it was highly likely that he had climbed aboard in Abidjan, and that he was probably a citizen of Côte d'Ivoire. The understandable, but nonetheless harsh, stateless person scenario was becoming more evident and plausible with every passing minute. I had terrible, nightmarish visions of the stowaway being on board No. 1 tug for the complete voyage to

Singapore unless he somehow managed conveniently to 'jump ship' in one of the intermediate ports during the trip. The company would then lose the high-value financial bond they would have to deposit with the immigration authorities of every country we visited en route to actively discourage such an event from occurring. We were caught up in a costly 'no-win' situation, unless some identification papers could be found, and found quickly.

Willem and Arno had repeatedly searched No. 1's engine room looking for the stowaway's documents, but it was like looking for a needle in a haystack and against the clock. Small pieces of paper in an engine room could be anywhere and time was steadily ticking by, with one and a half hours already gone. We had only another twenty-five miles to go before arriving off San Pédro. The VHF squawked into life once again. It was Pieter and he sounded much happier.

'Dave, the papers have been found. It is as I thought. He is from the Ivory Coast and not Ghana.'

'Okay, Pieter. I need the guy's name and any other information you might have on him, like passport number, age, the usual bullshit.'

'His name is, I spell for you. Mike-Bravo-India-November-Kilo-Alpha-Romeo – new word – Hotel-Alpha-Bravo-India-Lima-Alpha – new word – Kilo-Whisky-Alpha-Golf-Hotel-Bravo-Oscar. Mbinkar Habila Kwaghbo. His date of birth is eighteen March, nineteen-seventy-one. His place of birth is Yamoussoukro, Côte d'Ivoire, and his identity card number is 6594338478. He is also 'male' and 'single'. I don't think there is anything more than that.'

'Thanks, Pieter. I'll send these details to Jaap and the agents.'

No. 1 tug steamed in close to the headland to rendezvous with the pilot boat that had been arranged to transport the stowaway ashore and into police custody in San Pédro. In some respects I felt a little sorry for him and wondered whether he would later think it had all been worth it. He must have been quite desperate to leave Côte d'Ivoire for a better life somewhere else. Maybe he was a criminal on the run from the authorities and saw the *Oriental Tug No. 1* as his means of escaping from justice. Only Mr Kwaghbo could tell us that, and he was already handcuffed and sitting in the pilot boat awaiting the delights of San Pédro's police department and the local judiciary.

We drifted a couple of miles offshore while Pieter disembarked his unwanted and non-fare-paying passenger. The two tugs were together again an hour or so later, and course was set for a position a safe distance off Cape Palmas on the south-eastern coast of Liberia. Inevitably the topic of discussion for the remainder of the evening was the stowaway and what punishment was being meted out to him during the course of our conversation. We could only speculate as to his treatment; no one wished to be in his shoes, or rather flip-flops.

The honours for locating the vital documents should have been conferred on Captain Maung, the Myanmar. While Pieter had been on his bridge talking to me on the VHF radio, Maung had gone onto the main deck and had a quiet word with Mr Kwaghbo, possibly in broken French, or English, or even in Burmese. According to André, who had witnessed the meeting, the results had been quite dramatic. There might well have been a slightly threatening tone in Maung's voice, but what was said, only Maung and the stowaway will ever know. Mr Kwaghbo had started trembling and then shaking violently, obviously scared absolutely witless by the words, or by the tone of the voice he had just heard. His eyes had rolled upwards until only the whites were showing. The reaction was, apparently, as if Maung had delivered a deadly voodoo curse. And then, quite voluntarily and without any further persuasion, he had made some hand signals to Maung indicating where he had hidden his identity papers, close to his place of concealment. Willem found them almost immediately, stashed inside a small aperture behind a pipe just above where his hiding place had been inside the funnel. How he hadn't been asphyxiated or burnt in the fire the day before remains a total mystery.

The stowaway provided the perfect example of appeasement and the effects of such a mistaken and timorous policy. He instinctively knew, but had also probably been told, that his European captors would treat him fairly; he was aware he would come to absolutely no harm in our care. Our laws, whether they are right or wrong, just or unjust, require us to conduct ourselves towards such people with politeness and humanity, irrespective of the cost, or whether the circumstances contain a degree of self-inflicted misfortune. The unfortunate Mr Kwaghbo had, however, recognised his Myanmar interrogator as being someone very different, someone who would not hesitate to carry out his promises; someone from another society who valued human dignity and the sanctity of life on a totally different scale to his European colleagues. He became afraid, and with his fear, he accepted defeat. He had not been touched or bullied, or received any threat of physical abuse. It had been just a few simple words. Had he not revealed the location of his identity card, he might still have been aboard the tugboat today, such is the bureaucratic insensitivity towards stateless persons. A far more likely outcome would have been his escape in Las Palmas, one of the main stepping stones for illegal immigration into Europe from Africa. The company would have ultimately sustained a large financial loss, and Mr Kwaghbo would have made the first of his many underhand moves in integrating himself into a new and unfamiliar society.

His punishment from the local authorities would act as a temporary deterrent to his migratory aspirations, but I was convinced he would try to escape his country again in the not too distant future. It is the African way.

The ITCZ

The weather remained balmy and the seas rippled and slight as we made our way along the Liberian coast. A couple of days after our unscheduled and very brief stopover at San Pédro, we sailed past Buchanan, an indistinguishable speck on the distant horizon that would have remained unnoticed had we not known it was there. Both Shwe and I had absolutely no regrets at being unable to see the town, unanimous in our desire that Buchanan should never again reappear on our seagoing or working itineraries. As in the old carpenter's myth about the Shwe Dagon Pagoda in Rangoon, neither of us looked back over our shoulder to watch the barely visible coastline recede into the distance. Despite the passing of time, I still held a ridiculous but unshakeable misgiving that the unforgettable George H. Too Wesley Senior and his lady friend would suddenly emerge from over the horizon to come back and haunt me. Shwe's concerns were a little more realistic and closer to home. His worries were purely selfish and based on whether we would sail past the port without stopping to visit, and whether he would be able to retreat into cowardly obscurity by escaping an angry confrontation with his abandoned wife and their innocent, but 'fatherless', one-year-old daughter. Nothing was further from the errant Shwe's mind than seeing his African spouse or young child again. Liberia, to him, was already just a passing memory.

The weather reports we were receiving suggested our days of peaceful sailing were coming to an end. We were fast approaching the ITCZ, short for Intertropical Convergence Zone, the area in the tropics where the winds from the two hemispheres converge. Massive and spectacular cloud formations are often created, in which every shape and imaginary face under the sun can be seen and identified by those with fertile and inventive minds; it is also an area where the heavens can open in the most torrential of downpours that can only be matched by the sudden and violently heavy monsoon rains of the Indian subcontinent.

The morning saw the skies slowly surrender their shapely clouds to become threatening and heavily overcast. The winds steadily strengthened to force 5 from the south-west, and then the rain could be seen in the distance, a dark and heavy line advancing quite slowly, but relentlessly, towards our two insignificant little tugboats. A few minutes later the squall was upon us, a solid and unbroken wall of water that deluged down as if we were passing through the very centre of an immense and cascading waterfall swollen with the rains of many rivers in flood.

The puddles of water appeared indiscriminately all over the wheelhouse less than thirty seconds later. The soft rubber gaskets positioned between the steelwork of the bridge front and the brass frames around the wheelhouse windows had perished and were no longer watertight, and the steel deck of the open monkey island that had once provided the weathertight roof for the wheelhouse leaked like a rotten sieve. Rainwater poured in from every conceivable direction, seemingly with the specific aim of drowning our essential items of electrical equipment. The cloudburst couldn't have arrived at a more inconsiderate or unsocial time. The morning coffee break, our precious thirty minutes or so of trivial conversation and lighthearted banter, was hastily abandoned as we battled to protect our global positioning system navigator and our vitally important satellite communications transmitter from being damaged. The loss of either unit would make life incredibly difficult and complicated. Black plastic garbage bags, not only useful for protecting vulnerable ventilator heads against heavy seas, came into their own as plastic rain covers. Within minutes, the wheelhouse gave every appearance of being a garbage disposal site, black bags dotted around over the consoles and chart table, held in place by bits and pieces of lashing twine and strips of silver duct tape. Our efforts to protect some equipment were unsuccessful: we could do nothing to prevent the two glass protective bowls for the interior emergency lights that were mounted on the Formica-panelled wheelhouse deckhead from being slowly but surely filled with water, until the 24-volt light bulbs and fittings were totally submerged. I crossed my fingers and hoped we wouldn't have to resort to emergency power until the bowls had been emptied and the fittings dried out.

Dirty water, 20 to 30 millimetres deep at the deep end, depending upon its movement from the slight rolling of the boat, sloshed noisily around the deck. The sill to the wheelhouse door, and the small steel lip at the top of the stairs going down to the accommodation below, prevented the water from escaping. The psychedelic linoleum that Shwe had unkindly laid over the original ribbed non-slip floor covering was receiving a long-overdue rinsing. It mattered not, for dirty or clean I couldn't envisage the nipple-pink and lime-green squares surviving much beyond Las Palmas; with the boat moving around the shiny and skiddy surface was far too slippery and dangerous to stand on when wet. We struggled on, steering by the magnetic compass because we could no longer see the other tug in the heavy rain, maintaining a lookout, and continuously baling out the water in case it rose above the sill level and poured down the stairs to flood Remy's and my cabins one deck below.

After thirty minutes or so the rain stopped as quickly as it had started and the image-filled clouds returned in their billowing and flowery shapes to scud across the otherwise clear blue sky. The dark line of the rainsquall could be seen fading away into the distance behind us. Our essential radio and position-fixing instruments had survived inside their garbage bag covers and were still operational. One or two charts had become wet from water on the chart table, but would soon dry out. The magnetic compass on the monkey island appeared unscathed, its gently swinging compass card still vaguely visible from the periscope inside the wheelhouse, although we were now back to steering by following in the wake of our sister tug a few hundred metres ahead.

The consequences of being caught in just one heavy rain shower had resulted in the running repair lists for both the boats receiving yet more additions. Our stopover in Las Palmas for repairs was going to be considerably longer than anyone had originally anticipated.

Airs and repairs

Sleeping on what the ship's chandler in Abidjan had deceptively sold as a mattress hadn't become any easier with familiarity or practice. Despite my frequent and often very aggressive pummellings with whatever I could find to hand – usually only my fists, elbows or knees – the hardness, the knobbly bits, and the unevenness stubbornly remained. Sometimes the lumps, which had neither softened nor adapted to my body shape in the slightest, annoyingly appeared to be on the move as if having a life of their very own. Paranoia took over to the extent that sleep would be just a few seconds away when yet another hard and imaginary boulder would suddenly evolve and erupt from the dark blue patterned cotton surface beneath me. That one precious moment, the one we can never quite remember, of slipping into the blissful unconsciousness of a deep and much-needed slumber, would be denied by a sharp and spiteful prod in my back or side. The insomnia brought frustration, and with the frustration came more insomnia, until it became a vicious and unending circle that somehow had to be broken before I became completely and utterly exhausted.

Packing an airbed into my grip before leaving home had been a last-minute decision resulting from one of those hasty but absurd premonitions that a piece of inflatable moulded rubber normally reserved for a lazy day at the seaside might just be useful. Finding it again in my baggage so many days after the voyage had started, folded, limp and airless, and still patiently waiting to be unpacked, was as important to me as the discovery of Tutankhamun's tomb must have been to the Egyptologist Howard Carter. Forty long minutes later, flushed cherry red in the face and with lungs fit to burst, I had finally persuaded the unyielding rubber to adopt a ribbed but lump-free mattress-like shape with a spongy square pillow attached to one end. Given a bucket and plastic spade, a strip of sand, and a coloured handkerchief knotted at the four corners to keep the sun from my head, I could have been destined for a day on the beach.

The Abidjan African mattress was ceremoniously lifted from my bunk and stood on end in the corner of my cabin next to the wardrobe, like a mischievous child in disgrace, while the air mattress proudly took its place on the bed frame. I climbed on, gingerly and very carefully so as not to create any uneven pressure, and listened apprehensively for that unmistakable wet farting noise that would announce with a terrible finality that one of the compartment stopper valves or moulded seams had burst open with my weight. Silence, quite amazingly, ensued, and two hours later I awoke with a start from my desperately needed short course in death, still fully clothed, but refreshed and completely rejuvenated. Made up later with white cotton sheets and a light blanket, my air mattress had become a bed like no other bed I had ever slept upon. I found it just a little disappointing and inexcusable that the mattress designers had made no allowance for the fitting of a pillowcase to complete my very own creature comforts.

We passed Freetown in Sierra Leone during my unplanned yet most welcome afternoon sleep. The city was too far off to be seen, but its mere presence just over the horizon provided another point of reference on the chart to act as a measure of our slow but steady progress. Yet another unused port of refuge could be deleted from the somewhat pessimistic voyage plan we had made prior to sailing from Côte d'Ivoire.

In the early evening the wind strengthened and became westerly, causing the boats to start rolling in the more pronounced seas and longer swell. I hadn't realised the significance of my cabin being on the weather side until the first signs of moisture appeared on the vinyl covering of my bench settee located on the outboard bulkhead. It took me only a few seconds to trace the source of water to the window-box air conditioner and the ineffective seal between the unit and the crudely cut opening in the steel plating of the superstructure. I suspected the unit in Remy's cabin and the two aboard No. 1 tug would be exactly the same. No blame could ever be attached to the two Myanmar captains and chief engineers for fitting the units. Air conditioning had provided about the only degree of comfort available to them in the stifling and unbearable heat of an endless midsummer's day in the sheltered and airless harbour of Buchanan. Their one and only real concern had been the impossibly difficult living conditions confronting them at the time; the likelihood of the boats being employed elsewhere and the consequences of having to make a long sea passage to another port would never have been a consideration when the steelwork had been modified.

A more inquisitive look revealed that it wasn't only the non-existent seal between the air conditioner and the steelwork that was causing the ingress of water. Sea spray, caused by the occasional wave smacking heavily against the port bow, was climbing its remorseless way several metres up the superstructure and uncannily finding the gap under the unit where the condensate tray was fitted. Every time the boat rolled into a trough between the waves, the tray filled with seawater until the boat rolled back in the opposite direction. The contents were then emptied straight onto the bench settee, so that the tray could be conveniently available for collecting the next shower of spray from the following wave. There would be the briefest of respites when the boat became upright, before the rolling motion repeated itself with another tray full of seawater being deposited onto the settee and into the cabin. With the gradual deterioration in the sea conditions, the tray was being filled and emptied with increasing frequency, not a good omen for having dry and comfortable accommodation to return to at the end of my evening watch.

By placing a bucket in a strategic position just under the tray, I was successful in catching a significant part of the first two deposits, until the weight and water level in the bucket was too much to prevent it from tipping over with the ever-increasing rolling motion. There was absolutely no way of tying the bucket down: it had to be reasonably free for it to be quickly emptied into the bathroom across the alleyway. In any case, the problem of what to do with the bucket was purely hypothetical: four hours of steering and bridge watch in the wheelhouse would frustrate any attempt I made to keep my cabin from flooding. The ITCZ could do its worst for all I cared. There was very little comfort to be gained in knowing that Pieter on No. 1 tug would probably be experiencing exactly the same misfortunes, and that his cabin would be every bit as wet and uncomfortable as mine.

The rain showers were torrential during the evening watch. Four long and exhausting hours were spent baling and mopping out the wheelhouse and attempting to protect the electrical equipment from the leaks in the roof. Standing up on the treacherous surface of Shwe's psychedelic and wet linoleum became an art in itself, as did the steering by squinting at the magnetic compass card, or by following No. 1's flickering stern light whenever I could see it. Handing over the bridge watch to Marco at midnight was an extremely welcome relief, even if only to retire to my cabin for yet more mopping and baling. Thankfully the weather was showing signs of abating and the spray was no longer filling the air conditioner tray and spilling onto my settee. Finding seawater where it didn't belong was making me tired and irritable.

Despite the damp atmosphere in my cabin I slept well, no doubt mentally and physically exhausted from the unfamiliar exertions of handling mops and emptying

From left to right: Ex-Chief Engineer Tim Nyunt; Ex-Captain Shwe Myint and Ex-Captain Maung. Messroom Oriental Tug No. 2

buckets. Sleeping on the air mattress had obviously provided my subconscious mind with some additional life-saving comforts. I no longer cared if the weather took a sudden turn for the worse, for knowing that I could float off into the Atlantic Ocean if the water levels in my cabin were to rise unnoticed was immensely reassuring.

The situation in the lower deck accommodation was infinitely more unpleasant and uncomfortable than in the upper deck cabins. Mieke, Marco, Shwe and Tin were already suffering considerable discomfort from having to reside in damp and musty conditions inside the hull and below the waterline, and without the benefits of either air conditioning or fresh air from portholes that could be opened. With no ventilation entering the accommodation the atmosphere had become horribly fetid, damp and stale. Despite frequent mopping, puddles of water lay on the alleyway decks, fed by condensation dripping down from the Formica deckheads and painted steel surfaces. Mildew and green mould had replaced filth and ants. Seawater had been pouring in through leaking vents and through the supposedly watertight accommodation escape hatch that had to be kept closed during the bad weather. The compressed woodchip-type panelling used in the cabin and furniture construction was already swelling and becoming distorted from being continuously saturated with water. André spoke of living in his cabin on No. 1 tug as camping out in a 'tropical rain forest', with his clothes and bedding, like everyone's, becoming mouldy and damp. Upgrading the lower deck accommodation so that it became at least ventilated and dry would be essential in retaining our two crews for the onward voyage to Singapore.

The tugboat owners in Singapore had appointed our company to act on their behalf for the repairs in Las Palmas. Marco and I shared the tiresome responsibility of listing and numbering all the deficiencies being noted from both the boats and sending them by email on the satellite communications unit to our office in Holland. The repair lists being submitted by both Remy and Marco were extensive and detailed, unlike the surprisingly brief and cryptic list of defects being advised by No. 1 tug. Our sister boat appeared, on paper, to be in a far better condition than ours.

Replacing the window-box air-conditioning units with the original portholes proved to be an area of contention between Remy, Pieter, Willem and me. The persuasive viewpoint of having comfort in the heat of the Red Sea against the short-term discomforts of flooding in bad weather inevitably won the day. I bit the bullet and made no mention of reinstating the portholes into the superstructures in the defect lists being transmitted to Holland. The surveyors in Las Palmas would ultimately decide the issue. I suspected the units themselves would surely succumb in the not too distant future to the unfriendly effects of salt water periodically spraying through their electronic components, and then my argument would be won in any case.

A few more days of bad weather would probably end the debate once and for all and to my advantage.

A dash for port

Inside the accommodation Mieke and Larry the lizard, or chameleon, were having some success in our continuing battle against the ants. Larry apparently survived from eating ants, and had appeared one day completely out of the blue, or green in his case, to set up home in the mess. His sudden appearance had caused considerable debate as to whether he was a chameleon or not, for no one had actually seen him changing colour. He seemed to be permanently green, not a good colour with which to disguise himself against the creamy white Formica bulkhead and ceiling panels. Perhaps he was seasick, in which case his lack of colour-changing ability from speckled green to whatever other colours chameleons proudly display could be easily explained; in reality Larry was probably only a common or garden seagoing lizard that had stowed away with the stores in Abidjan.

In our predominantly male society on board we had always assumed Larry to be male rather than female. The female names Lorraine or Lillian lacked the impact he so richly deserved; Larry the lizard falls off the tongue far more easily. Larry was an accomplished expert in catching the ants, patiently waiting for them to appear on the mess bulkheads, totally motionless and silent until they came within striking range, and then zap, tongue out and bye-bye little ant. The ones he missed, which happened only very rarely, fell foul of an equally motionless but sometimes not so silent Mieke armed with her deadly aerosol spray. The ant population was quite definitely on the decline, and not far from being entirely eradicated. Flies were another target for Larry; he seemed to appreciate them more when he was hungry and when there were no ants to be found. Larry had become a most welcome guest; it was to our lasting regret that he was unable to find a shipmate of the opposite sex. A brood of little Larrys to carry on his good work would have been much appreciated.

The weather continued to slowly moderate as we left the ITCZ and its tropical rainstorms behind us. After two very long and claustrophobic days of being entombed inside the accommodation, we were able to open the watertight doors, ventilators and the escape hatch from the lower deck, and life aboard the two boats returned to some degree of normality. The flow of naturally warm air from outside helped in starting to dry out the surface moisture from the cabins and alleyways, but dehumidifiers would be required to be working for many days before all the condensation and humidity in the spaces below the waterline was completely removed.

Six days after sailing from Abidjan we passed Dakar, the capital of Senegal. Our track took us a couple of miles to the west of Cape Vert, the promontory that forms the protective bay in which the city shelters, and so we were able to use our cellphones. Telephoning home is always a considerable morale booster, and on this occasion it helped to brighten an otherwise gloomy and depressing day.

Our continued good progress was being threatened by No. 1 tug having some severe mechanical problems. During our morning VHF radio conversation Pieter had informed me that not only had one generator expired completely with an unidentified electrical fault, but that the spare machine was overheating mechanically. To add to their engineering problems, Willem had also discovered water in the oil sump of the main engine, and more than 600 litres of precious and expensive lubricating oil lying wasted and useless in the engine room bilges after the lubricating oil purifier had inconveniently failed. Our sister tug appeared to be close to coming to a grinding halt with Las Palmas less than a thousand miles away.

Remy had been in the wheelhouse when Pieter was imparting his tales of woe. Knowing Remy only too well from our previous voyages together, I quickly realised from his grim and ominous expression that the unwelcome news on the VHF radio was not the only cause of his unhappiness. Apparently both our generators were in a similar fragile state with mechanical failure imminent. Not yet broken, I was told, but well advanced in the breaking process. With no spare parts of any description on board, I optimistically reassured myself that Remy had surely meant days rather than just a few hours when assessing the machines' projected lifespans.

Pieter and I discussed the possibility of having to tow one another, although the question of which boat would be doing the towing was tactfully left unanswered. With less than four days' steaming to the repair facilities in Las Palmas, completing the passage using our own respective engines was first and foremost in both our minds. Although we were on board tugboats, the amount of usable towing equipment we had found in our cursory inspection of the cluttered and untidy deck store in Abidjan was barely sufficient to make up an adequate towline, and that was with combining the resources from both the boats. Towing one another would quite definitely be a last resort.

The additional comments in our noon position report advising the company of both the boats' mechanical problems and the loss of lubricating oil on No. 1 tug must have made for some miserable reading in Holland. I just wished that on such occasions the satellite radio equipment had either been duplicated, or more appropriately, the set had been placed on the other tugboat so that Pieter could have sent his own tales of gloom, doom and despondency. Knowing that No. 1 tug would soon be provided with her own communications unit in Las Palmas made my task of having to report their misfortunes no easier. I took absolutely no delight in having to transcribe the tales of our sister boat's troubles onto the keyboard ready for transmission. For some strange and inexplicable reason I felt as if I were acting as an underhand whistleblower or spy, taking great pleasure in reporting our shipmate's unfortunate setbacks. Nothing could have been further from the truth, but it left a bad taste in my mouth.

With only two days to go to reach the Canaries, our progress was again being hindered by strong northerly winds. As we passed Cape Blanc, marking the boundary between Mauritania and West Sahara, both boats were pitching heavily and shipping seas and spray straight over the bows. The lower deck accommodation was awash with seawater again, and any progress that had been made in the past couple of days in drying out the cabins had been completely lost. At times it was as if the escape door leading onto the main deck didn't exist, with the cross-alleyway at the bottom of the vertical ladder having to be regularly baled and mopped dry. The cabin deckheads continuously dripped seawater, which was entering from the main deck through corroded and leaking air vents. The lower deck had become virtually uninhabitable again within a few short and soul-destroying hours.

Two decks above, spray was once again pouring through the air-conditioning units, only this time Remy was sharing the benefits as well. It was as if the weather had sided with my viewpoint that the portholes in our cabins should be reinstated at the earliest possible opportunity. Attempting to mop out our cabin decks and to keep our personal possessions dry was proving to be a futile and wasted effort, and one in which both of us admitted defeat within a few exhausting minutes. The conditions we were experiencing had deteriorated to the point where I expected a mass exodus straight back to Holland as soon as we arrived in Las Palmas.

With the pitching and rolling came the usual cacophony of sounds to be heard when a ship is being tossed around, only this time it was to the accompaniment of the whooshing noise of slopping seawater. We reduced our speed in an attempt to ride the head seas more comfortably and to decrease the volume and weight of water being shipped over the bows, but both Pieter and I were mindful of the very serious problems within our engine rooms and the possible consequences of extending the passage time. The poor condition of the two boats dictated that we should minimise the risks of incurring any structural damage: a compromise somewhere between speed through the water and the delay in our arrival time seemed the only sensible solution.

To add to our frustrations on No. 2 tug, our one and only real luxury, the pink toilet seat, made a successful bid for freedom during the night from the back of the lavatory. A combination of the thin rope lashings and a cracked piece of twenty-seven-year-old porcelain at the back of the toilet bowl had finally proved to be of insufficient strength to withstand the out-of-the-ordinary lateral pressures of someone's weight counterbalancing against the motion of the boat. A timid and cowardly silence was the name of the game. No one claimed any credit for the damage, no one had sought medical treatment and, quite unbelievably, not a sound had been heard. Any cries of anguish had been effectively smothered by the other very loud bangs and crashes echoing from inside the housing.

With only one day to go to reach the shelter and safety of Las Palmas, Remy proudly announced that he was sixty years old. No one could understand why he should have chosen a day of being bounced around in steep and heavy seas to reveal that he was now a proud and distinguished sexagenarian. Birthday celebrations were postponed in retaliation for his inconsiderate and thoughtless timing. To cheer him up and to show just a little conciliatory respect and admiration towards his old age, Mieke told him that, when the conditions were quieter in the galley, she would cook him one of her very special meals in recognition of his achievement and his undoubted tenacity for life. We sang a remarkably tuneful and heartfelt Dutch-English-Myanmar version of 'Happy Birthday' during our morning get-together in the very damp wheelhouse and raised a congratulatory toast to him with our half cups of coffee. With the slipping and sliding around on Shwe's wet linoleum, and our holding on against the boat's unsteady movement, it was the best we could possibly hope to achieve in the difficult circumstances. He seemed to be more than appreciative of the fuss we made of him.

Two hours later, and just in time for inclusion in our daily position report with its update on any mishaps either boat might have encountered in the previous twenty-four hours, Remy announced that the main engine was now using between 100 and 150 litres of fresh water an hour; nearly 3 tonnes a day. He thought that either a cylinder liner had cracked, or that some of the tubes in the cooler for the engine's cooling system had failed. We were very fortunate in having sufficient fresh water in our tanks to sustain the loss until we arrived in port. Had it happened in the middle of the Pacific Ocean and miles from any help, we would have been faced with, potentially, a very serious situation. Tugboats neither have the tank capacities nor requirement to carry large reserves of fresh water.

Early in my evening watch and with the dubious benefit of fading twilight, I chased, stamped upon many ineffectual times, and eventually killed two of the largest cockroaches I have had the misfortune to come across for many years. They appeared positively huge in the poor light, at least 5 centimetres in length, and looked as if they might have come straight from one of Spielberg's *Jurassic Park* movies. As far as I was aware, they were the first cockroaches we had discovered on board. It was an absence we had all found a little peculiar given the ideal breeding conditions provided by the two boats during their lengthy stay in West Africa. Where they had come from I had not the slightest idea: perhaps, with all the water that had been swilling around inside the wheelhouse, they had been flushed out from their hall of residence. I just hoped they were an isolated pair, for the last thing we wanted was a cockroach infestation. Cockroaches have proved to be resolute and resilient survivors despite the modern aggressive chemicals and the deadly fumigation methods pitched against them. Eliminating the ants, even with the untiring efforts of Larry the lizard and Mieke, had been difficult enough.

The weather started easing during my evening watch, but the respite was only temporary, the lull before the storm. By 2 a.m. the next morning the wind had veered to the north-east and had increased to a force 8 gale. Our speed dropped to less than four knots as we battled against the headwinds, making our promised arrival time of midday off Las Palmas an impossible and illusionary target.

Less than two miles offshore we struggled up the featureless and barren east coast of Gran Canaria and passed the busy airport close to Punta de Gando. Despite the inclement weather the planes were landing and taking off with regular monotony. The top of Pico de las Nieves, the extinct volcano near the centre of the island rising some 1,900 metres above sea level, lay hidden under a grey tablecloth of low and dense cloud that extended towards the north of the island and the capital, Las Palmas. We continued our slow passage northwards, eventually arriving off the Dique del Generalismo, the huge granite breakwater protecting Puerto de la Luz, by mid-afternoon. Our eleven-day sea passage had been achieved at a far better average speed than we had ever thought possible, but it would surely be remembered for all its mishaps and disasters and the appalling living conditions that both crews had endured since sailing from Côte d'Ivoire. We gave the Port Control the tugboats' details, and in return received our instructions for entering the port.

Placing my command alongside the main quayside in Puerto de la Luz, the Grande Muelle, should have been a straightforward and simple ship manoeuvre, but after just a few days at sea I had lost my touch and managed to get it horribly wrong. I hadn't properly allowed for the wind, which was still quite strong within the port and blowing off the berth. It was a nightmare that left me mortified and upset. I finally succeeded in getting the stern alongside on the third attempt, the only damage being to my severely injured pride and the acute embarrassment of my crew. It hadn't helped that Pieter and No. 1 tug had made a textbook landing a few minutes earlier.

I wish every port adopted the arrival formalities of the Spanish at Las Palmas. The ship's agent visited thirty minutes after we had docked and collected three copies of the crew list to pass to the appropriate authorities. I found it hard to accept that no further documentation would be required and that there were no official papers or forms to stamp. There would be no raids on our storerooms, and no tokens of our esteem to be proffered. Port officials, in all their guises, were conspicuous by their absence, proving beyond all doubt that we were back in civilisation once again.

A couple of hours later service technicians boarded and took away all the fire extinguishers for testing and recharging. It was 6 p.m. and the first of what were to be our many repairs had already started.

4

LAS PALMAS

Muggers and meetings

I could recall having visited Las Palmas only once before, as a second voyage deck cadet, and that was for a fleeting few hours while the ship in which I was serving took on bunkers, fresh water and a few fresh provisions. My watch-keeping rota had allowed me some time off duty to go ashore with a couple of the junior engineers to buy souvenirs and telephone home. My parents never received their call, and a present from the Canaries was conveniently forgotten. Being a teenager who knew it all and a bit more besides, I had been perfectly confident that drinking Bacardi and Cokes in the hugely intoxicating measures served by the Spanish could be easily handled and could do me no harm. Learning the hard way comes to all of us at various times in our lives. Bacardi and Coke both entered and left my life in just a few short hours, and remained off my drinks list for many a long year. I have no clear recollection of being carried back to the ship, only the memory of being severely admonished by my stern and unsympathetic chief officer the next morning, who told me in no uncertain terms that not only was I a disgrace and a failure to him, but also a disgrace to my ship, to my shipping employers, and to the entire Merchant Navy. I was informed that my irresponsible and misguided behaviour during the course of one afternoon ashore had caused more than enough disgrace to last my whole seagoing career. With shore leave banned, I was to spend two long and lonely weeks standing at the head of the gangway gazing longingly at the sights of a forbidden Cape Town and watching my shipmates go ashore to enjoy themselves. Bacardi and Coke had cost me dearly.

Despite my miserable experience of many years ago, I was looking forward to revisiting Las Palmas. Shwe, Tin and Maung volunteered to remain on board the two boats to keep gangway watch, assuring us that they had absolutely no interest or desire in going ashore for the first night in port. The remaining nine of us strolled down the quay in a group, conscious that every step and move we made was being closely scrutinised by small groups of itinerant Africans lurking half-hidden behind the stacks of empty pallets stored untidily in front of the warehouses. I was convinced that other unseen eyes remained concealed and out of view, but ready to pounce out from their hiding places at the slightest opportunity to attack or rob us. We had the comfort of numbers, but the threatening and very unnerving presence of the illegal immigrants brought home the agent's stark and shocking warning that Puerto de la Luz could no longer be considered safe at night for the foreign crews of visiting ships.

I had been told that robberies and muggings were frequent occurrences inside the open port, no doubt encouraged by there being no restrictions on movement and neither gates nor security checks for visitors entering or leaving the area. According to the agent, the local police had been singularly unsuccessful in apprehending the muggers and thieves, and were being openly criticised for paying only lip service to a very real problem that was rapidly escalating beyond their control. I vowed to myself there and then not to step ashore on my own at night: the Africans' presence felt not only uncomfortable, but also frightening and intimidating. It went to show that, had the stowaway, Mr Kwaghbo, remained hidden aboard No. 1 tug for the duration of the passage, he might well have been able to jump ashore unnoticed after our arrival in port. Becoming a member of one of the feral and roaming gangs in their lawless pursuit of innocent seafarers and their worldly possessions would have been his next inevitable step. History will judge one day whether Europe has been sensible, or not, in relaxing its border controls and welcoming a different society onto its shores.

Unsurprisingly, the walk towards the town brought back no distant memories of my youthful misadventure some forty years earlier. I recognised neither building nor street. One or two nameless members of our group insisted they knew where we were going but, as is all too often the case in such circumstances, didn't know how to get there. We wandered around aimlessly, meekly following our forgetful guides, until the almost unanimous desire to quench the thirst became overwhelming and brought the aimless route march to a halt at the nearest bar. A couple of beers later, we made a prolonged stopover at a hole-in-the-wall ATM outside a local provincial bank, where we did our very best to empty the machine, and then on once again. We had no idea as to where we were going, but were determined to keep on going until we arrived there. The benefits of taking a long stretch of the legs after a voyage of being confined, albeit willingly, in the small and restrictive constraints of a harbour tug can never be argued: a few hours away from the two tugboats would do us all a power of good. After yet another stopover for some more liquid refreshments, we ventured upon La Playa de las Canteras which, unbeknown to the silent majority, had been our intended destination since leaving the docks some two hours earlier. Our haphazard wander and lengthy meander had finally come to a welcome end.

The huge selection of restaurants and bars made the choosing of a mutually acceptable venue exceedingly difficult, and with nine different tastes, almost impossible. After a further seemingly endless and frustrating stroll down the length of the promenade, we eventually agreed on an establishment at the north end of the bay with a large outside seating area and a varied and comprehensive menu that would suit every palate. Hunger pangs had played no small part in our eventual choice.

Bram, one of our company's superintendents, had checked into a local hotel earlier in the evening. He would be remaining in Las Palmas for the duration of our stay to oversee the repairs and to assist us with the various surveys and inspections required for the issuing of the trading and safety certificates. A short while later he joined us for a drink and our late evening meal. The discussions around the restaurant table confirmed our suspicions that we would be staying in Gran Canaria for at least fifteen days, and possibly longer. The Singaporean owners had adopted a surprisingly realistic attitude and had agreed to carry out every single repair we had detailed in our lengthy reports. The problems we would probably encounter in sailing the two rather neglected and tired old tugboats the 8,500 miles to the Far East had obviously been fully appreciated. We split up into smaller and more manageable groups after our meal. Remy, Mieke and I remained together for the walk back to the docks. The streets were quiet and almost deserted, and twenty minutes later we had cautiously negotiated the hidden dangers along the length of the Grande Muelle and were back aboard, safe and sound. The distance from the beach to the docks wasn't that far once we had established the correct direction in which to walk.

The meeting in the mess of No.1 tug with the managers from the ship repair company lasted for most of the next morning. Priorities had to be decided and work that would involve technical labour identified. We agreed to defer the starting of small jobs for a few days in order to concentrate on the larger repairs that could only be carried out in properly equipped workshops ashore. Removing the oil and seawater coolers from the engine room of No. 2 tug, and then transporting them to a specialist company for re-tubing, was estimated to take the best part of two days, and would have to commence immediately in order to have the work completed within our two-week timescale. Watertight doors and door openings that would have to be enlarged for the coolers' removal onto the quayside had already been identified. Work was hastily scheduled to start in the afternoon.

Shortly after lunch, and while we were seated outside awaiting the arrival of the shore labour, there was a huge commotion on No. 1 tug, accompanied by angry and very loud shouting. A few seconds later, André, Arno and Marco could be clearly seen running hell for leather down the quayside towards the city chasing after a black person. They never got within a whisker of the fugitive, and, after 100 metres of desperate sprinting, the gap between pursued and pursuers had widened considerably. The chase was abandoned shortly afterwards and the three totally winded and out of condition Dutchmen returned to the boats to tell their story.

They had been talking together on the stern of No. 1 tug when the African, who had been nonchalantly seated with his legs over the edge of the quay watching them for quite a few minutes, had suddenly stood up and unexpectedly jumped aboard. He leapt into the accommodation through the open watertight door and returned out on deck less than ninety seconds later and before anyone had time to properly react. They managed to grab him before he could climb back onto the quayside and wrestled him untidily to the deck. At that stage it all went horribly wrong. Their grip on him somehow relaxed, and with him being slippery and wet with perspiration, he wriggled from their half-hearted clasp and made good his escape. He was away with a gazelle-like jump from the deck followed by the Olympic sprint down the jetty.

He had succeeded in stealing one hundred or so euros from each of the open cabins of Arno and André in less time than it takes to blink. Despite a perfunctory search in the dock area for a few days afterwards, he was never to be seen again.

An unwelcome lesson in security had been given to all of us. Our cabins had to be locked at all times, day and night, and access into the accommodation restricted to one door only, with someone positioned outside it whenever possible. The whole unfortunate episode left an unpleasant taste in everyone's mouth. We couldn't say we hadn't been warned: some of us had simply chosen to ignore the warnings.

Later on in the afternoon the inflatable life rafts were landed ashore for survey. Technicians boarded to commence work on repairing the radars and the VHF radios, which had started to suffer from intermittent and crackling transmissions a couple of days before our arrival. Perhaps our black plastic garbage bags hadn't been entirely effective in keeping out the rainwater and sea spray from the leaking wheelhouse deckhead!

The repair contractors brought a small mobile crane down to the jetty and loaded a 10-foot container and some large electrical transformers onto the aft deck of each tugboat. The containers were packed with tools, welding and cutting equipment, and all the essential paraphernalia needed for commencing the repairs in earnest in the morning. We borrowed the crane to load some 200-litre drums of lubricating oil for the generators and main engine. Changing the oils in all the machinery would be just one of the many smaller jobs for Remy and Tin to contend with during our lengthy stay in port.

Bram, Pieter and I went ashore with the agent shortly after the end of the Spanish siesta to collect a hire car. Bram would be using it to get to and from his hotel every morning and evening, leaving it free for Pieter and me to use during the working day. We had already determined that the cost of the hire car would be more than offset by the savings we would make from not using taxis or appointing a ship's chandler to supply our provisions. It looked as if I would be indulging yet again in one of my favourite seagoing pastimes: shopping for ships.

In the evening Remy and I enjoyed a quiet dinner and a bottle of wine on our own in one of the more salubrious and expensive restaurants just off the Playa. The location and the refined and stylish interior provided the perfect setting for the belated celebration of Remy's sixtieth birthday. The special occasion not only allowed me to share in his overdue celebrations, but also to drown my sorrows. My window-box air-conditioning unit had fallen silent, no doubt finally succumbing to the terminal effects of seawater entering its most sensitive of places. Since the majority decision of my senior colleagues had been to retain the units, I decided, perhaps rather hypocritically in view of my singular opinion, to add its repair discreetly to the contractor's list in the morning. I could see no reason at all why I should be the one to lose out on the comfort zone.

Tiredness and old age brought an early end to our evening of relaxation. We successfully ran the gauntlet past the hidden African muggers and thieves, and were back on board just before midnight to take 'one for the road' before calling it a day.

Remy's snoring was, unfortunately, no less sonorous now that his sixtieth birthday had been officially celebrated.

The rot sets in

Shortly after 8 a.m. all hell broke loose when the ship repair gangs boarded for their first day of work. Their singular objective in life appeared to be to start every job on our repair lists within the hour. There would be no escaping the deafening noises that reverberated around the boats and the adjacent quayside: the swooshing roar of the high-pressure gas of the oxyacetylene cutting torches; the staccato tap-tapping of hammers on steel plate; the deep throaty throb of diesel-engined road compressors providing the air for some of the equipment and tools; the distinctive rattle of pull-chains on chain blocks as heavy items were either raised or lowered; the shouted instructions, the curses, the laughter, and then the sudden moments of silence, which in their own way were just as deafening as the noise, as if the stillness had been mysteriously orchestrated by a hidden conductor.

Instead of the usual emptiness and the peace and quiet of a rust-streaked and uncluttered deck, there were the unfamiliar sights and fevered activity of many people at work: of cables and hoses untidily criss-crossing the decks; of the blinding, eye-searing flashes of welding electrodes arcing against the steel to be welded; of the paint on the steelwork suddenly blistering and burning, traces of smoke spiralling upwards in neat little whorls as the heat from the cutting nozzles seared it from its original faded colour to a smouldering black; of the safety barriers of rope and hazard tape stretching across a section of deck or alleyway warning of danger ahead; of the fire extinguishers and fire blankets standing by like unmoving sentries ready for instant deployment; of scaffolding being assembled and stagings being carefully lowered by ropes to provide access to unreachable parts.

With the sights and the sounds came the smells: the pungent and sometimes suffocating acrid stink of burning paint; the familiar stench of diesel exhaust fumes hanging in a pall like an invisible shroud over the deck; the unmistakable reek of steel being welded and the chemical fumes from electrodes being arced; the odours of human sweat as the perspiration flowed more freely with the heat of the morning sun. We were no longer living aboard two old harbour tugs in need of repair: they had suddenly, almost magically, been transformed in less than an hour into floating workshops, buzzing with workmen and technicians and reassuringly alive with the sounds, the sights, and the smells of work in progress. Our repairs were underway.

During our stay in Abidjan the windlass, the winch on the foredeck used for raising and lowering the anchor and its chain to and from the seabed, appeared to be lacking in both power and speed. A specialist firm of local hydraulic engineers arrived in the middle of the morning to test it under working conditions and to ascertain if it was operating correctly. We gathered on the foredeck to let go the anchor into the harbour, and then to heave it back up while the technicians with their fancy pressure gauges, flow meters and instruments could monitor its performance.

After disengaging the clutch Remy applied his strength to the long steel bar screw-handle that would open the brake band and allow the gypsy that supported the chain to turn. A loud splash a few seconds later announced that the anchor was on its way to being buried in the mud and sand just a few metres below the hull. The anchor chain followed, rattling noisily with an ever-increasing momentum over the spinning gypsy and down through the hawse pipe. Remy frantically tried to apply the brake by turning the handle to tighten the steel band onto which the fibre brake lining was riveted: a disaster was in the making. The band chose that precise moment to disintegrate into two or three pieces of perforated and badly corroded steel: with the brake no longer in existence the chain could run freely without restriction, and with nothing to hinder its free-fall to the harbour bottom.

The seawater appeared a few seconds later. During the bad weather the chain lockers, which we suspected hadn't been cleaned for many years, had unavoidably become partially filled with seawater that had leaked in through the rotten protruding sections of the spurling pipes leading from the main deck into the lockers. Their repair had already been detailed in our repair lists. The Spanish engineers, Bram, Marco and I all managed to nimbly dodge out of the way, but Remy had absolutely no chance of escaping, standing behind the windlass itself. The foul-smelling stagnant and rusty water came up from the lockers with the rapidly moving chain links and drenched him from head to foot. Rust particles and lumps of black stinking mud accompanied the deluge. We stood well clear, close to the boat's side, and watched it all happen, aghast and totally helpless: there was nothing we could do. The chain continued running noisily, throwing water and mud in a parabolic arc over the hapless Remy, the windlass and the foredeck, until it jerked suddenly and violently to a shuddering stop. The bitter end, the nautical term for the securing pin that passes through the end link of the chain and onto a steel pad eye welded at the back of the locker, had done its job and held firm. Had it failed the complete chain, all one 160 metres of it, would have ended up on the harbour bottom and would have required the services of a diver to help get it back on board.

The deathly and uneasy silence on the foredeck lasted for only a few seconds until our half-choked sniggers became hysterical laughing. Remy peered out at us through a mask of black and foul-smelling mud, his unblinking and angry eyes staring from the centre of two flesh-coloured spectacle-sized circles that had remained only partially clean when he had screwed up his face defensively against the onslaught. He looked as if he had received one of those skin-cleansing facial mudpacks, complete with sliced cucumber eye patches, on which small fortunes are spent in exclusive health farms. The obscenities that accompanied the frequent globs of muddy saliva and rust he was spitting in all directions were words from the Dutch language I had never had the privilege of hearing before. I don't think I had ever seen my friend quite so annoyed or agitated. Our heartless and unsympathetic amusement only aggravated his acute discomfort. He stormed off furiously towards the accommodation, leaving a muddy trail of footsteps behind him, and wasn't to be seen again until lunchtime, when we all sat down together for a beer and acted as if nothing untoward had happened.

The hydraulic engineers connected their pressure gauges and instruments into the appropriate pipes so that diagnostic readings could be taken during the hoisting operation. We heaved the anchor slowly back on board until it was hanging just clear of the water's edge. Its speedy and dramatic descent had caused the chain to become hopelessly twisted and knotted, with the heavily rusted swivel link connecting the anchor shackle to the chain seized solid and unmovable. A mobile crane would have to be hired to put the anchor either on the quay or on the deck so that the swivel could be freed and the chain untwisted. Testing the windlass had proved to be a costly exercise for the tugboat owners, and, for Remy, an experience he would never wish to repeat.

According to the Spanish engineers the hydraulic machinery was performing within its design parameters, although where their data was gleaned from I had not the slightest idea. I didn't believe them, but had no basis upon which I could present any further argument. Having watched the windlass's interminable struggle to heave up the chain and to lift the anchor, it seemed to me that even a layman would have questioned its working capabilities. Bram had no choice but to accept the engineers' findings, and I had no choice but to quell my misgivings and to vow silently that the anchors would only be used in an emergency, and as a last resort.

Shortly after lunch we said goodbye to Arno. He had agreed to join No. 1 tug in Abidjan at very short notice, providing the company relieved him in Las Palmas for the holiday he had booked earlier in the year. I didn't think he would forget his short voyage as second engineer on No. 1 tug for a long time. With the financial sting he had suffered in Africa and the robbery from his cabin the previous afternoon, it had hardly been a rewarding voyage from a monetary point of view. Only time would tell if the experiences he had gained in his two and a half weeks aboard would outweigh the losses he had incurred. He seemed wholly delighted to be jumping into the taxi to take him to the airport. His relief, another young Dutch second engineer, arrived in the early evening, and made a cursory but highly critical inspection of his damp and mouldy cabin and the general chaos associated with the repairs, before demanding that he, too, be relieved at the earliest opportunity. Pieter and our superintendent, Bram, were advised, in no uncertain terms, that he had absolutely no intention of sailing in such appalling and unhealthy conditions. The telephone lines to Holland would be hot in the morning.

The rot I had predicted just a few days earlier was already setting in.

A move to the Virgin Pine

The repairs continued unabated, and with varying degrees of success. As had been anticipated at the planning meeting with the ship repair managers, disconnecting and extracting the large heavy cylindrical oil and seawater coolers from the depths of the engine room had been far from easy. Two steel watertight doors and a doorsill had to be removed before they could be squeezed into the accommodation cross-alleyway and out onto the main deck. A mobile crane was brought in to lift them onto the quay ready for transporting to the engineering workshops. The process had taken two labour-intensive days and had defied the pessimists, who had voiced their doubts about whether their removal would ever be possible at all.

Due to many unforeseen difficulties, jobs that had originally been considered to be simple and straightforward were progressing more slowly than predicted. In some instances the already tight schedule had to be reprogrammed to accept additional and quite extensive work. A fire hose water test on the messroom, galley and bathroom portholes on the main deck had revealed them to be leaking despite the fitting of new sealing rubbers and their steel retaining strips. The circular steel porthole frames that the rubber is pressed against to form a watertight seal when the portholes are closed and bolted down were found to be heavily corroded and distorted. The rough steel edge being presented against the surface of the rubber was so heavily indented and uneven that a proper seal could never be made. It was a case of having to renew the frames, a major repair involving steel prefabrication, cutting, and welding.

The testing of the windlass a couple of days earlier had shown the need for a complete overhaul. The seized swivel links on the anchors required freeing to prevent the chains from kinking, and two new brake bands with the fibre brake linings riveted to their insides had to be manufactured and installed. The chain lockers would have to be inspected and cleaned out, and the spurling pipes leading from the lockers onto the main deck renewed to make the lockers watertight for the long sea passage ahead. Most of it was extra work that hadn't been expected, but would have to be completed before we could sail. With additional jobs being added to the list by the hour, the original estimate of fifteen days for our stay in port was already appearing to be a little optimistic.

The personnel problems on No. 1 tug didn't finish with the second engineer. Mark, the cook, had been suffering from a pronounced limp since our arrival in Las Palmas. The doctor had diagnosed either blood or food poisoning, and recommended he should abstain from alcohol and acidic foods for three to four days to help reduce the painful swelling on his ankle. I clearly recall having received similar medical instructions for an agonising attack of gout in my big toe many years ago. Placing him on light duties, which in effect meant no work, the doctor advised him to keep his sore foot up and rested whenever possible, and to avoid standing for any length of time. André, No. 1's chief officer, never an advocate of the subtleties of diplomacy, suggested quite bluntly that Mark had been on light duties since joining the boat in Abidjan, and that self-inflicted food poisoning was, without question, the most likely cause of his uncomfortable ailment. I gained the distinct impression that all was not well with the catering department aboard our sister tug.

With cooking and food poisoning temporarily withdrawn from Mark's agenda, the galley and mess on No. 1 tug were left to their own devices. Breakfast, lunch and dinner were no longer on the menu. Two chairs were placed on deck outside the accommodation door, one for Mark to sit on and one to rest his swollen ankle on. His unfortunate and untimely incapacitation had resulted in him being officially appointed as No. 1 tug's gangway watchman, a bit like closing the stable door after the horse had bolted. The indisputable fact that he could hardly walk, let alone run, had not been a consideration in his controversial selection. I failed to see how a lame and immobile watchman with a clearly visible and heavily bandaged ankle could possibly respond to any undesirable attempting to enter their accommodation, although it was suggested later that his seated presence outside the door would be an effective deterrent to any opportunist thief and was marginally better than having no watchman at all.

Dirty clothes and bedding and a lack of laundry facilities had become an issue. We had been using buckets for the hand-washing and rinsing of small items such as tee shirts, socks, shorts and underwear, but bed sheets, towels and boiler suits were a little more demanding. Having no hot water apart from the little that could be boiled in a kettle or saucepan exacerbated the problem. On the passage from Abidjan we had rigged washing lines for drying our clothes on deck, but these had been transferred to the engine room when the weather had become too bad. With the African thieves and the repair work in progress, our drying facilities had been lost, and the question of how we could wash our bedlinen and larger items of clothing had been raised. Bram agreed that the services of a local *lavandería* could be utilised.

Our laundry, in clearly labelled individual plastic bags, was collected from the boat in the morning. A couple of large bundles strung together were returned in the early evening accompanied by an extortionate bill of nearly 300 euros. We spent more than an hour trying to sort out the confusion on the messroom table. While bed sheets, towels and boiler suits were of little consequence, the same could not be said of our personal items of clothing. With memories of our recent voyage together on the *Justine* still indelibly printed on my mind, Remy's vivid green boxer shorts patterned with jumping frogs were instantly recognisable, but identifying everyone else's less eye-catching and very ordinary jockeys, shorts and tee shirts was far more difficult. Mieke had no such problem. She had been sensible in keeping her underwear entirely separate from ours, safe and secure behind the locked door of her cabin, and completely removed from our inquisitive eyes and frantically scrabbling hands. We agreed that a washing machine for each boat should be purchased when our shopping trips started.

After four days alongside, the port authority decided that we had outstayed our welcome at the Grande Muelle. Two foreign harbour tugboats moored alongside the main commercial jetty and occupying an important cargo-handling berth to undergo lengthy repairs could hardly be described as the best utilisation of the port facilities. As it was Saturday, the morning shift had stopped work at midday, the owners unwilling to pay the costly overtime rates to continue the repairs into the afternoon. Moving to another berth over the weekend would cause only minimal disruption to our repair schedule. Since our engines had been immobilised, the agent arranged for two small rope-handling towboats to come in the early evening and take us away, one at a time, to our new berth in the outer harbour. Muelle del Virgen Pino, the Quay of the Virgin Pine, was far more suited to our ship repair activities, with a large, uncluttered, yet accessible quayside some distance away from the main port and cargo-handling area. Used principally as a grain berth and a lay-by berth for ships not loading or discharging, it had the considerable benefit of being relatively quiet and peaceful, and of little attraction to the gangs of thieving illegal African immigrants who appeared to be able to roam and plunder the main jetties with surprising ease and impunity.

For some inexplicable and very obscure seafaring reason, our short and trouble-free voyage of being towed across the harbour was celebrated in grand style later. With Mark forbidden to stand over a hot kitchen stove and Mieke disinclined to do so, we treated ourselves to a slap-up meal in one of the Italian restaurants on the Playa before retiring to a salsa club somewhere in the back streets. We managed to sit together in a long line at the bar where, deafened by the throbbing music, blinded by the strobe lighting, and stunned by the overpriced beverages, we could admire the young revellers perform the athletic and gymnastic gyrations that are often referred to as modern dancing. I think it was about 4.30 in the morning when we retired to our respective boats at the Quay of the Virgin Pine. The Myanmars and Mark had sensibly given up waiting and hidden the keys in the usual place before going to bed.

A brace of days

The spontaneous decision to take a Sunday sightseeing trip had its beginnings when taking a stroll down the quayside to clear the effects of the late-night-cum-early-morning at the salsa club, and I noticed that Bram had very thoughtfully parked the hire car under the grain elevator at the end of the jetty. The desire to escape the port and to see the countryside for just a few hours was enthusiastically supported by both Pieter and Willem, but declined out-of-hand by everyone else. They preferred the austere surroundings and solitude of their damp and darkened cabins to nurse their hangovers. I was sure that, in the absence of workmen or repairs, their need for monastic silence and calm tranquillity would be theirs to savour.

We headed out of Las Palmas on the three-lane *autovia* towards Aeropuerto de Gran Canaria in the heavy mid-morning Sunday traffic. The internationally accepted aeroplane logo on all the road signs helped us in our speedy escape towards the south. Once past the airport we turned off inland towards Ingenio and the Pico de las Nieves, the extinct volcano forming the highest point on the island. The contrast in the weather from five days earlier, when we had been out at sea battling our way north in a force 8 gale, couldn't have been more pronounced. Then the crests and peaks of the distant mountain ranges of Las Canadas and Montana de las Tierras had lain hidden under a grey and threatening veil of mist and rain; now we could see them in all their grandeur: magnificent rocky and barren slopes sparsely covered in clumps of thin and spiky spruce trees and patches of lifeless and sun-bleached scrub. In the distance, to the south, lay the scattered clusters of the white buildings of Risco Blanco and La Culata. The conditions couldn't have been more perfect – just a few whispery feathers of cirrus cloud high in the otherwise clear blue sky, and a hint of a cooling breeze to deflect the baking heat of the summer sun.

We passed through Ingenio and drove on, entering the National Park as we climbed steadily upwards following the signs to Pico de las Nieves. The views to the south and the east of the island were breathtaking in their clarity and detail. The altitude sign at the side of the narrow road proclaimed we were at a height of 2,000 metres when we came across the original centre of the extinct volcano, a grassy hollow in the terrain that formed a plateau no more than a few hundred metres wide. Had there not been a tourist information placard marking the spot, we would have been none the wiser and driven straight past. Unlike the huge deep craters with sheer cliffsides and dramatic vertical drops that are normally associated with extinct volcanoes, Gran Canaria's centre of volcanic eruption was very much an anticlimax, a nothingness that would never earn a place in my 'must see again' list of memories.

Our disappointment was soon forgotten a few kilometres down the road when we came across a *restaurante* where we could sit outside on a veranda and admire the spectacular scenery and panoramic views. We must have stayed there for a couple of hours or more, quietly soaking up the warm afternoon sunshine and enjoying our dishes of savoury *tapas* and the refreshing glasses of *tinto de verano*, the 'wine of summer'. Every windblown tree, every nook, cranny and shadowy gully that decorated the scrubby and rocky landscape below was painstakingly studied. Occasionally we talked, just a few muttered words here and there, perhaps a brief exclamation and a finger pointed towards a partly hidden ruin or a distant *cortijo*, but mostly we sat in silence, absorbing the scenery, the peace and the solitude. The two boats could not have been further from our minds; it was just the break we needed.

My two passengers directed me back to Las Palmas on a different and more rural route from the one we had taken in the morning. The quieter road was a pleasure to drive on after the busy *autovia*. We enjoyed a traditional Spanish meal in a café-bar we found quite by accident in a side street hidden somewhere within the depths of the city, a place we would never find again had we searched for a month of Sundays. Shortly after nightfall we had parked the car and were back on board our respective boats, only to find the forever conscientious and uncomplaining Shwe, Tin and Maung sitting together on the main deck at the side of the accommodation of No. 2 tug keeping watch. The others, including Mark, whose ankle must have made a sudden and most unexpected recovery, had gone ashore, supposedly for an evening meal. I thought it far more likely that their ultimate objective would be a second visit to the salsa club to further their studies into some of the more intricate steps of Latin American dancing.

In the morning we were back to the noise and the bustle of a floating shipyard and repairs resumed with a vengeance. The peace and quiet of our sightseeing tour the previous day had been instantly relegated to a not so distant memory. Little did I realise that within the hour, I would be sitting behind the steering wheel for a second day running, but this time accompanied by Mieke. Thanks to the need to replenish some of our provisions, my unvoiced concerns for commencing the shopping were to be realised sooner than expected. Bram had determined, a little unfairly in my biased opinion, that Mieke and I should be responsible for the storing of both the boats. I suspected that Mark's apparent incapacity in daylight hours, and his complete lack of interest in all matters of a catering nature, whether it be day or night, might have been influential in Bram's controversial decision. He had also decided that Mieke should act as the treasurer and bookkeeper for both Pieter and myself. I didn't complain too loudly, for although it is traditionally one of the Master's duties to account for the ship's cash, it would save me many anxious and nail-biting hours of mathematical confusion and financial jugglery. If anyone wanted cash they would be knocking on Mieke's door and not mine: in that respect, it suited me down to the ground.

The Carrefour in Las Palmas is a very large store, or hypermarket, to which I took an instant dislike. I have yet to discover what possible pleasure can be derived from pushing a shopping trolley up and down unfamiliar aisles comparing the prices of one product against another, yet women, for some incomprehensible reason, appear to thrive upon such delights. Despite her many years as a seasoned seafarer, Mieke's femininity rose to the occasion. Her face was one of enraptured happiness and elation as the automatic doors swung silently open in their gesture of welcome. I tried very hard, but unsuccessfully, to share her obvious enjoyment and enthusiasm. We each had two trolleys; I was shopping for Pieter, and Mieke was shopping for Mieke. She was absolutely resolute and inflexible in her determination that we should show no favouritism between the two crews: there was to be no preferential treatment and no personal preferences. I relinquished command and did as I was told: what Mieke put into her trolley, I had to put into mine, the identical product and in exactly the same quantity. She worked through her list, five tins of peas for tug No. 1, and five tins of peas for tug No. 2; six tins of peaches for one and six tins of peaches for the other; and so it went on, tin after tin, product after product, and trolley after trolley until every single line on the tin section of her computer-generated company shopping list bore her pencilled mark as having been purchased. I could remember my mother painstakingly going through exactly the same rigmarole when I accompanied her on her shopping trips as a child. It seems as though technology still has no answer to the simple little shopping list and a stubby pencil with a chewed-up end.

We returned to the *muelle* at midday, the car boot jam-packed with tins for our shipmates, and the back seat and footwell with tins for ourselves. Our purchases were carefully passed from hand to hand in a human chain down the respective gangways and stowed into the storerooms. I was permitted a brief respite from shopping to eat a lunch of bread and cold meats, and then had to head back to Carrefour in the afternoon for another full load. It had been tins in the morning, and would be packets in the afternoon. We hadn't thought about bottles, or fruit, or meat, or bread, or the thousand and one other items we would need for the voyage ahead: I had visions of spending many more hours yet in the Carrefour aisles.

The personnel problems aboard No. 1 tug had escalated while Mieke and I did the shopping. A meeting involving Pieter, Willem and André had been convened in the afternoon and, by two votes to one, they had decided that Mark, their cook, should be sacked immediately and sent home. While the actual outcome had probably been inevitable, I thought it had been a momentously sad day. To allow what in effect had been a 'kangaroo' court to sit in judgement, and to pass a ruling that should have been the Master's decision, and the Master's alone, I found to be not only incredibly bizarre, but contrary to everything I held good in our seagoing traditions.

In the evening I went ashore on my own. The events of the afternoon had left me depressed and with a confusion of conflicting and puzzled thoughts. Meeting up later with Mieke and Remy in the Parque Santa Catalina for a couple of drinks and a bite to eat did nothing to lift my downhearted mood. We were back on board before midnight: the shopping had done more than its fair share of making it a truly bad day.

Privies and problems

Mark said his farewells shortly after breakfast. Hauling himself slowly up the gangway for the final time, he appeared remarkably calm and resigned to leaving. Everyone waved and wished him a safe journey home as the taxi set off down the quay to take him to the airport. If there had been any grudges to bear, they didn't seem obvious to those not involved.

Shortly after his departure, and before it became too hot, Mieke and I were back in the Carrefour hypermarket to buy all the soft drinks and bottled water. We both found it physically exhausting lugging cases of coca-cola, orange, lemonade and bottled water from display to trolley, from trolley to cashier, from cashier to trolley, from trolley to car, and finally from the car down the gangways and into the storerooms. Handling nearly 300 litres of bottled drinking water and 100 litres of soft drinks for each boat in two separate trips was not really my idea of fun. The novelties of being one of the three nominated drivers for the hire car, and of being a glorified shopping assistant and ship's chandler, were wearing just a bit too thin. To my mind, my responsibilities lay with checking and overseeing the repairs on board my command, not gallivanting around the busy side streets of Las Palmas in a hire car attempting to find the least congested and quickest route between the port and the supermarket. Mieke had done her level best to convince me I was much more suited to shopping than my colleague, but I think her mistaken conclusion was based on female intuition rather than fact; as far as I was aware, Pieter's shopping skills had yet to be tested. I put her convictions down to nothing other than a strong personality and her knowledge that she was the only cook for the two boats.

As we unloaded the car after the first trip of the day, I guessed that Mark would be already airborne and probably looking down at us from 35,000 feet with a drink in one hand and bearing a smug and hugely contented smile. We would never know if he had been exceedingly clever and had beaten the system: as he had been sent home, the company would be paying the costs of his repatriation, a far less expensive option for Mark than demanding to be relieved and having to foot the bill for not only his own travel, but also that of his relief.

I wasn't to know that the arrival of two pieces of shiny white porcelain and the plumbers to install them could create such furore and such bad feeling. The repair list we had sent to Holland had included the renewal of the lavatories in both the bathrooms: the four years in Liberia had taken their terrible toll, leaving them heavily stained and encrusted and, with the pedestals and bowls cracked and chipped, totally unhygienic. They were, quite irrefutably, no longer acceptable, or capable, of being used for their designated function. 'Not fit for purpose', as today's jargon would have us say. The plumbers set to immediately with their unpleasant and appalling task of disconnecting and removing the last of our grotty African mementoes.

The acrimonious feuding that flared up within a few minutes between three responsible persons and so-called seafaring friends over the installation of a couple of toilets was quite dumbfounding. André, who had remained aboard our tug after taking his lunch, was incensed at seeing the plumbing work, and demanded to know the schedule for replacing the toilets on board his boat. Bram checked and double-checked the repair lists and company orders before confirming my initial fears that none had been purchased for No. 1 tug. The reasons behind our sister appearing, on paper at least, to be the better of the two boats were suddenly becoming only too apparent: defects that had been there for everyone to see had either not been noted, or had been deleted from the lists in the mistaken belief of being unworthy of further attention or repair. It was a questionable policy of economy that would win no friends and do very little to keep an already malcontent and unhappy crew on board.

Remy and Mieke were vehemently opposed to André's insistent demands that the new toilets be shared, despite the bathrooms on both the boats being equally appalling. I was glad on this occasion not to be able to converse in the Dutch language, finding it quite bad enough to be a somewhat biased, but dumbstruck and silent bystander. The voices became raised and angry, the argument heated and bitter. Bram intervened by hurriedly agreeing to the ordering of two additional toilets, and instructing the puzzled plumbers to take one of those already delivered down the quayside and into the bathroom of Pieter's boat. A sensible compromise had won the day and given us all a temporary reprieve from the highly vocal disagreement.

The quarrel continued to simmer, albeit in a more civil manner, for most of the afternoon until it was quietly forgotten and we climbed ashore for our habitual evening stroll to the Playa de las Canteras. With the plumbing not yet reconnected on either boat, the spotlessly clean and immaculately presented *servicios* facilities of our regular and friendly restaurant would have to be utilised for a little while longer.

The Lloyds surveyor attended the following morning for the first of many visits to inspect the steering system and to issue the appropriate class certificate. Despite our thorough and rigorous testing the previous day, an unfriendly electrical gremlin prevented the rudder indicator in the wheelhouse from cooperating. With the shoreside electricians unable to resolve the problem quickly, the surveyor refused to issue the certificate and left the boat a short while later. It had become suddenly all too clear that the age and condition of the boats would make some of the mechanical and electrical repairs far more wide-ranging and comprehensive than initially planned.

The generator that had failed on No. 1 tug during the voyage from Abidjan was proving to be a far greater problem than had originally been envisaged. The rotor, one of the main components of the generator itself, was discovered to be so badly worn as to be irreparable in the Canary Islands, and it would have to be air-freighted back to the manufacturers in the UK to be rewound. With the repair predicted to take anything up to fourteen days, an alternative solution had to be found. We knew that a further delay of two weeks or more in port would not only be commercially unacceptable to the Singaporean owners, but would also cause immense frustration to the two crews: after only eight days, tempers were already becoming tense and frayed.

As a temporary measure only, Lloyds, the classification society, agreed to the hiring of a portable generator for the passage to Malta. The conditions of continuing to sail in convoy, and of reinstating the rewound rotor back into the original generator before leaving Valletta, were both practical and realistic. Unfortunately it didn't end there: the proposal would have been implemented immediately had the power take-off for the emergency air compressor not been mechanically linked to the engine of the generator under repair. No generator meant having no spare air compressor, a prospect for the Mediterranean passage that neither Willem nor Pieter was willing to consider for safety reasons. The hiring of a generator was left in abeyance, but arrangements were made with the agent for air-freighting the damaged rotor back to the manufacturers for rewinding. It would have to be repaired at some time during the voyage to Singapore, irrespective of the decisions yet to be made in Las Palmas.

The angry and rancorous falling out the previous day between André, Remy and Mieke hadn't ended as peacefully as we had first thought. After leaving our boat later in the afternoon, André had returned to No. 1 tug to air his strong feelings with Pieter. The undeniable fact that many of the difficulties and defects that existed on No. 1 tug were not being dealt with due to their deletion from the repair lists had upset him far more than anyone had initially realised. He considered the frugality to be misplaced and unreasonable, and to be at the expense and continuing discomfort of both himself and his shipmates. He could see no reason at all for their exclusion. The owners had, he rightly argued, sanctioned the repair of every defect and problem of which they had been made aware.

The embittered altercation that followed ended any remote possibility of Pieter and André remaining together for the ongoing voyage; the Master and chief officer have the challenging responsibility of ultimately respecting one another's decisions and of working closely as a team. The professional trust they might have previously shared in one another's capabilities and conduct had hopelessly unravelled in a few heated words that would be remembered by both parties with nothing but sorrow and regret.

Later in the evening, having already given them both twenty-four hours to reconsider their positions, Bram reluctantly accepted André's request for immediate repatriation on the grounds of an irrevocable breakdown in personnel relations. The second engineer, who had relieved Arno just a few days earlier, had already flown home to Holland; Mark, the cook, had left the day before; and now André, the chief officer, was due to leave in the next few days: my colleague was experiencing an unenviable nightmare with his crew. I would never have thought such a situation possible in such a small boat with so few persons involved.

I sincerely hoped the disease wasn't infectious, and that the good and happy working relationships we had been carefully nurturing aboard No. 2 tug would be sufficiently robust to resist all the pressures around it.

Shopping and leaks

The technical wrangling between air on the one hand and electricity on the other looked as if it might be amicably resolved in favour of air. The final decision to purchase a diesel-engined air compressor for No. 1 tug, instead of hiring a portable generator, was made after further consultation with the appropriate authorities. As compressed air was essential for the starting of the main engine and its continued running at sea, the buying of an emergency air compressor seemed both sensible and entirely logical. Telephone enquiries with a Dutch company confirmed that one could be despatched almost immediately to the Canaries, and would hopefully be delivered to the quayside within a few days. Both Pieter and Willem appeared delighted with the outcome of what might have been leading towards an insuperable problem.

The proposed installation outside would be relatively simple and avoided the difficulty of finding space in the already cluttered and congested engine room. Plans were drawn up with the ship repair draughtsman to weld bed-plates to the deck on the towing winch platform in a position protected from the elements by the funnel casing and winch housing. A combination of high-pressure pipes and flexible hoses would be piped directly from the new machine into the engine room and to the air-storage cylinders that act as a reserve in the event the main air compressor should fail.

No. 1 tug would make the eight-day passage from Las Palmas to Valletta with the one generator, which was in the process of being completely overhauled, backed up by the emergency batteries. It was a workable compromise that Willem had reluctantly to accept as being the best that could be done in the circumstances. The rewound rotor for their second generator would be awaiting our arrival in Valletta, where it would be installed and commissioned by shoreside fitters and electricians.

Bas, the third person to sail as second engineer in our sister tug since sailing from Abidjan, signed on at lunchtime. He was accompanied by Albert, a cook in his mid-sixties, who was already well known to both Mieke and Remy as one of the company's few remaining true and lasting characters. The introductions were made in an endless round of denture-less and jaw-dislocating smiles that would have done them proud in the finals of a seaside gurning competition. With their firm and sincere handshakes and their jovial and lighthearted attitudes, our gloom-and-doom moods of the past twenty-four hours were instantly lifted. They were like not one, but two breaths of life-saving fresh air, the morale booster we all so badly needed.

They had already been shown the uncivilised and grim conditions on board both the boats, and had grudgingly accepted them with a resigned shrug of the shoulders and an obvious determination that the situation could only improve. If my first impressions were anything to go by, I had the feeling that both Bas and Albert were here to stay, and would still be with us at the end of the voyage.

Despite spending most of the morning shopping, I was more than happy to take Shwe, Tin and Maung to the supermarket in the afternoon to buy some clothing, toiletries and gifts for their families. Their excursion ashore would be only the second time they had stepped onto dry land since sailing from Liberia many weeks earlier, although that had been their choice and certainly not mine. Their obvious delight in seeing the sights as we drove through the city was a joy to behold.

The expressions of total awe and disbelief as they entered the hypermarket were something I will treasure for a very long time. The immense size of the building with its several sales floors and seemingly endless aisles and displays boasting every possible type, colour and size of commodity one could ever wish to buy, left them standing motionless and open-mouthed. They must have remained by the entrance for four to five minutes, totally spellbound, eyes darting from one point of interest to another, completely oblivious to anything but their immediate surroundings. It was blatantly apparent they had never seen anything quite like it before. Daw Aung San Suu Kyi, the Nobel Peace Prize winner in 1991 and female political leader of the main opposition party to Myanmar's repressive and unpopular military regime, had just won another three converts to her electoral dream. I could see from the envy on their faces that our three Myanmar shipmates would be totally supportive of her electioneering pledges to modernise and improve their impoverished country.

Friday's National Holiday gave us a welcome break from the noise and hassle of the repair work, and the opportunity to safely bunker 60,000 litres of gas oil while there was no burning or welding work in progress. The additional fuel would be sufficient for us to steam for some eighteen or nineteen days at economic speed, a distance a little short of 4,000 nautical miles. The temporary break from not having the shore labour, fitters and technicians around, allowed us the time to try and assess the progress of the repair programme, and to make our plans for the ongoing voyage. While a major part of the repair work appeared to be nearing conclusion, some additional items would have to be completed during the coming week for our ambitious schedule to be maintained.

The arrival of Bas and Albert, and the imminent departure of André had, once again, brought to our attention the very real and pressing problems of the lower deck accommodation. Despite the warm and sunny weather and repairs to the outside vents, the cabins remained damp, musty and decidedly unhealthy spaces in which to live. It had to be said that in the ten days we had been in Las Palmas, we had made little effort to address properly the unacceptable conditions that existed in the dank and fetid atmosphere below the waterline.

The theft from No. 1 tug shortly after we had arrived had exacerbated the already serious problem by preventing the cabin doors from being left open to air the spaces inside. Although we had seen very few Africans since our move to Muelle del Virgen Pino, there were still one or two very suspicious hobo-type characters lurking around the quayside. Whether they were thieves or merely interested bystanders we would never know, but it was only human nature on our behalf that we should tar them all with the same brush. We were trying to keep a vigilant watch on the main deck access into the accommodation, but it was inevitable that there were moments when no one was around. With the benefit of hindsight, our security attempts were nothing more than paying lip service to the problem: had we suffered the ultimate indignity of being robbed again, none of us possessed either the stamina or the fitness to be able to chase after the fleeing robbers with their ill-gotten gains. The more I thought about it, the more futile and pointless it all became.

Our original intention had been to purchase one or two dehumidifiers for each boat for drying out the cabins, but it transpired that the ship's generators were producing an electrical current with a frequency incompatible with the appliances available in the Canary Islands. Not being electrically minded, I have absolutely no understanding of this voltage, frequency or cycle business. Remy explained, in very simplistic terms, that to feed a machine with the wrong frequency would generally make most machines run a little faster: for appliances such as dehumidifiers, which are dependent on sensitive electronics, supplying the incorrect frequency would be tantamount to providing an electrical 'coup de grâce'. As a result, we couldn't justify buying dehumidifiers, and the cabins had stayed damp and unhealthy.

With Carrefour and most of the other shops closed for the national holiday, Mieke had no excuses for dragging me ashore to do more shopping. Instead, I took the opportunity to spend some time studying the charts and navigational books for the onward passage to the Straits of Gibraltar and eastwards down the Mediterranean. I found the chartwork enjoyable and time-consuming; my first intimation that the sun had long passed its zenith and had dipped into mid-afternoon was the water dripping from the deckhead above straight onto the books and the chart table.

Marco and Shwe had taken the opportunity to wash the boat down with a fire hose to clean away some of the accumulated filth and debris from the repair work. Starting from the highest point, they were quick to discover that the waterproofing of the monkey island deck above the wheelhouse had clearly not achieved its intended purpose: the wheelhouse roof still leaked. Having abandoned the fire hose, we turned our attention to testing the steering gear, only to find that the rudder indicator, the cause of our failing the initial survey, remained stubbornly inactive. The electricians would have to return on Monday, as would the contractors to fix the roof. Perhaps our overall progress was not going as well as we had thought.

We were told it would be party time in the streets and plazas with the national holiday. Revellers would abound, sights would be seen, and we would have a night to remember. I have experienced and enjoyed a few Spanish fiestas and Mardi Gras with having a second home in Nerja on the Costa del Sol. I well know that most festival celebrations don't normally commence until a very late hour, and will then continue uninterrupted until the new day is born.

Despite my protestations that our stepping ashore was far too early, we set off at the usual hour, six of us together, dressed up to the nines and ready to sample and experience the delights. There were few people around and, if anything, it seemed to be quieter than usual. Disappointed, we headed for our regular restaurant at the end of the Playa, where we were greeted like long-lost friends by *los camareros*. We ordered our usual rounds of drinks and our favourite meals, and stayed there until late in the evening, when the lack of activity persuaded the impatient majority to abandon the night, disillusioned and deflated. My impulsive shipmates had made little or no effort to understand the finer points of Spanish festivals and their unpredictable and spontaneous timekeeping. Not wanting to walk back or to stay out on my own, I stayed with the party poopers to return to the boats.

The music and fireworks started shortly after we had climbed aboard and were to continue sporadically throughout the night. As the sun rose slowly above the horizon for the start of yet another day, the celebrations drew to a gradual and unwilling close: from all accounts, we had missed a very good night.

Another weekend

I awoke early after the anticlimax and disappointment of missing the fun and the festival frolics. In the hope of having neither rain nor fire hose to interrupt my work, I retired to the wheelhouse to continue with the chartwork and the preparation of the passage plan for the next leg of our voyage. My concentration went largely unhindered until the irresistible and hugely distracting smell of frying bacon and eggs lured me away from the chart table, and unerringly towards their source.

I had no idea that my 'full Monty' breakfast, complete with freshly percolated coffee, was to be a blatant and duplicitous culinary bribe. Shortly after finishing my meal, I found myself being briskly frogmarched down the quayside towards the grain elevator and the hire car parked conveniently underneath: the forever demanding Mieke and Albert had audaciously shanghaied me for yet another chauffeuring trip to Carrefour. My displeasure was made known to them both only too clearly: it was neither my intention nor my desire to spend my holiday weekend shopping for ships. With Mieke's familiarity of the store and its layout, and with Albert's much-ridiculed propensity for doing absolutely everything, including talking, at breakneck speed, there was little to delay us. Less than one hour later, we were back on the boats with the weekend lunches. I would have had no just cause for complaining if every trip to the hypermarket had been achieved with equal enthusiasm and speed.

The unprecedented luxury of an afternoon nap was to follow our lunch of baguettes and beer. Suitably refreshed, we gathered in the early evening for what had become our routine and unhurried stroll along Calle de Juan Rejon, and then on to our regular restaurant on La Playa de las Canteras. After a leisurely and very enjoyable meal, we set off down the esplanade, stopping off at one or two café-bars where we could sit outside in the evening twilight, drink our beer, and watch the holidaymakers and local family groups promenading and taking the night-time air.

André was flying home to Holland in the morning and was, quite naturally, determined to make the most of his last night in Las Palmas. We moved slowly away from the peace and quiet of the seafront before ending up, I'm sure not by accident, in the salsa club of which he had become a regular and quite familiar patron. Marco and André were soon in the thick of it, leaving the rest of us to sit quietly at the bar and absorb the atmosphere and the thunderous noise. A taxi took us back to the docks in the early hours, leaving our tirelessly energetic and salsa-loving chief officers to follow on later.

We bade our farewells to André at midday. Judging from the state of both his and Marco's eyes, extensive 'roof damage' had occurred at some point during or after their salsa dancing. From the extent of their dehydration and hangovers, I felt not the slightest regret in having abandoned the goodbye party sooner rather than later. Somewhat unsurprisingly, Marco declined my invitation to join Remy and Bas for an afternoon's drive out into the mountains. He obviously considered that a few peaceful hours of quiet meditation would far outweigh the benefits of exploring the island that had been our host for the past twelve days.

It was another glorious and sunny day for sightseeing, with just a few traces of high cirrus cloud. With Remy acting as my navigator, we set off through the city and found one of the main roads that climbed steadily towards the centre of the island. We paused only briefly at one or two panoramic viewing points as we headed towards the Pico de las Nieves. Taking the mountain road towards Camaretas and Ayacata, the scenery became familiar, only for me to realise a little later that we were retracing the route I had driven with Pieter and Willem the previous Sunday.

The very forgettable volcanic centre of the island appeared once again, but despite my protestations that there was little to see to justify stopping, Remy insisted upon taking some pictures. I couldn't complain; I knew that, with his keen and time-consuming interest in all things photographic, we would inherit a comprehensive and interesting record of our experiences together, whether they were on land or on sea.

Shortly after leaving the grassy volcanic amphitheatre, we found the same *restaurante* with the same table outside, vacant and free. Our *tapas* and 'wine of the summer' were just as enjoyable as before, and although only seven short days had elapsed since I had sat on the identical seat and admired the same breathtaking vista, I found new points of interest to study and some familiar ones deserving a second look.

We resumed our trip down the mountain road and joined the main highway towards San Bartolomé de Tirajana and south to the tourist town of Maspalomas. As we descended the meandering switchback above Fataga, the countryside became one of amazing and magnificent contrast, barren and moonscape in appearance, totally void of vegetation or scrub, but with the distant views to the south and the Atlantic Ocean unparalleled for their rugged and awesome beauty. Passing a herd of camels and a flock of ostrich, we questioned how they could possibly survive in such inhospitable and arid surroundings, and how they had come to be there in the first place. It was only a little later that we realised how close the islands are to mainland Africa, from where the animals had probably originated several hundred years earlier.

Maspalomas has provided many happy and memorable holidays for countless thousands of tourists seeking the sun and the glorious beaches, but, having just travelled down from the mountains and the real Gran Canaria, the attractions appeared both demeaning and tasteless. We didn't stop long. The 'Royal Oak' bars, the 'Jolly Roger' tattoo shops, and the dozens of garish outlets selling tee shirts, flip-flops, sunglasses, and the rubbishy overpriced knick-knacks that almost invariably end up decorating grandmother's mantelpiece for want of a better home, failed to impress us.

Our journey north on the *autovia* to Las Palmas was slow and tedious in the heavy holiday traffic. Finding a parking space close to the Playa was to lead us, as creatures of habit, to an evening meal at our regular restaurant. We returned to very quiet boats: the excesses of the night before had taken their toll. Our fiesta weekend was drawing finally to a close, and we would be back in the morning to the hustle and bustle and organised chaos of two tugboats undergoing repairs.

A Serrano for sailing

Bedlam announced the resumption of repairs. Monday can never be a good day, being at the beginning of the working week. Everything seems to happen on Mondays and with the two tugs it was no exception. The repairmen were having a field day: rejuvenated after their three-day break, they set about the funnels on both the boats with their cutting torches, burning one-metre-square holes into the external faces so we could climb inside the large oval-shaped steelwork to check the insulation and lagging, and attempt to discover the reason behind the fire on No. 1 tug shortly after we had sailed from Abidjan. We could find nothing: all the exhaust pipes from the main engine and the auxiliaries appeared to be in good condition, with the lagging and insulation free from oil or other combustible substances. There seemed to be no reason for a similar fire to occur on board our tug. We left the access hole open in case the surveyors wished to confirm our lack of findings.

Antonio, or Ton, as he prefers to be known, appeared on the quayside at the same time as the diesel-engined air compressor from Holland. Ton was to be No. 1 tug's new chief officer, a large man with a prominent corporation to match his build and a walrus-like moustache that successfully hides his upper lip and extends down either side of his mouth towards his chin. A heavy smoker, he breathes not only nicotine, but also likeability and sincerity. Having taken early retirement as a captain, Ton took up ship delivery work on a part-time basis rather than swallow the anchor completely and sit at home either twiddling his thumbs or waxing his moustache. Choosing to sail permanently as a professional chief officer, he is quite content to leave the responsibilities and hassle of being the Master to the younger generation. Been there, done that and got the tee shirt was his succinct reply to being asked whether he would like to sail as a captain again.

Failing not only the radio but also the engine surveys provided us with the first major setback of the week. During his couple of hours on board, the surveyor, who was polite and courteous but uncompromising in the exacting thoroughness of his inspections, managed to uncover sufficient defects to be able to write a precise and unambiguous report of his findings that covered two sheets of paper and made unpleasant reading for all those involved with the repairs. Until all the problems in his lengthy report had been resolved, we wouldn't be going anywhere. Las Palmas was clearly going to be our home for a little while longer.

With the majority of the mechanical and structural repairs completed, we had the painstaking task of checking every item on the original and additional defect lists to ensure the work had been carried out as specified and that the remedies had been effective. Directing a fire hose at the portholes on the main deck and the watertight doors leading into the accommodation revealed the second setback of the week: like the monkey island deck, which acted as the roof of the wheelhouse, water was still appearing where it had no right to be. While only of a minor nature in most cases, the leaks would have to be fixed before we sailed. The lower deck accommodation and its four occupants had already suffered more than enough from the ingress of seawater during the first leg of the voyage.

As part of the radio survey, the surveyor had tested the 24-volt electrical system supplying not only the radio installation, but also the navigational instruments in the wheelhouse, and had found one of those awkward and aggravating intermittent faults that baffles even the experts. The repair company's electricians were having considerable difficulty in persuading it to work properly. Fed from a large bank of car batteries, which are continuously charged by the boat's generators, the supply was proving to be erratic and unreliable. During the twenty-seven-year life of the boats, basic wiring and switching had deteriorated to the point that in extreme cases it was no longer functional. The situation was further aggravated by the plans and drawings of the original installation being either incomplete or so faded as to be no longer legible. The bridge instrumentation and radios depend upon the fail-safe system that is designed to provide operating power for a limited number of hours in the event of a total failure of the boat's electrical generating plant.

In the afternoon I left the electricians to mull and puzzle over their faded and tatty plans for yet another run up to Carrefour, supposedly for the last-minute bits and pieces. The galley radios on both boats, the starting point for almost every rumour, whether it be good or bad, had intimated that we might be sailing in a couple of days, although I would like to have known from where that idea had originated. Remy took the opportunity to accompany Mieke, Albert and me in the hire car, although he kept strangely quiet about his reasons for wishing to go shopping.

The truth was there for all to see when he rejoined us at the checkout forty-five minutes later. Clutched in his sweaty left hand was the largest Serrano ham I have ever seen, a thigh so succulent and meaty that undoubtedly it must have originated from the most overweight and overfed boar to have been bred in the whole of Spain. No wonder he had been reticent about his intentions. I had the distinct, but mischievous, impression that he was hoping to somehow sneak the back end of the beast secretly aboard so that he could hang it behind his cabin door where he could quietly carve off a slice whenever it took his fancy. My hunch could never have been more correct, although he dared not admit it. He did indeed hang it behind his cabin door, and his fancy was such that only the bone, picked absolutely clean as if it had been thrown to a school of piranha fish, remained a fortnight later; no one but Remy could be held responsible for its brisk and efficient despatch.

Smiling electricians and a brand-new battery charger permanently wired into the 24-volt system provided the boat's radios and navigational instrumentation with uninterrupted power and a new lease of life. Everything had been checked, plans and drawings stowed away, and Shwe's psychedelic linoleum taken up and removed to allow the original and undamaged non-slip ribbed deck matting underneath to be scrubbed clean. We were brimming with confidence as we discreetly watched the Lloyds surveyor walking down the quayside the following afternoon. There were no apparent reasons why we should fail the surveys a second time: every defect on his list, and more besides, had been rectified and double-checked.

Sadly, the generators had not been included in our plans to impress. At the precise moment the surveyor stepped onto the gangway, as if the weight of one of his feet had activated a hidden switch on one of the steps, they spluttered and coughed once or twice before falling into total silence. The lack of mechanical noise was eerie. We sat in the unlit messroom and waited for something to happen. Nothing could be done to persuade either of the generators to provide power to the distribution panel; the fault, we were told, gave every appearance of being identical to the cooker problem on No. 1 tug in Abidjan three weeks earlier. The surveyor kicked his heels impatiently for a few minutes before calling it a day and agreeing with Bram to return in the morning. It was not the most auspicious start to obtaining the vital certificates we required for continuing the voyage.

A glimpse into the fortune-teller's crystal ball must have been behind the port authority's request the previous day for us to moor the tugs alongside one another. The fact that another vessel needed No. 2 tug's berth was extremely fortuitous, to say the least. The trusty power cable that Tin had been using in Buchanan was rigged again between the two boats so that No. 1 tug could provide us with electrical power until such time as our generators could be made to run. We left the engineers and electricians working overtime, and took our usual wander down Calle de Juan Rejon and onto the Playa for what the optimists considered might be our last evening meal in Las Palmas. I remained undecided about whether I should share their obvious enthusiasm. Unpredictable setbacks seemed to have been ruining our week.

The surveyor boarded again in the morning to the reassuring sound of the generators running and the lights glowing brightly. The cause of the blackout the previous afternoon had finally been traced to a small mechanical problem with the governors on the generators, ably assisted by a loose wire inside the switchboard that had resulted in one of those intermittent faults that are frustratingly difficult to find. The optimism for sailing suddenly seemed as if it hadn't been misplaced after all.

The surveyor had got out of bed on the right side and one hour later a safety radio certificate, loadline and safety exemption certificates, and interim class certificates for the engine room had all been issued. What a difference a day can make. He had either not noticed, or had chosen to ignore, the two air-conditioning units boldly protruding from either side of the housing on both of the boats. For me, it made little difference. Despite my less than subtle pleadings, Bram had regrettably decided there was no justification in repairing my unit when the surveyor might have insisted upon its removal prior to our leaving. Fortunately I still had a forward-facing porthole that could be opened to catch any breeze if the weather should become unbearably hot, unlike the four cabins two decks below that still smelt damp and stale, and had had absolutely nothing done to them during our lengthy stay in port.

Our departure plans were hastily activated. The hire car was returned to its depot and the inspection holes in the funnels welded up. The port clearance papers were arranged with the agents, who were able to book an early evening flight for Bram back to Holland. After sixteen days in Las Palmas, the impossible had been achieved: both boats had undergone extensive repairs and trading certificates had been issued permitting us to complete the long voyage ahead to Singapore. We would sail after lunch.

The author Dave Creamer. Master Oriental Tug No. 2

Renewing distorted porthole frames, Las Palmas

The wheelhouse of No.2 tug

'Dad's army recalled'. The crew of Oriental Tug
No.1 *ready to repel boarders*

Oriental Tug No. 2 *alongside Muelle del Virgen Pino, Las Palmas*

Oriental Tug No. 2 *in calm waters*

Laid-up stern trawlers, Las Palmas

Oriental Tug No. 1 *being towed to Muelle del Virgen Pino, Las Palmas*

Captain Pieter Van Noord. Master Oriental Tug No. 1 *with 'catch of the day'*

Oriental Tugs No. 1 & No. 2 *alongside Muelle del Virgen Pino, Las Palmas*

The two tugs moored together steaming off Malta.
Swimming pool can be seen on the aft deck No. 2 tug

From left to right: Ex-Captain Shwe Myint;
Ex-Captain Maung and Ex-Chief Engineer Tin Nyunt

Air conditioning unit removed for repair, Valletta

Oriental Tug No. 1. *Cook Albert ('Appie') filleting a fish on deck*

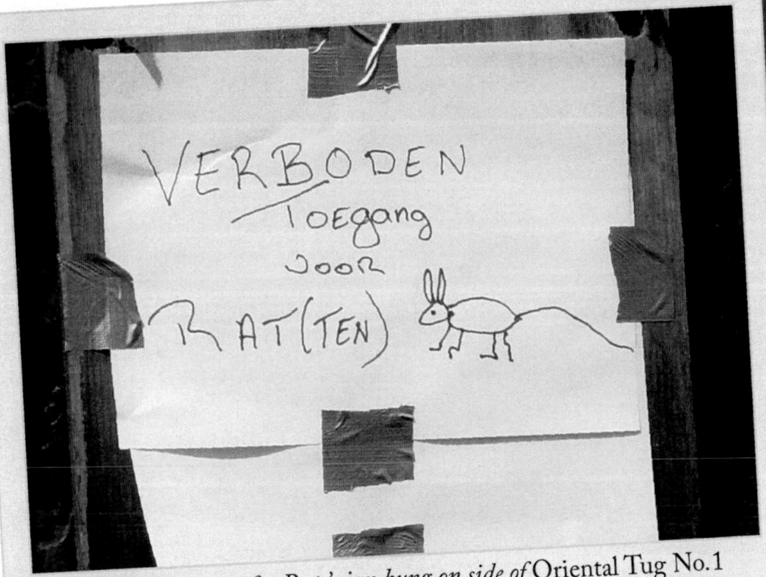

'Forbidden Entry for Rats' sign hung on side of Oriental Tug No. 1
when two boats berthed alongside each other off Malta

Oriental Tug No. 2 *in the Indian Ocean*

5

LAS PALMAS TO VALLETTA

Back to sea

Slipping the mooring ropes and being able to point the bows in the general direction of the harbour entrance brought a huge and welcome sense of relief to us all. The boat surged impatiently forward, almost willingly it seemed, as we headed towards the outer breakwater. Bram, who had stood on the quayside to witness our safe and long-awaited departure, left at the same time to head in the opposite direction towards the airport and an early evening flight back home to Holland. As he climbed into his waiting taxi, I couldn't help noticing the envious looks from one or two shipmates as they jealously watched him make good his escape. With a final wave from the vehicle's back window he was soon out of sight. We were on our own once again.

The open waters beckoned invitingly beyond the imposing granite-block sea wall to which dozens of laid-up deep-sea trawlers had been moored double and triple banked so as to use the limited quayside space efficiently. Clearing the breakwater, we slowly powered up the engines, ever conscious of all the repairs that had been carried out and the need to slowly nurse the boats back to their normal working condition. With No. 1 tug adopting her usual position in the lead, we started pitching and rolling very lazily to the low and long incoming swell of the Atlantic Ocean. The most welcome, yet barely perceptible, movement brought home the reality of that very special and respectful relationship every sailor has developed with the sea. To experience the motion of the waves after being ashore for so many days or weeks provides the seafarer with a lighthearted, almost relaxed, feeling of being at home once again. We were back to where we truly belonged, back with the sea and back to all the challenges it would bring.

Our course was set to pass to the west of Lanzarote and on towards the distant Moroccan coast and the Straits of Gibraltar. Gran Canaria and the Pico de las Nieves slipped slowly away behind us to become little more than a darkened shadow on the hazy horizon. I handed over the navigational duties to Marco and retired to my cabin to catch up on paperwork.

The pen had barely touched the paper before Remy was knocking at my open door. Perspiring heavily, his facial expression was one of total and abject misery. I could immediately sense his utter and complete dejection before he spoke. The main engine seawater-cooling pipe had failed in two places, and his attempts at making temporary repairs to reduce the flow of escaping water hadn't been successful. I insisted upon seeing the damage for myself, not that I didn't believe him, but so that I would be able to describe the scene accurately should I ever be asked.

The leaking section of alloy-type pipe gave the appearance of having become corroded and porous with age. The small holes from which the two jets of seawater were harmlessly squirting were unhelpfully located on the outside of a right-angled bend in an awkward and barely accessible position. As Remy had already discovered, it would be almost impossible to bandage the pipe to render it watertight. As the leaks looked relatively inconspicuous, I momentarily questioned his concern, until I realised that if the whole pipe were to fail suddenly, the main engine would have to be shut down and the ship's side valves closed to prevent the engine room from flooding. The prospect of my hapless command sinking slowly and perhaps not so gracefully beneath the surface on her way to an ignominious and early grave was not one I relished. Turning back and returning whence we had just come, despite the obvious cost in terms of morale, was really the only sensible option. I left Marco to advise Pieter and Ton of our situation on the VHF radio, while I called Bram on my cellphone. Fortunately I still had a signal and managed to catch him in the airport departure lounge shortly before he boarded his flight.

The few seconds of dumbfounded silence were quickly followed by rapid-fire expletives in both Dutch and English, before self-discipline and a degree of constraint took over. He would return to the city and make contact with the agents and the ship repair firm, while we steamed back slowly towards the port. No. 1 tug would anchor in the bay off the breakwater to avoid being charged for additional harbour dues. There was no reason to suspect that the pipe repair would take too long, and there was absolutely nothing our colleagues on our sister tug could do by way of providing assistance once we were back alongside.

The port authority instructed us to proceed to the same berth on the Muelle del Virgen Pino, the Virgin Pine. Bram and the ship repair people were waiting for us on the quayside as if we had never been away, although a welcoming party would have been putting too fine a point upon it. We were all considerably disheartened at having to return to the port just a few hours after leaving. Having spent sixteen days alongside undergoing repairs, we found it difficult to accept that further remedial work should be needed within such a short space of time. With the main engine shut down and the seawater intake valves located at the ship's side closed to stop the leaks, the defective section of alloy cooling pipe was disconnected and transported ashore to the contractor's workshops for patching and rebuilding.

No one could face traipsing up the road again and having to make yet another round of *adios mis amigos* farewells to the friendly and attentive staff of our adopted *restaurante*. Besides, we had no idea how long the repairs would take. Instead, our evening meal was prepared by Mieke and eaten in the mess. The atmosphere was similar to that of a happy death party, but without either the alcohol or the nostalgic recollections of those gone before us. We might as well have been summoned to the Last Supper, such was the mood of gloom and doom among my dining companions.

The pipe was returned on board in the late evening, but by the time it had been reconnected and tested, it was well past midnight. The decision to sail at first light after everyone had been fully rested was taken for reasons of both safety and convenience. Having managed to rebook his flight for mid-morning, Bram retired to his hotel for the night, while we retired to our bunks to dream yet again of soon sailing away.

Breakfast in the half-light of dawn was a subdued and solemn affair and no more cheerful than our evening meal had been the night before; our bacon and eggs were eaten in total silence, almost as if it were the quiet before the storm, the very last act before the final curtain. No one had the courage or temerity to say a few words, however irrelevant, just to break the spell. There was an air of expectancy, as if we were in anticipation of something else going wrong, but had not an inkling of what it might be. Sailing from Abidjan had been quite different. There, we had accepted the challenge of reaching the Canary Islands knowing full well that the boats were in a neglected and extremely poor condition. Undergoing extensive repairs for sixteen days had brought about change: we were back in class, fully certificated and deemed by those in the know to be capable of safely making the voyage to Singapore. In the harsh and cold light of day our concerns were intuitive rather than factual, but instinct can often play a decisive role in our lives. Time would be the ultimate judge as to whether perception or reality would prove correct on the day.

Bram acted as linesman and let go our moorings before waving a confident goodbye. For the second time in two days he set off towards the airport, while we proceeded towards the breakwater and the dozens of laid-up rusting trawlers. Pieter and his crew, who had been patiently waiting all night for our departure, started weighing their anchor as we headed out of the port and towards the open sea. We set our course once again to pass to the west of Lanzarote, proceeding slowly so that No. 1 tug could overtake us and lead the way after raising and stowing her anchor. Nothing had been changed in the convoy order; our sister tug was proving to be an invaluable aid to our steering by hand.

Looking astern and back towards the anchorage, there appeared little or no indication that No. 1 tug was making an effort to join us. There was no response to our calls on the VHF radio, and no disturbance in the water at her stern to indicate her propeller was turning and that she was getting underway. Altering course, we headed back towards the bay. As we drew closer I could see through the binoculars a great deal of frenzied activity on her foredeck. The VHF radio crackled into life shortly after we had slowly steamed a full circle around her. Pieter sounded none too happy. A hydraulic coupling had blown on their windlass, leaving their starboard anchor still hanging in the water; no spare couplings could be found and the voyage obviously couldn't be progressed with the anchor and 3 metres of heavy chain dangling outside the hull and trailing along behind them. They would have to return to the repair berth to seek shoreside assistance to replace the coupling and a length of badly corroded hydraulic pipe. If our troubles hadn't been so serious, our attempts to escape the clutches of Gran Canaria would have been quite amusing.

Bram, seated at the café in the now familiar airport departure lounge, was completely lost for words, totally silent and speechless. At first he thought I might be joking. It was only after the third repetition that I eventually succeeded in convincing him I was speaking the truth, although I could understand and sympathise with his evident reluctance to believe me. It is, so I am informed, one of the penalties of possessing a not totally undeserved reputation for mischievous wind-up humour. He left the airport for a second time without managing to board an aircraft. No. 1 tug headed slowly back into port, trailing the short length of chain and anchor down her starboard side, while I elected not to anchor, but to drift around in the anchorage area using the engine as and when necessary to maintain our position. The specialist hydraulic engineers with their fancy gauges and instruments hadn't reassured me one bit that our windlass was capable of reliably performing its designated purpose in life. I had already determined that our anchors would only be used as a last resort and when all other options had been exhausted.

A couple of hours later saw the repairs to No. 1 tug completed. If the spares had been available, either Willem or Remy would have been more than capable of carrying out the work. As it was, she appeared in all her glory outside the breakwater shortly after lunch, anchor stowed and ready for the voyage. We manoeuvred into position five cables behind her and, once again, set our course for Lanzarote and beyond.

I tried telephoning Bram to thank him for his help, and belatedly to wish him a safe journey home. For some very peculiar reason I received no response: his cellphone had been switched off. It seemed a little too early for his rescheduled evening flight to be airborne, but who could really blame him for making himself unobtainable after the events of the previous twenty-four hours?

No longer for Larry

I always find it difficult to sleep properly for the first night when I'm back at sea, whether it is after a few days in port, or after a few weeks ashore at home. Sailing from Las Palmas was no different. Disturbed by the usual mechanical noises and vibration from the main engine and the occasional, but very irritating, sharp knock or rumble from an unsecured domestic item rolling around with the movement of the boat, my hours off watch from midnight until eight in the morning were reduced to a series of worthless and frustrating catnaps. I also had to contend with some worrying and unusual noises from my air mattress, unfamiliar rasping and flatulent-like sounds that were emitting from beneath me with every restless movement I made. Giving mouth-to-rubber resuscitation to some of the panels that appeared to be no longer airtight and were slowly but surely deflating seemed only to prolong their agony, and to exhaust me physically in the process. I had an awful foreboding that my hours of sleeping on a cushion of air were strictly numbered, and resigned myself to accepting that the unforgiving and rigid contours of my rock-filled West African mattress would be imprinted upon my back within a few days, whether I liked it or not.

Much to everyone's joy, Larry, our seagoing lizard, reappeared two days after sailing. He had vanished shortly after our arrival in Las Palmas, and hadn't been seen since. Our pessimistic fears that he had probably fallen foul of the unseeing boot of one of the Spanish repair contractors had proved unfounded. He had obviously been driven into temporary hiding, or a short hibernation, by the intrusion of strangers and the incessant noise of the ongoing repairs. I suspected that food during our stay in port might have been a problem for him: the very few ants remaining on board prior to our arrival had abandoned ship after our berthing on the Grande Muelle. Thankfully they were no longer to be seen and Mieke's deadly insect spray had been returned to the messroom drawer, hopefully to remain there for the rest of the voyage.

Larry had taken the opportunity of being in port to climb up a deck, and had settled in the more salubrious surroundings of the recently renovated bathroom that Remy and I now had the pleasure of sharing. He had shown commendable tastes in selecting his new abode, one that had been refitted with a pristine, shiny white lavatory that fulfilled all its designed functions without the assistance of buckets or balers, and a shower that provided hot and cold water at the turn of a tap. Shutting his eyes would have helped the illusion, for there was no escaping the dingy and rust-streaked paintwork and the cracked and scarred concrete that had been laid many years before as a protective non-slip coating for the steel of the bathroom deck.

My delight in finding Larry was somewhat tempered by his sickly appearance. Looking lethargic and desperately thin, he didn't possess the strength to acknowledge my presence. A few hours later he was in the same position, but lying on his back, legs stiffly outstretched and with his little green toes curled tautly inwards: rigor mortis had already set in. I scooped him up on a piece of cardboard and gave him a quiet and dignified burial at sea without any service or ceremony. His spectacular success at exterminating his very own food stocks had obviously brought about a premature death from starvation: he was to be sorely missed. We were never to know if he had lived his life as a simple seafaring lizard, or as a chameleon in disguise.

The oil-drum water butts that had fulfilled such a vital role in preserving fresh water stocks in Liberia had been removed from the bathrooms and were now lashed down on deck ready for use as either incinerators or barbecues. A cheap and cheerful washing machine took pride of place in the main deck bathroom. Wrong electrical cycles and consequently a washing speed that was far in excess of what its designers had ever intended would ensure a limited but exciting life. As it had cost less than half the outrageous price the local *lavandería* had charged for the two bundles of laundry sent ashore, we calculated it would be a sensible and worthwhile purchase if it lasted for longer than a week. Our domestic facilities were now every bit as good as the age and general condition of the boat would permit.

Two and a half days after leaving Gran Canaria we were thirty-five miles off the Moroccan coast and passing Casablanca, too far off to see even a hint of coastline. The weather had been reasonably kind and we had made good progress. Ahead lay the Straits of Gibraltar and the unwanted forecast of an easterly gale that would be right on our bows. The narrow entrance into the Mediterranean, with the high land of the European and African continents on either side, acts like a constricting funnel for both wind and sea. Tarifa, the Spanish town at the western edge of the Straits is well known in the sporting fraternity as a location for the almost perfect windsurfing conditions, a long and shallow sandy beach and strong westerly winds coming in off the Atlantic Ocean. During the hot summer months, the campsites behind the beach are brimming with tents and camper vans, and the white-crested seas dotted with the triangular and colourful sails of speeding surfboards.

Cape Spartel, the north-western tip of Morocco, was passed halfway through my evening watch. The wind increased to north-easterly force 6–7 as we rounded the headland. We started pitching and rolling heavily as we turned into the Straits and joined the traffic separation scheme that acts as a nautical highway in keeping the easterly and westerly shipping routes apart, with an exclusion zone, or central barrier, located between the two lanes. I followed Pieter in making my mandatory position report on the VHF radio to Tarifa Tráfico, the Spanish Coastguard station at Tarifa responsible for monitoring all the shipping movements through the busy Straits of Gibraltar. Our two tugboats would now be tracked on the shoreside radar screens as we slowly progressed through the narrow and normally bustling waterway.

The Straits were unusually quiet and almost devoid of shipping. Short and steep seas were breaking over our bows and onto the main deck. Sheets of spray, urged on in the howling wind, climbed up and over the wheelhouse, rattling noisily against the bridge windows before cascading down in gushing waterfalls over the strengthened glass. The second attempt at waterproofing repairs on the monkey island seemed to have proved effective, and mopping puddles of water from the wheelhouse deck while slipping around on a wet linoleum surface appeared to be a hazardous chore of the past.

We reduced speed with the strengthening wind. Slamming head-on into the heavy seas would only increase the risk of damage, cause unnecessary discomfort to everyone, and waste expensive fuel for little or no gain. The forecasters, to our detriment, had got their predictions exactly right. The further east we steamed into the Straits the stronger the wind became, until it was blowing a full easterly gale, a typical summer Mediterranean depression that would quickly blow itself out. While it wasn't the best of conditions for two old and hard-worked harbour tugs, experience reassured me that once we had passed the Spanish enclave of Ceuta on the Moroccan coast, both the wind and the sea would quickly moderate and life aboard would return to normal.

I was very glad to hand over the bridge watch to Marco at midnight. I had found it quite exhausting hand steering continuously for four hours in the heavy seas. Trying to follow the stern light of No. 1 tug as it moved around, fading and sometimes momentarily disappearing altogether behind the sheets of water frequently drenching the wheelhouse windows, had made my eyes tired and weary. As I left the bridge, the shore lights of Gibraltar and Algeciras bay could be seen twinkling in the distance just forward of the port beam. I couldn't help remembering the many days of trial and tribulation both Remy and I had spent in Gibraltar on the *Justine* just a few months earlier. It was pure conjecture whether our current voyage on the *Oriental* tugs would be remembered with such clarity and misplaced affection.

Pallets and pools

Sunrise saw us well into the Mediterranean. Two hours later, as I was taking over the watch from Shwe at eight o'clock, the easterly wind dropped away until it was virtually calm with a bank of sea fog clearly visible in the distance. We watched it make its unhurried approach, a white mass of rolling vapour, an impenetrable fluffy cloud that steamed off the surface of the water as if the very sea itself was boiling. The abrupt change in the weather in such a short space of time was as dramatic as it was sudden. Just a few hours earlier we had been battling our way against steep, white-crested waves and a full-blown gale; now the sea was flat and barely rippled, with an enveloping shroud of dense and clammy fog hanging over us like a huge opaque curtain that reduced the visibility so that we could no longer see even the bows of our boats just a few metres away.

Shwe remained on the bridge with me; I didn't have to ask him to stay for he already appreciated the impracticalities of simultaneously hand steering and keeping a careful radar watch. He continued with the steering while I kept my eyes glued on the dozens of targets scattered like confetti on the circular radar display. I found it almost hypnotic tracking the much faster eastbound vessels as they overhauled us at a great rate of knots before blindly and casually overtaking, sometimes quite closely, with all the confidence and accuracy that modern electronics and anti-collision systems can provide. Fortunately Shwe's extended duty didn't last too long. The fog was burnt off by the strengthening sun and, by our mid-morning coffee break, the visibility had sufficiently improved for everyone to join me in the wheelhouse for our daily attempt at putting the world to rights.

Pieter and I chose the same morning to have our first professional difference of opinion. Sailing together in convoy made it inevitable that we should think differently and individually at some stage of the voyage. Our argument was a trivial, perhaps even laughable, matter of adjusting our speeds so that we could arrive off Valletta at daybreak on the Sunday. It was a stupid and churlish disagreement over a decision about whether we should slow down immediately or maintain our present speed and slow down a day before our arrival. The root cause of our senseless quarrel appeared to be based on the degrees of confidence we had in our engine rooms. We agreed to disagree and to keep on sailing at our present speed for a further twenty-four hours before raising the matter again.

Later in the morning, the office in Holland conveniently resolved the issue by instructing us to slow down to a minimum speed so as to arrive off the Fairway buoy at Valletta, not on the Sunday, but at the beginning of the new working week. The Singaporean owners had made the decision that the financial benefits of avoiding the high and unproductive cost of dockyard overtime far outweighed those of voyage expediency. Further repairs and reinstating the refurbished generator rotor for No.

1 tug would be carried out only in normal working hours. Our nonsensical dispute had been amicably settled without loss of face to either party. We could stay good friends for a little while longer.

Shortly before midday, Remy joined me in the wheelhouse to catch a glimpse of the Chaparil mountains that soar majestically above the coastline close to Nerja, the Spanish seaside resort on the Costa del Sol. Being eastbound and heading for the coast off Tunisia, we were too far from the land to be able to see anything but a vague and shadowy outline darkening the distant and hazy horizon. Nonetheless I had a deep yearning to be back in the town where I have my second home and many friends and acquaintances. During our last voyage together on the *Justine*, Remy and I had been able to pay Nerja a short weekend visit when the boat had been undergoing repairs in Gibraltar. The fact that our two days away had coincided with the annual *carnaval* had made our impromptu sojourn one of those remarkable and unforgettable occasions. Despite the passionate longing on both our faces, Nerja wouldn't be receiving a visit from either of us on this particular voyage. We continued on our way eastwards, following in the wake of our convoy leader.

Now that we were sailing into the warmer and sunnier Mediterranean weather off the Algerian and Libyan coasts, Mieke decided to construct a wooden sunlounger upon which she could sunbathe in the afternoons. Shwe, always the chivalrous and perfect gentleman, watched her cack-handed and clumsy struggles with a wood-saw, hammer and nails for only a few minutes before politely offering his assistance. The positions were quickly reversed as the uncomplaining Mieke gratefully accepted her new role as an observer, pupil and part-time carpenter's mate. Shwe proved to be not only a master mariner, but also a carpenter-cum-cabinetmaker extraordinaire. He had obviously learnt the traditional woodworking skills by closely understudying the same Chinese carpenters who had made the captain's teak bedroom suite in Rangoon so many years ago. At least Shwe's furniture-making efforts wouldn't be destroyed by the drying effects of aggressive air conditioning.

Like the Chinese chippies, he was able to use his seemingly double-jointed and splinter-resistant toes as vices to hold the wood he was cutting. In no time at all, he had fashioned a robust and very presentable sunlounger from lengths of rough planking salvaged from some of the second-hand broken pallets we had acquired from the quaysides in Las Palmas. Most people would have discarded the splintered scraps of timber as mere firewood for the incinerator. The sunlounger's design was undoubtedly revolutionary in that the non-adjustable height of the fixed legs would give it the dual purpose of serving as a counter or high table for the barbecues we were planning once the warmer weather was upon us. He continued his carpentry for the rest of the afternoon by making a wooden bench and a table to join the two steel benches that Tin had welded together from scrap metal during their stay in Buchanan. The end result was a seating area on the stern with tables and benches every bit as good as those at a roadside picnic area and a slatted sunlounger minus its all-important access ladder, which could be instantly converted to an additional table should the need ever arise.

A day after Shwe had finished his carpentry, Remy and Marco announced that they were going to construct a swimming pool. While I didn't doubt their sincerity, having a pool on board a tugboat was something I had neither seen nor experienced before. I have many recollections of permanent swimming pools on deep-sea ships, including the distinct and unhappy memory as a deck cadet of having to scrub one from top to bottom with my toothbrush. I thought the punishment for splashing the deck-golf course that surrounded the pool shortly before the captain and his guests were due to tee or 'puck' off in their early evening round of golf to be particularly draconian. Several afternoons and many toothbrushes later, and with a face and neck sunburnt and blistered from the unrelenting tropical sun, I had learnt my lesson the hard way, but that is another story.

Remy and Marco hadn't been joking. Using the towing frame, the aluminium gangway and the two ex-bathroom oil drums filled with seawater as pillars to support the remainder of the stolen pallets, they cordoned off the rounded section of bulwark on the starboard quarter to produce an almost oval-shaped enclosure. Numerous rope and wire lashings were secured around the drums and the gangway to prevent them from being displaced once the pool had been filled. The reason behind a large plastic tarpaulin mysteriously appearing on my Carrefour shopping list in Las Palmas now became clear. Once the pallets had been checked to ensure there were no protruding nails or sharp edges, the tarpaulin was unfolded and positioned within the space. Marco stood inside the slowly filling pool and carefully kick-stretched the plastic sheeting as the seawater from the fire hose poured in. Within an hour, we had a very acceptable swimming pool well over a metre deep. To circulate and refresh the water, the fire pump was started and the permanently rigged washdown hose fed seawater into the bottom until the pool overflowed onto the deck and the pump could be switched off. I had learnt in just a few hours that my Dutch colleagues not only have the ability to keep water out, but also to keep it in. The pool was an exemplary model of their dyke-building skills in reverse. I rejected the idea of painting a deck-golf course next to the pool: we had neither the pucks, wooden mallets nor sufficient toothbrushes for the pool cleaning the captain inevitably would demand if his course should become the slightest bit wet.

As the ambient temperature increased with our easterly passage, gatherings by the pool became a social event for all those off duty. With the cabins still being relatively airless, sitting outside and having the luxury of being able to take a cooling dip when it became unbearably stuffy and hot made living on board just that little more acceptable. Thankfully the sea conditions remained reasonably kind. If the pitching or rolling became more than gentle, the internal wave pressure on the plastic tarpaulin would prove too much for the lashings holding the drums and pallets in place and the pool would cease to exist.

Perhaps my half-deflated air mattress would have a second life after all, but my hopes that it could be reincarnated as a lilo-waterbed upon which I could relax in the pool were swiftly dashed. The few remaining airtight panels lacked sufficient buoyancy to keep my head above the water. In a fit of childish frustration and temper,

I threw the limp and deflated remains into the still smouldering incinerator in which we had recently burnt our bags of rubbish, only to realise a couple of minutes later that the dark clouds of acrid black smoke billowing from the burning rubber could be interpreted as a signal of distress if seen by any passing ships. Fortunately, no offers of assistance were received, and a few minutes later all traces of my faithful inflatable friend had disappeared forever. Fait accompli: I was back to my African mattress.

Roland the rat

Six days after leaving Las Palmas, Algiers lay on our starboard beam some forty miles beyond the horizon. With a gentle east-north-easterly wind and clear blue skies unmarked by even a hint of cloud, the Mediterranean was having one of its more compassionate and hospitable days. I paused from my leisurely strolling and leaned on the bulwark to stare out at the sea. The dazzling strobes of sunlight being reflected in the shimmering wavelets were mesmerising and almost blinding. A long and barely noticeable swell casually rocked the boat as gently as a young mother would her newborn child. Circling above the housing at masthead height, a couple of seagulls soared patiently and effortlessly, ever watchful for the unwary fish that might incautiously leap to the surface to escape the disturbance of our passing wash. Ignoring the steady throb and vibration of the main engine and generator, it was, quite simply, a beautiful day for being at sea.

During my morning bridge watch I had made the irrational and ill-conceived decision to resume my physical exercising while the weather was balmy and not too hot. As with my previous voyage on the *Justine*, I resolved once again to pace the main deck every afternoon in a futile attempt to keep my ever-expanding waistline under strict control and within the limits of medical acceptability. A critical self-appraisal of my sideways egg-on-legs shape had convinced me that I could derive some benefit, and probably come to little or no harm, from participating in some form of casual exercise, providing it was neither too energetic nor too challenging. Persuading my strict and not-so-impartial shipping federation doctor that my so-called obesity is really only a relaxed muscle disorder that comes with age has become a visionary and impossible dream. Finding an original excuse, or an acknowledged medical ailment for being just a little overweight is becoming more difficult by the year: my doctor has heard it all before.

I find walking at sea to be quite a pleasurable exercise, irrespective of whether it may be beneficial. To most people, the act of strolling continuously around a steel deck for a couple of hours would appear rather mundane and tiresome. There can never be a destination, and reaching a target is impossible, unless it is one of hours or minutes spent walking. Completing a specified number of laps of the deck can never provide the same personal sense of achievement as having hiked the measured distance between two set points, or walking along a recognised route that has been clearly mapped out in a rambler's guide. A maritime walk can, quite simply, be very monotonous. Occasionally there might be a point of interest, a passing ship, a school of dolphins or porpoise, perhaps a faint dark shadow of distant land, but generally there is nothing: only the sea and the sky, and the deck that is being walked.

I enjoy the solitude of taking a nautical stroll; the brain can be switched off and the mind set in neutral. Dreams can be dreamt and plans can be made. The scenery remains unchanged: just the solitary straight line of the horizon clearly visible in every direction, below the line the darker hue of the sea, and above the line the lighter blue of the sky. Apparent, Sensible or Visible horizons, Rational and Artificial horizons are all names I learnt in my navigational lessons at marine school for that distant horizontal and level line that will always show that most, if not all, floating objects will still be gently rolling or pitching even in the smoothest of waters. Walking at sea is not merely about the forward and backward movement of the lower limbs that we discover as young children, but also about bracing and balancing against the continuously changing angle of the decks upon which we walk, an extra effort that can quickly tire the legs and exhaust the muscles. Stepping onto dry land will soon reveal every sailor's 'battleship roll'. He has to learn all over again how to walk on the still and unmoving surface of the terra firma upon which he has come to land.

My shipmates said very little after watching me take to the deck for the second consecutive afternoon, but the questioning looks in their eyes revealed their obvious anxiety for my mental health. Only I was to blame for their heartfelt concerns: I had absolutely no intention of divulging my exercise strategy or intentions to them and ending up being the target for their non-stop ridicule and merciless barracking. I already knew I was being talked about behind my back. I suppose the sight of their Leader walking aimlessly round and round in circles, whether they be diminishing or not, was providing them with understandable cause for bewilderment and concern.

Marco had also become a man of habit. He had taken to sitting outside in the evening after his meal to enjoy a cigarette before retiring to his airless and stuffy cabin for two or three hours' sleep prior to his midnight watch. It was a routine that was to cost me dearly. The sun had already dipped below the horizon and twilight was slowly succumbing to the approaching nightfall, when Roland determined it was safe and sufficiently dark for him to venture from his hiding place to search for his supper. Life would have been so much easier had he only left it a little later and been more circumspect in selecting his time for his daily constitutional. For Marco to observe the rat scurrying across the aft deck close to the towing winch and not far from where he was sitting was the match that finally lit the slow-burning fuse of discontent. He stormed into the wheelhouse shortly after I had started my evening watch to angrily voice his unhappiness at not only discovering we had rats onboard, but also to complain bitterly about the appalling and unacceptable conditions that still existed in the lower deck accommodation. I was just as perturbed and shocked as Marco to learn that we were playing host to vermin of the four-legged variety. From our recent rat experiences on the *Justine* in Bahrain, I already knew that Remy would be particularly dismayed and concerned at hearing the news. Like all seafarers, he has an abhorrent dislike of any shipboard occupation other than that of his fellow humans.

There were no legitimate excuses for the dreadful environment in the lower deck accommodation. Despite our sailing into the warmer and much calmer summer Mediterranean weather, the cabins below the waterline remained damp and musty. While the bathrooms had been repaired in Las Palmas and most of the seawater leaks into the accommodation had been rectified, absolutely nothing had been done either to address or to eradicate the continuing problems of the damp in the cabins. Seawater that had entered the housing during the voyage from Abidjan had been absorbed into the fibreglass insulation that had been glued to all the steelwork of the hull and the underside of the deck behind the decorative Formica panelling. Short of completely dismantling the whole accommodation, there was little that could be done without the moisture-extracting process of air conditioning or dehumidifiers to prevent the water constantly dripping from the sodden insulation into the cabin interiors. The airflow into the lower deck depended upon the forward-facing escape door being left wide open, but the slightest hint of spray shipping over the bows meant that the door had to be closed to prevent the ingress of yet more water. I knew that drying the cabins by natural ventilation would take considerably longer than the estimated five weeks that remained of the voyage.

Our coffee break in the wheelhouse the next morning was a strained affair that revealed the joint strength of feelings for the unacceptable living conditions on board. Marco, Mieke and the two silent but quite clearly supportive Myanmars were adamant that their very justifiable complaints could no longer be ignored. There was never to be any argument, for the evidence was clear to see: I was shown leather shoes that had gone mouldy, and clothes and bedding bearing stains and a smell that could only come from never being quite dry. I couldn't help agreeing with their viewpoint that the cabins were not the healthiest of places in which to relax or sleep.

The unwelcome appearance of our four-legged friend, and the possibility that he had companions, had further exacerbated the ongoing problem of ventilating the lower deck spaces. Remy and the others had declared that the messroom portholes on the main deck and all the doors leading into the accommodation must be kept closed at all times to prevent an adventurous Roland from seeking sustenance from within the housing. Our coffee morning ended a little later than usual with my promise of sending an email to the office with the news of the rat sighting, and a request for dehumidifiers to be supplied in Valletta to dry out the cabins. A reply was received later in the day from Holland confirming arrangements were in hand to deal with both the problems.

The sea and air temperatures were becoming noticeably warmer as we headed further into the Mediterranean. My air conditioning was already being sorely missed, but in the circumstances I had no just cause for complaint. The slight breeze that entered through my forward-facing porthole two decks up from the main deck was complete and utter luxury compared with the oppressive atmosphere of the cabins down below, which had become stifling hot with all the doors and main deck portholes being kept closed to prevent Roland's entry. Sleeping or relaxing in the lower deck accommodation had become virtually impossible.

The reckless and impulsive burning of my airbed a couple of days earlier had proved not to be the sad mistake I had initially feared. My West African mattress, with all its unforgiving lumps and boulders, seemed a little less hard the second time round, and I found myself sleeping reasonably well. Perhaps my daily exercise regime was proving to be beneficial not only to my waistline but also in tiring me out.

During the night our track took us close in to the Tunisian coast and past the city of Bizerte and the headland of Cape Bon. Rounding the Cape saw us turn onto a south-easterly heading towards the two islands of Malta and Gozo, just over a day's steaming away. Shortly after lunch, the exclusive Italian holiday island of Pantelleria could be seen in the distance. I have sighted Pantelleria on many occasions: it lies directly on the route between Gozo, the island immediately to the north-west of Malta, and Cape Bon. With an area of only thirty-two square miles, its conical shape is capped by Montagna Grande, an extinct volcano. During the Second World War the heavily fortified island was bombed without respite by the Allies for more than a month until finally surrendering to a single Allied soldier just a few days before a major amphibious landing was planned.

At the northern end of the island lies the capital and port of Pantelleria, in which nearly one third of the island's population live. The masts and funnel of the ferry that operates a regular service from Trapani in Sicily can often be seen behind the large and impressive breakwater built to shelter the harbour. From the sea, the town itself appears to be a haphazard collection of two or three-storey white-painted buildings surrounding a church or cathedral. A road can be seen heading away from the town with clusters of farms and dwellings in a long drawn-out line marking its south-easterly route towards the opposite end of the island. Dirt tracks branch off like tributaries from a river and point towards some of the more isolated buildings lying closer to the sea, or higher up into the mountains towering into the distance.

We passed a couple of miles off the steep rocky coast at our unhurried speed of eight knots. My leisurely afternoon stroll was frequently interrupted by leaning on the starboard bulwark to study the scraggy and sparsely vegetated slopes. Aerials and antennae could be seen reaching skywards from the highest mountain peak in the centre of the island. I have vowed to myself that one day in the not too distant future, I will actually pay a visit to Pantelleria rather than sail past its shores as a wistful but disappointed observer. There seems to be a particular tranquillity and peaceful air about the place that holds a special, but unexplained, attraction for me.

By the end of the afternoon, the last distant shadow of land had slipped below the horizon, leaving us to follow in the wake of our sister tug towards Gozo and Malta, and some promised remedies to our pressing problems of rats and musty cabins.

A feast off Filfla

We arrived off the marine nature reserve surrounding the barren outcrop of rock named Filfla, a low-lying islet positioned about two and a half miles off the south coast of Malta, shortly after breakfast on Sunday morning. Passing the islet, we turned towards the mainland and the drift position Pieter and I had selected off the picturesque little hamlet of Il Hinejja. Despite the early hour there were already quite a few cars parked around the sheltered bay, and a number of small sailing yachts and speedboats darting around close inshore. With the clear blue skies and the merest whisper of a cooling breeze, we couldn't have been blessed with either better weather or a more idyllic location for drifting around and passing the time of day.

Our very best efforts to run at a minimum speed so as to reach Valletta at the beginning of the working week had proved fruitless and we had arrived off the Maltese coast nearly twenty-four hours early. The engineering difficulties associated with turbochargers, critical revolutions, and the impossibility of running our main engines for prolonged periods at very slow speeds had successfully put paid to our manager's cost-saving plans. The day we had gained, or hadn't lost, would not be wasted. Pieter and I had already agreed we should manoeuvre the boats alongside one another to allow everyone to get together, to enjoy the swimming pool facilities on our boat, and to share a barbecue in the early evening.

The handwritten notice 'Verboden toegang voor Rat(ten)' on the back of a cancelled chart that had been taped to a piece of plywood and then hung over the side of No. 1 tug for us all to see as she inched her way alongside, brought howls of protest from Marco, Mieke and Remy. The slightly ambiguous warning, 'Forbidden Entry for Rat(s)', was to be the springboard for an entertaining afternoon of childish banter, reminiscence, and shared anecdotes between the two crews, and when the sun became too hot, for relaxing and cooling off in the shallow waters of our home-made swimming pool.

We took it in turns to keep a bridge watch, to check our position regularly and to move the two boats together as one unit further off the coast when the current and tide started to sweep us inshore. Every so often we became the centre of attraction for local yachts, which would motor past us on a tour of inspection as if we were visiting dignitaries receiving a naval salute. Our chauvinistic and childish attempts to draw some of the bikini-clad crew members that little bit nearer with our cheerful waving and raucous whistling were spectacularly unsuccessful: I suspect that age and the less than inviting display of grotesquely distended beer bellies and spindly lily-white legs might have had something to do with our visitors' total lack of enthusiasm for cementing international relations further.

The barbecues were lit in the early evening. With Mieke and Albert pitting their culinary skills against one another to produce the tastiest and most original side dish, we were all assured of a thoroughly enjoyable feast. Marco and Bas, No. 1 tug's second engineer, appointed themselves the two chefs-de-charcoal. It wasn't too long before the aft deck became heavily scented with the smells of barbecued kebabs and steaks, and shrouded by the smoke from burning and blackened sausages that would never have been eaten had they been cooked to perfection in the galley. The party continued until after sunset, when Pieter and his crew called it a day and returned to their boat, sated and exhausted after a day of much leisure.

We kept the two boats secured alongside one another for the night, drifting together to pass five miles to the south of Marsaxlokk. Like so many other ports in the world, what was once a small and peaceful fishing harbour not so many years ago has now succumbed to the twenty-first century with an extensive development that has turned it into a large and thriving deep-water container terminal serving the island and some of its nearby Mediterranean neighbours. Just after six o'clock in the morning we let go the mooring ropes and, with No. 1 tug in the lead, headed around the Outer Munxar Rock buoy and onto a north-westerly course that took us up to the Fairway buoy off Valletta port, where we arrived exactly on schedule.

A fishing boat occupying our intended berth kept us waiting for over an hour outside the entrance into the Grand Harbour. I spent the time peering through the binoculars at the forts and bastions that represent centuries of Maltese history. Many of the defensive battlements that still proudly exist today were designed and built four or five hundred years ago during the Knights of St John era, bearing testament to the incredible skills of the engineers and stonemasons responsible for their construction.

All too soon we were underway again and proceeding slowly inwards, steering between St Elmo's lighthouse and the breakwater on our starboard side and Fort Ricasoli on our port side. A gradual turn to port and the immense size of the Grand Harbour, with all its creeks and defensive walls, becomes apparent. We were heading for Laboratory Wharf, a berth with which I was familiar from my last visit to Valletta. Proceeding down the harbour we came to Fort St Angelo, built in a strategic position not only to defend the inner harbour, but also to protect both Kalkara Creek and Dockyard Creek. On the opposite side of the narrow waterway and within the city walls, I could make out the Grand Master's Palace and St John's Co-Cathedral. Magazine and Laboratory Wharves could be seen ahead of us, a short distance beyond the massive steel gates of the huge China Dry Dock built at the side of French Creek.

No. 1 tug berthed first, and a few minutes later we were securely moored to her outboard side and our engine shut down: another leg of our long voyage to Singapore had been safely completed.

6

VALLETTA

A trip down memory lane

After dealing with the clearance formalities on board No. 1 tug, our shipping agent, Joseph Azzopardi, and the three uniformed port officials climbed over the bulwarks to repeat the process for our boat. The procedure involving the checking of a crew list, customs declarations and a stores list was dealt with efficiently and quickly: the combined effects of perspiration and of the lack of ventilation made the messroom an oppressive and uncomfortable place and one in which no one wished to linger. I chose not to look the Port Health Inspector in the eye when passing him the International Maritime Declaration of Health. The document not only records any crew sickness, but confirms the Master's sincere belief that there are no diseases from, or pertaining to, any rats on board. How the Master is meant to establish this strange and somewhat outdated requirement has never been made clear. I was, however, more than confident that no one in my crew had suffered from any debilitating sickness since Roland's untimely appearance two days earlier. I was also equally aware that if the presence of our furry friends on board were made known to the local health authorities, the ensuing bureaucratic furore would make our life extremely unpleasant. Joseph, who had been informed of our delicate problems by the company prior to our arrival, succeeded in distracting the inspector's thoughts sufficiently long for the slightly less than honest document to be filed away unchecked into the official's open briefcase. A hastily consumed round of soft drinks and a couple of mucky after-dinner jokes helped pass the time of day until our official entry into the port of Valletta had been sanctioned by the imprint of the all-important rubber stamp. The officials left shortly afterwards, leaving Joseph and me to abandon the messroom for the outside deck, where we could discuss the arrangements for our stay in port in a little more comfort.

I had first met Joseph on my previous voyage, when the *Justine* and the *Martha* had stopped off in Valletta on their way to Trinidad from Bahrain. It had taken me only a few minutes to recognise him as a conscientious and extremely experienced ship's agent with an immense local knowledge and an impressive list of contacts. He is a friendly, respectful and confident man with an outgoing manner and an envious ability to adopt a calm and considerate approach to any difficulty. During the *Justine*'s troubled stay, he was presented with many pressing and sensitive issues involving both boat and crew and saw them through to a successful conclusion.

I like to think that in those two or three short and hectic days, we managed to develop a mutual respect for one another, and a solid and businesslike relationship that could be easily renewed with any subsequent visit. Our quiet but serious conversation on the deck outside instantly confirmed my initial opinion: our brief working friendship established several months earlier still existed and had survived the passage of time.

Joseph had made most of the arrangements to deal not only with our problems, but also with those of our sister boat. As we spoke, the well-travelled and rewound rotor from No. 1 tug's damaged generator appeared on the quay in the back of a shipyard truck ready to be manhandled into her engine room and reinstated by shipyard fitters and electricians. Later in the morning the ship's chandler, another old acquaintance from the *Justine's* visit, arrived with some fresh vegetables and fruit, and a new fridge-freezer for our galley. The old one had inconsiderately expired shortly before our arrival in Valletta after suffering what had clearly been a long and hard life in West Africa. At least it had given up the ghost where a replacement could be conveniently purchased, rather than in the middle of the Red Sea. Had that happened, the intense and unforgiving heat of the Arabian summer would have made the provision of our meals a particularly daunting challenge.

As of late, Mieke had been suffering with her catering equipment. While the unfortunate loss of the all-important refrigerator for two or three days had made her culinary role a bit more demanding and awkward, it paled into insignificance when compared with the problems of the galley cooker. A heavy-duty industrial model that gave every appearance of having been built at the same time as the boat twenty-eight years earlier, it had developed an irritating and extremely unfriendly habit of giving an occasional short sharp electrical shock to whoever should have the misfortune to touch its main frame when it decided to misbehave. The unfortunate Mieke was more closely involved with the cooker than anyone else, and we became quite used to hearing her suffer from the painful jolts of being half-electrocuted. We chose to ignore the loud and sometimes quite prolonged and angry outbursts that reverberated throughout the accommodation whenever she received her electric shocks; to the outsider, we might have appeared rather callous in choosing not to console her, but old and traditional maritime habits die particularly hard. Throughout many generations of seafaring, 'salty sea-dogs' and 'sympathy', although appearing relatively close to one another in the pages of an English dictionary, have never been the most natural of companions. We have learnt to look after ourselves and not to expect any understanding or commiseration from our shipmates. We also learnt, from observing Mieke's discomfort, not to go near or touch the cooker without first ensuring it was switched off at the mains.

The electrician who boarded just before lunch to rectify the fault learnt the hard way, despite our jocular but friendly advice to keep well away. Two shocks and some bad language later, the problem had been located to a faulty circuit for the hot-plate indicator lights. A carefree snip with his trusty wire cutters, some bandaging with insulation tape, and the cooker once again became user-friendly, but minus the lights that warned that the upper surface of the stove might still be hot. I vowed there and then that Mieke should have the sole and exclusive rights to the entire galley with all its pots, pans, crockery and cutlery, and the various other ancillary bits and pieces that went to make up her catering domain. Promising myself never to help Mieke or to enter her galley again was, perhaps, a little impetuous and chauvinistic given the feeble excuse that the stove might be hot. I decided to review my promise in a few days' time, although being a kitchen assistant was never my intended vocation in life.

The man we all wanted to see, the rodent exterminator man, arrived on board carrying just a small bag. He brought no assistants, yappy terrier dogs, wire cages, or any of the other paraphernalia that might normally be attributed to the art of shortening the lives of unwanted rats. He wandered around outside for a few minutes, eyes staring long and hard at the rust streaks and bubbly corrosion on the steel deck, no doubt in the hope of spotting a giveaway ratty footprint that might lead him directly to where they were hiding. The towing winch area between the two funnels became his centre of attention and it was there that he placed several blocks of poison, discreetly hidden under ropes and other items of nautical miscellany that had been collected over the years. He showed me his hiding places and asked that I report to Joseph in the morning with the number of blocks that had disappeared. From the quantity of food that had been eaten, he would be able to estimate the number of rats we had residing on board. I couldn't help recalling my voyage on the *Justine* and our time spent in Bahrain with the rat-catching man from Mumbai, and Remy's absolute horror at finding the stiffened remains of one such unwanted guest still firmly clutching between its teeth the electrical cable of the chest freezer we were throwing away. I just hoped the unassuming and nonchalant rat-man from Malta would be every bit as successful as his counterpart from Mumbai in ridding the boat of our *ratten*.

In the early evening, the taxi collected Remy, Mieke and me from the dock gate at the base of the Corradino Heights to take us on what Remy and I had determined would be a trip down memory lane. Our first stop was to be the Osborne Hotel in St John's Street, which held poignant memories for us both. It was to this hotel that Joseph Azzopardi, our agent, had booked the *Justine*'s entire crew for two nights so that we could rest and recuperate in clean and hygienic accommodation after a particularly unpleasant voyage to Malta living in disgusting and primitive conditions without either fresh water or toilets. The lounge bar had changed little from just a few months previously. Our pre-dinner drinks of pints of cold beer tasted just as refreshing as they had done then, and had there been flies on the wall to listen to our conversation, I suspect that very little would have changed: talking about ships and the sea seems to be endemic among sailors. We passed a very pleasurable couple of hours drinking and chatting before setting off on another step down memory lane to find the Cocopazzo restaurant, a small, homely and delightful bistro-like establishment Remy and I had had the good fortune to discover when we had previously been wandering the Valletta streets looking for somewhere to eat.

With Remy's nose for detecting a fine catering enterprise, and my navigational sense of direction, it was only a few minutes' walk before we were standing once again under the restaurant's swinging street board that proudly proclaims 'The small place to eat for a big treat'. The seafood platter and local wines were every bit as delicious and unforgettable as the restaurant's hoarding boasted. Our memories had spoken true. Satiated and fatigued, we called it a day and returned by taxi to the questionable delights of Laboratory Wharf and the *Oriental* tugs. We had work to do in the morning.

An unfriendly seizure

Having just awoken, I thought my eyes were deceiving me when I peered out of my forward-facing porthole shortly after the sun had risen. I couldn't recall having consumed such an excessive amount of alcohol the night before to have caused a visionary malfunction. The foredeck to the port side of the windlass two decks below me had been transformed from being a rust-streaked deck into an untidy and cluttered camping site, with pieces of cardboard and a couple of the bench seats from the stern laid out in positions where their occupants hoped they might catch whatever breeze existed during the long hours of darkness. The exhausted residents of the lower deck accommodation had taken up new lodgings outside. The cool night airs had clearly been sufficiently tempting to overcome not only the discomforts of sleeping on the steel deck or on the narrow confines of the bench seats, but also the possible risks of sharing their temporary abode with a half-poisoned Roland or one of his mates.

The street board for the Cocopazzo restaurant, Valletta, Malta

I couldn't blame my shipmates in the slightest: their cabins, for want of a better name, had become virtually uninhabitable in the oppressive heat of the Mediterranean summer. Their patience in waiting to see what action the company, in liaison with the owners, intended taking to rectify the almost impossible situation had been severely tested. It was pleasing to see that the men had been magnanimous in their sleeping arrangements and had positioned Mieke safely within their midst, where she might be afforded just a little protection from an attack by a crazed or hungry rodent. I was sure Erik, Mieke's husband, would have been very appreciative of his fellow seafarers' concerns for his wife's continued good health and well-being.

The road tankers drove down onto the quayside shortly after breakfast. The visit to the boat the previous afternoon by the oil company representative to discuss the plan for taking bunkers the following morning had ended in a long and impassioned argument. Arrangements had been made for our fuel to be supplied from a bunker barge without our knowledge or agreement. Both Remy and I were convinced, and no amount of reassurance would persuade us otherwise, that the very same barge had supplied, albeit unknowingly, biologically contaminated fuel to the *Justine* and the *Martha*. The bad fuel had caused the crews of both boats endless amounts of hassle and an eight-day stay in Gibraltar spent pumping contaminated gas oil into sludge tankers, steam-cleaning fuel tanks to kill the bacteria, and fitting additional in-line fuel filters to the main engines. Once bitten, twice shy – we were adamant we weren't going to be caught out again. Our unwavering persistence in refusing to accept the arrangements eventually paid off and, after a lengthy telephone call, the oil company relented and agreed to supply both the boats with gas oil from road tankers. Their welcome appearance signalled a victory for common sense.

While Remy and Tin connected the bunker hose and oversaw the filling of our fuel tanks to capacity, I checked the winch housing and all the places where the blocks of rat poison had been carefully hidden. My search, which I repeated in case I had missed one of the hidey-holes in my enthusiasm to discover the truth, revealed absolutely nothing: not a single poison block remained, which indicated to my very limited experience in the finer points of vermin control and rat-catching that Roland was not only extremely hungry, but that he had also managed to procreate in spectacular fashion in the very short period he had been in residence. The other possibility, which I found difficult to even consider, was that Roland was merely the leader of the pack and that the *Oriental Tug No. 2* was playing host to a far larger rat occupation than we had originally thought. Joseph attempted to calm my concerns during our telephone conversation and assured me he would pass on my lack of findings to the pest control company.

The radar technician boarded a few minutes before the air-conditioning expert. They both set to work in the wheelhouse, the former to look at the radar, which had failed again shortly after the fog in the Gibraltar Straits, and the latter to look at the bridge air-conditioning unit, which had been repaired in Las Palmas, but had decided for some unknown reason to dispense hot air rather than the cold air we had come to expect. The opportunity was simply too good to miss. Ten minutes after the bridge unit had been recharged with freon gas, the window-box air conditioner that had occupied pride of place in my cabin was outside on deck and being dismantled, a trail of flaking rust particles showing the route in which it had been carried. From the debris left behind, I was surprised that the machine was still in one piece and considered to be worth repairing.

A gaping rectangular hole, through which I could see a cruise ship moored to Pinto Wharf on the other side of the harbour, had taken its place, my cabin bulkhead providing a perfect picture frame for the floating hotel. The crudely cut opening into which the unit had been positioned provided all the evidence I needed to see why the seawater spray had been pouring into my cabin when we had been passing through the rough weather in the Intertropical Convergence Zone on the passage from Abidjan to Las Palmas. The uneven and jagged edges in the steelwork verified my initial doubts that the opening could never be made watertight without major refurbishment. A couple of hours later, my picture-frame porthole had been closed and my cabin was once again being cooled by air conditioning, confirming that miracles can indeed occur when least expected. Any guilt I might have had about claiming some creature comforts at the expense of my colleagues was swiftly forgotten with the long-awaited and welcome news that more air-conditioning units would be supplied in the early evening to be installed on both the boats the following day. It had been decided by those in the know that air conditioning would be more effective than dehumidifiers in removing the moisture from the lower deck accommodation. The added and very real benefit of having a much cooler atmosphere in which to live had obviously been an important additional consideration to the pressing need for drying the cabins.

Remy, Marco and Mieke decided to go ashore in the late afternoon, leaving me to catch up with them later once the rat-catcher had been with more poison. He appeared in the early evening to replace all the missing blocks, and to advise me of his uncertainty as to how many rats might be living with us. He was, however, confident that the heavy consumption of poison the previous night could only bring about the beginning of the end for our unwanted occupants. I just wished I could share not only his enthusiasm, but also the one and only portable air conditioning unit available on the island that was delivered to the quayside shortly before nightfall. Despite my loud and vociferous objections, there was nothing I could do to prevent the occupants of the lower deck cabins of No. 1 tug from hastily grabbing the unit. First come, first served. I was unable to resolve the issue of how a single machine could possibly be divided between the two boats. Unbelievably, we were back to the saga of our ship's electrical frequency not only being different to the current being generated ashore, but also being unsuitable for many of the electrical appliances available in the shops. The same problem had occurred in Las Palmas.

To say I was completely and utterly disillusioned would have been the under-statement of the year: I could already visualise the arguments and bad feelings that would exist between the two crews when it became apparent that one boat would be sailing towards the Suez Canal and beyond without benefiting from any of the promised remedies for improving the conditions of the cabins below the waterline. I quickly realised the absolute futility of arguing with Ton, Bas, Albert and Maung. Their claim to the portable air-conditioning unit was, unfortunately, every bit as valid and legitimate as that of Marco, Mieke, Shwe and Tin, and possession is nine-tenths of the law. I would have done exactly the same had I been in their shoes.

In fear and trepidation at being the bearer of the bad news, I left the boat to meet the others. The taxi dropped me off at the edge of the city so that I could walk down Republic Street towards the Great Siege Square, where they had told me they would be waiting. I stopped to read the marble commemorative plaque bearing the inscription of the famous message from King George in Buckingham Palace to the Governor of Malta on 15 April 1942 awarding the George Cross to the Maltese nation. Next to it was the message from President Franklin Roosevelt to the Maltese people at the end of 1943, commending their resolute fortitude and indomitable courage during the unending aerial bombardment. The heroism of the local population made me feel exceedingly humble, and brought home the stark reality that I had been born into a generation of very ordinary and insignificant people. My mission to relay the sombre tidings that our colleagues on No. 1 tug had claimed the one and only air-conditioning unit seemed very foolish and trivial when compared to what the inhabitants of Malta had bravely endured some sixty years previously. There was a new and carefree purpose to my stride as I approached the table in the plaza where I could see them quietly reading their one-day-old Dutch newspapers and enjoying their beers.

The stunned and deathly silence that greeted my news lasted for only a few seconds. Perhaps, with hindsight, I was just a little too casual in choosing to take the direct approach by telling them everything in a matter-of-fact manner and without any attempt to soften the blow. I was acutely conscious that having my own air conditioning repaired earlier in the day could be interpreted as being slightly less than diplomatic. My bluntness was rewarded by the conversation reverting to the Dutch language, which, for the second time in the space of just a few weeks, I was really quite happy not to understand. The mention of a few names and the ill-humoured tone in which they were spoken was more than sufficient for me to get the gist of what they were saying: the telephone airwaves to Holland would be hot in the morning.

After a couple more beers, the subject of air conditioning had been exhausted and was temporarily off the agenda. We left the plaza and walked down Strait Street, once known as the infamous 'Gut', which can still be recalled with either aversion or affection by the thousands of seamen and service personnel who visited its hostelries many years ago. Renowned for its sleazy bars and for the dozens of amicable hostesses offering 'short time' female hospitality to those suffering from lonely hearts and holes in their wallets, it now bears all the hallmarks of respectability and decency. It is a sad fact of life that its colourful history will soon be irrevocably forgotten with the passing of time and the loss of a generation whose memories have kept it alive.

The swinging advertisement board for the Cocopazzo restaurant was there in front of us as we entered South Street. For the second consecutive night we were treated to a truly wonderful meal, made all the more enjoyable by the attentive and amiable staff who greeted us like long-lost friends as we stepped over the threshold into the tastefully decorated and atmospheric dining area. The wine and conversation flowed freely. All too soon the evening ended and we were heading in our taxi back to the Corradino Heights and, for Mieke and Marco, another restless night with Shwe and Tin on the foredeck of the *Oriental Tug No. 2*.

Breakfast was a solemn affair, with the conversation reverting once again to the damp, hot and appalling conditions in the crew cabins, and what should be done with the one and only portable air-conditioning unit of the right electrical frequency available on the island. I sensed it was only a matter of hours before someone would throw in the towel and demand to be relieved, quite understandably in my opinion. Exchanging members of the crew would not resolve the problem: at best it would only provide a very limited short-term solution, as No. 1 tug had already experienced with the second engineer who had relieved Arno in Las Palmas only to go back home a few days later. With the voyage heading towards the Suez Canal and the exhausting heat of the Red Sea in the height of summer, it was entirely unrealistic to suggest that anyone should have to put up with living below the waterline in dank and airless quarters that had little or no ventilation.

Hoping to avert a major crisis, I agreed to telephone Jaap Smit, our manager, straight away after breakfast. The wind was immediately taken out of my sails with his assurance that an order had just been placed for the urgent supply of a large split air-conditioning unit to be installed on board our boat. Joseph, our agent, had already made him aware of the impossible and sensitive situation the previous afternoon when he had learnt that only one portable unit would be delivered. I applauded and thanked Jaap, and the owners, for their decision. The jealousy roles were instantly reversed and within a few minutes the news was out that we would be receiving a large and permanently fitted air-conditioning unit with sufficient cooling capacity to service not only all the cabins in the lower deck accommodation, but also the main deck mess and cross-alleyway. Ton, Bas and Albert instantly made their unhappiness known, but sympathy was off the agenda: a few hours earlier they had been content with a single portable unit that would have to be wheeled from cabin to cabin in the hope of slowly drying out the whole of their accommodation.

With the installation and testing of the rewound generator rotor completed on No. 1 tug, Pieter and I decided to reverse the boats' positions later in the morning. We would take pride of place secured alongside the quay, with our crestfallen and furious friends moored on our outside. This would allow us to land some more cooling water pipes for repair, to load twenty drums of lubricating oil and the new air-conditioning unit, and to take the rest of our provisions order from the ship's chandler.

The unwelcome occupation of Roland and his fellow rodent squatters had still not ended. Another four blocks of so-called 'deadly poison' were discovered missing, either eaten or dragged away under the cover of darkness to wherever the rats had set up home. Joseph Azzopardi, who had visited us to see the problem for himself, agreed to invite the rodent company to attend the boat once again with a further supply of blocks. He shared the rat-catcher's confidence that the poison would eventually take its toll and that we would soon be rid of our vermin. I remained unconvinced and preferred to await the sight and sounds of the Pied Piper of Hamelin, only this time, unlike in the centuries-old legend, I would ensure he received payment in full for fulfilling his contract, rather than face the threat of his returning the following year. At least our moving alongside the quay had made it that much easier for him to pipe his four-legged followers down the gangway and away ashore.

Shortly after switching the boats around, the air-conditioning company arrived to commence work on the installation. Their hastily agreed contract demanded that the work be finished within twenty-four hours so as to keep the delay to the two boats to an absolute minimum. The lower deck accommodation soon resembled a scene of devastation and chaos, with the deckhead panels in the alleyways and cabins being removed to facilitate the running of ducting and pipework. There had been no time for the preparation of drawings or plans: the installation design stayed one step ahead of the work and appeared to originate entirely from the experience and expertise of the air-conditioning engineer, who was also owner of the small company supplying the unit. The work continued unabated throughout the day and into the early hours of the evening, when Remy, Marco, Mieke and I decided to return once again to our adopted Cocopazzo restaurant for what would probably be our last evening meal ashore in Valletta. To show there were absolutely no hard feelings between the two crews, we welcomed Bas, No. 1's second engineer, into our party.

For the third night running, the meal and the service were both outstanding. The restaurant is owned by an ex-purser, who had served many years with one of the large cruise ship companies before starting his business ashore. His natural ability to deal with people and to cater to their every whim and need has rubbed off onto his staff, who have succeeded in emulating him in the friendly and attentive way they conduct themselves with their customers. After several bottles of 'house wine' and complimentary liqueurs at the end of our meal, the evening seemed to have ended before it had begun. The taxi ride back to the port in the early hours of the morning, and the short walk from the dock gate to the boats, brought us sharply back to reality. Despite the hour, the air-conditioning fitters had returned on board with the hope of completing their work later in the morning so that we could sail on schedule.

A main deck mutiny

The day started badly with Pieter coming to see me shortly after breakfast to tell me his crew had called a meeting and were refusing to sail beyond Port Said unless they received a second air-conditioning unit either in Malta or in Egypt. There was little I could say in the circumstances: both the boats had suffered from having seawater enter the accommodation during the passage from Abidjan and we were now paying the price for giving the problem less than lip service during our long stay in Las Palmas. It was unfortunate, or fortunate, depending on which deck you were standing on, that one boat was receiving a different level of remedy to the other. Had the boot been on the other foot, I suspected I would be telling Pieter a similar story to the one he had just told me. The final decision would rest with the company, but over the years I have developed a great respect for my office colleagues in Holland, and I knew they would already be treating the ultimatum, however unpalatable, with the utmost importance and urgency. The situation was made that little bit easier with both our manager and superintendent having spent many hours on the two boats and being able to appreciate and visualise for themselves the difficult conditions on board.

My bad start to the day continued with Remy accompanying me on my daily investigation into the overnight consumption of rat poison. Roland and his associates obviously possessed cast-iron constitutions and had managed either to devour or to filch several more blocks of their less-than-nourishing food. Remy, with his morbid dislike and phobic aversion to vermin, became exceedingly distressed at seeing the evidence that the rats were still very much alive, and warned me in a very hesitant and stammering voice that he was considering whether to call it a day and go home. Having sailed with Remy on two previous occasions, and being familiar with his occasional moods of despondency and depression, I offered neither opinion nor advice, well knowing that he would arrive at his own decision in his own time and without my help. I left him alone to ponder his difficult dilemma while I telephoned Joseph to ask the rodent company to provide a different and stronger poison: I sympathised with Remy in his concerns, and shared his opinion that, to date, the results of the rodent company's efforts to rid us of our *ratten* had been less than impressive. Patience has never been one of my virtues. In no time at all I was the worried and reluctant caretaker of enough liquid rat poison to last for more than two weeks, sufficiently strong and deadly, so I was informed in an almost clandestine manner, to exterminate half the world's population of rats, give or take a few million. I received precise instructions to distribute it on a daily basis in small non-corrosive beakers – the bottom of plastic water bottles would be entirely suitable – and to wear goggles, rubber gloves, wellie boots and whatever other protection I could find when decanting it from the unmarked and unlabelled 10-litre plastic container I had been given. Washing my hands or taking a shower after administering the 'medicine' was strongly advised, and would delay the adverse effects on my own health if I accidentally came into contact with any of the poison. I thought it just a little too flippant to ask whether insanity would be one of the first recognisable symptoms of being poisoned.

Since our arrival in Valletta the venue for our traditional morning coffee breaks had moved from the wheelhouse to outside the accommodation on the main deck. We found it quite a pleasant interlude from our work to sit for half an hour on the bench seats in the fresh air and sunshine, and absorb some ultraviolet rays while drinking our coffee and discussing whatever came to mind. I had no reason to suspect that this day would be any different from the previous two mornings. Everything was going, or had already gone, to plan. Amazingly, the air-conditioning installation was on schedule and due to be completed shortly before lunchtime. All the other repairs had been completed, our fuel and fresh water tanks were full, and we had sufficient provisions for the voyage to the Suez Canal and down the Red Sea to Djibouti, which had been nominated as our final port of call before steaming across the Indian Ocean and on to Singapore, our ultimate destination.

My casual observation that we would probably be able to depart after lunch was met with a stony silence and with heads bowed towards the deck. Mieke was the first to move, coughing quietly to clear her throat before advising me in a remarkably calm voice that they had no intention of sailing until there was clear evidence that the *ratten* had been completely exterminated. They were determined to have the proof that Roland and his friends and family wouldn't be accompanying us on our onward voyage to Egypt, or anywhere else for that matter.

I had never, ever, been confronted with such a situation before: the archaic word 'mutiny' came instantly to mind. I readily appreciated how Captain Bligh of the *Bounty* must have felt when faced with his little problem, but quickly realised I was in the far more enviable position of being able to step ashore onto a quayside in Valletta, rather than being forcibly cast adrift into a longboat with thousands of square miles of empty ocean to welcome me. On this occasion, the inhabitants of Timor would be denied the questionable pleasure of greeting either me or the survivors of a second epic voyage in an open boat.

I could recall reading in some nautical publication after the last British seamen's strike many years ago that 'mutiny on the high seas' was still technically a capital offence, punishable by hanging. Although the Act of Parliament dating back to the nineteenth century has never been repealed, the phrase 'industrial action' has been adopted as being more appropriate and in line with modern thinking, but the vessel must be in port and moored alongside for it to be classed as industrial action. The rebellion by my shipmates was probably not, therefore, a mutiny in the strictest of legal terms. I realised that trying to recollect my Shipmaster's Business lectures from some thirty-five years ago when I had been studying for my Master's certificate would be a futile exercise: the *Oriental* tugs were registered in Monrovia and were subject to Liberian law. English maritime law would be irrelevant in this particular instance, and I had already sensed that my Dutch colleagues would pay scant attention to any aspects of law with which I might foolishly threaten them in the heat of the moment, whether it be jungle, maritime or other.

I did the only thing possible and lost my temper, which was undoubtedly not the best or most diplomatic course of action in such circumstances, but at least it made me feel better and helped in relieving the considerable mental pressure I was under. An embarrassed and deathly silence was the answer to my not unreasonable demand to know how many rat bodies would have to be sighted to be considered a successful extermination. Would one body be sufficient or would I need to have five bodies, or even ten perhaps? I fired off question after question in rapid succession, to which there were no responses. What was the difference between sailing with rats at sea and living with them in port? Had it been appreciated that we were moored quite close to a granary with the likelihood of our rat population increasing rather than decreasing? Were they aware that I had sufficient poison onboard to kill all the rats in the northern hemisphere, and probably more besides? What did they hope to achieve by refusing to sail? I considered them all to be immensely sensible questions, to which I was receiving nothing in the way of logical and convincing answers. In fact, I was hearing no answers at all: it was as if a religious order of silence had suddenly been adopted. No one was prepared to look me in the eye. Shwe and Tin, obviously not wishing to be part of the proceedings, tactfully stood up and retreated towards the stern, leaving the others to shuffle their feet nervously, and to stare uncomfortably towards No. 1 tug moored alongside us.

I decided to take the bull by the horns, and handed my cellphone to Mieke with the suggestion that she telephone the office in Holland and explain why the two tugs wouldn't be sailing from Malta. She accepted the challenge and spoke for a few minutes to Bram, our superintendent, who had been with us in Las Palmas, before passing the phone back to me. I was instructed to telephone Jaap, our manager, in the early afternoon, but also to be fully aware that the management was becoming rapidly disillusioned with what was going on and with the demands and ultimatums being placed upon them. I was also informed that while our office colleagues had every sympathy for the conditions on board, they considered a distinction had to be made between reasonable and sensible requests and those that were clearly unreasonable and ill-advised. It was a viewpoint I shared unreservedly.

I took the time while waiting to make the call to Jaap to consider my own personal position. I felt my role as the Master would become completely untenable if the industrial action continued, and that I would be left with no realistic alternative but to pack my bags and go home. A captain commanding neither authority nor respect effectively becomes merely a figurehead blessed with a meaningless title.

Unlike me, Jaap took the softly-softly and far more sensible diplomatic approach and listened, without interrupting, to my version of events and my decision to leave the boat if the situation remained unresolved. He asked to speak to Remy, who moved away out of earshot only to return a few minutes later, grim and red-faced, to tell me we could sail as soon as port clearance had been received on board. I had not the faintest idea what had been said on the phone, but decided that seeking to find out would only rekindle the already tense and uneasy situation. Likewise, I could only guess as to who had been behind the protest in the beginning. Joseph responded to my call with advice that the clearance would be with me inside the hour.

Slipping No. 1 tug's moorings and then letting go our own ropes from the quayside was like a great weight being lifted from my shoulders. Waving goodbye to Joseph, who was probably equally pleased to see us heading towards the harbour entrance and St Elmo's lighthouse, finally convinced me that we were actually underway and sailing from Malta. The fact that we still had over five and a half thousand miles of our voyage remaining seemed of little consequence as we cleared the breakwater and set course to follow our sister boat towards Port Said and the Suez Canal and, hopefully, another air-conditioning unit for No. 1 tug.

7

VALLETTA TO PORT SAID

Broken again

Being back at sea and experiencing once again the gentle vibration of the engine beneath my feet had never felt so good. I was still trying to come to terms with what had happened during the course of the day and why it should have occurred so suddenly and without any prior warning. Up until that ill-fated moment at coffee time I had always considered my relationship with everyone as being friendly, cordial and businesslike: my door had never been closed to anyone wishing to discuss or resolve any personal or professional difficulties. The turn of events had been like a kick in the teeth. Self-pity suggested that, somewhere along the line, the special association and the high morale of my crew that I had been proud to display in Las Palmas when No. 1 tug had been suffering from its unforgettable personnel nightmares and problems, had been irrevocably broken; trust between myself and the others had been sacrificed with a few ill-chosen words and an immature and misconceived display of petulance that had achieved absolutely nothing but a few hours' delay in our departure from Valletta.

The four hours of my evening watch, in which no one came to the wheelhouse to help pass the time of day, allowed me the opportunity for further self-appraisal and to try and determine where events had gone wrong, and how I might have done things differently had I been made aware of the strength of feelings on board. I knew that the presence of Roland and his mates was extremely abhorrent to everyone, but I also considered that every reasonable attempt had been made to end their occupation. I had been entirely open in revealing the daily consumption of 'food blocks' and how ineffective the rats' special diet appeared to be; hopefully their days of sailing with us would be strictly numbered now that I was in possession of a more lethal poison. I could find no sensible or plausible answers as to why the others had taken the action they had, and concluded that 'least said, soonest mended' would probably be the most judicious way forward in re-establishing the bond between myself and my colleagues.

Oversleeping was the last thing I would have thought possible given the circumstances, but my first night back at sea became a short course in death that fortunately ended with my sudden and rude awakening barely five minutes before I was due to relieve Shwe. Dishevelled and contrite, I raced to the wheelhouse, only to be greeted by a cacophony of instrument alarms indicating a loss of mains electrical power and the sight of the battery-powered emergency lighting faintly flickering in the already bright sunshine. It wasn't long before the standby generator was running and Remy appeared on the bridge to tell me that No. 1 generator had failed electrically and that, from his very brief and preliminary investigations, he doubted that there was anything he could do to rectify the fault. We had been at sea for less than fifteen hours, and already further repairs would be needed before the voyage to Singapore could be completed.

The generator wasn't the only failure to have occurred in the short time we had been sailing. During the night both the rudder and propeller indicators had stopped working. The former, which had taken up so many hours of the electrician's time in Las Palmas and had caused us to fail our first survey by the Lloyd's surveyor, became stubbornly stuck in the one position despite the rudder angle being frequently adjusted to maintain our course, and the latter had come to the surprising conclusion that the propeller was no longer turning despite our steady progress through the water at around eight knots. The failure of the rudder indicator particularly annoyed me. I had travelled several thousand miles on the *Justine* hand steering for eight hours a day without having a clue as to the angle of the rudders. Although the three of us who had been involved with the steering had eventually mastered pointing the bows in the right direction without the instrument's help, its absence, especially during bad weather or a heavy swell, had made the task of maintaining a straight course all the more difficult. Perhaps we were fortunate that the Mediterranean was being remarkably kind, with not a ripple or wave in sight to throw us off course.

To add to our sorry and lengthening tale of woes, the radar technician in Malta had been unsuccessful with his repairs. The radar had been run for only a few hours and had developed an identical fault to the one he had supposedly repaired. After sending an email to the office advising of our latest difficulties, and having consulted with Pieter on No. 1 tug, we agreed to reduce our speed in case the decision was made by Holland to return to Valletta for further repairs. The Maltese shipyards have an enviable reputation in the Mediterranean for competitive prices, a skilled labour force and easy access to materials and spare parts.

Our traditional mid-morning coffee break took place in the wheelhouse as if nothing untoward or unusual had occurred twenty-four hours earlier. Since, by their silence, the others had obviously agreed not to mention the subject again, I was content to let sleeping dogs lie. I had already come to the conclusion that there was absolutely nothing to be gained from resurrecting the ill-feelings and anguish. Our lively conversation revolved around a possible return to Valletta for generator repairs and answering some technical questions that had been asked by the office in Holland. We decided to manoeuvre alongside No. 1 tug immediately after lunch to allow Bas, their second engineer, to come aboard. We hoped that, as he had been an electrician for a large part of his working life, he might be able to assist Remy in identifying the problem and, perhaps, to make a temporary repair.

Luck was not on our side. Bas spent more than two hours investigating the fault but arrived at the same conclusion as Remy, that the generator was producing only two of the designed three-phase output. One particular component was probably to blame, but without the appropriate spare part, they had no way of confirming their diagnosis. Shortly after informing Holland of our frustrating failure, we received instructions to proceed at our normal economic speed towards Port Said, where the repairs would be carried out. I could think of no punishment more severe for the industrial action in Valletta than the prospect of undergoing repairs in Port Said.

Smelling a rat

My evening watch was spent hand steering by following the lights of No. 1 tug and generally feeling miserable and down. Surprisingly, in view of the uneasiness still existing between us, my shipmates openly shared my dismay and anxiety at the prospect of spending an unknown period of time undergoing generator repairs in Port Said. Shwe had led a sheltered career and had transited the Suez Canal only once before and could remember very little of the occasion, while Tin had never experienced the pleasure and was, therefore, none the wiser. The only solution I could see to avoiding the stay in Port Said was either for Remy to come up with an unexpected miracle cure, or for us all to declare that the sudden loss of electrical power had been a figment of everyone's overactive and wild imagination. I thought it highly unlikely that we would be the beneficiaries of either option.

Defying the general mood of depression, I slept well. The air conditioning in my cabin was proving to be exceedingly effective, to the extent that I had to sleep under a blanket, while the new machine for the lower deck was slowly winning the battle in reducing the temperature and, hopefully, also the moisture content of the cabins below the waterline. The messroom was another story. Despite my request that they be kept closed, the outside doors to the housing were continuously being left open, which meant that the space suffered from being unbearably hot and humid, and especially uncomfortable for the enjoyment of our meals. The desire for fresh air apparently outweighed the discomforts of ineffective air conditioning.

The highlight of my day occurred a few minutes before going to the bridge for my morning watch, when I realised that all the rat activity appeared to have come to an end. The few remaining poison blocks had survived a night intact without being eaten or moved, and the liquid levels in the bottoms of the water bottles I had been using as non-corrosive containers seemed to be exactly as I had left them the previous night. Perhaps the rat-catcher from the rodent company and Joseph, our agent, had been perfectly correct after all. They had always implied that I was being far too impatient in expecting to see Roland and his mates flat on their backs and stiff from rigor mortis a few hours after they had hungrily devoured the first night's poison.

Coffee time in the wheelhouse was the scene for minor celebration. I chose to ignore my original promise never to mention the word *ratten* again to my colleagues, and happily announced the morale-boosting news of our victory over the vermin. The others were positively overjoyed at hearing my revelation and conceded, in an indirect manner, that their initial refusal to sail from Malta might have been unreasonable and a little impetuous. I wondered, rather impishly, whether a subtle apology was being made in a roundabout and non-committal way. I opted not to linger any further on what I considered to be water under the bridge. The fact that the battle against the rats had been won within thirty-six hours of sailing was of far greater consequence, despite my unspoken concerns that not a single victim had been sighted. Perhaps the poison was similar to that put down by the rat-man from Mumbai on board the *Justine* in Bahrain, when I had been assured, very convincingly it has to be said, that there would be 'no bad smelling of dead rats': the poison was such that they would have all jumped over the side in their thirst-deranged search for water.

The weather continued to be balmy with traces of white cirrus cloud barely visible high in the sky. With the seas calm and rippled, and the wind non-existent, we made steady progress at our economical speed towards Port Said for what we all knew would be trying and testing times ahead. I resumed my afternoon walking on the main deck, first in a clockwise and then in an anti-clockwise direction, head down and eyes searching for any possible clues as to where Roland and his mates might have been hiding, or where they might have selected for their final resting place, but not a trace of their occupation was to be found. The continuous strolling around the deck, with absolutely nothing to see but No. 1 tug in the distance ahead, was becoming far too aimless and boring, and the temperature a little too hot for the exercise to be healthy. The sun was increasing in warmth by the day and even Mieke, with her love of absorbing the ultraviolet rays, was finding that stretching almost lifeless on her wooden sunlounger-cum-table for much more than an hour at a time was uncomfortably sweaty and exhausting, and conveniently ignored the old aphorism that only horses sweat, but ladies glow and men perspire.

Marco decided to resurrect the swimming pool. We knew it would have to be dismantled again for the Suez Canal, but the benefits of having somewhere to cool down for the two or three remaining days of the passage far outweighed the effort of putting it back together again. It was not to be my lucky day after all. Roland made a break for freedom as Marco moved the gangway. Speeding up the main deck on the starboard side towards the bows, he went to ground hidden under the inaccessible bedplate of the windlass. He remained safely concealed, never to be seen again. No amount of cajoling would persuade him to venture out from his hiding place to face the music and a certain execution either by bludgeoning or drowning.

My evening meal was one of mixed comforts. Suspicious glances from all and sundry at the messroom table warned me that my joyful announcement in the wheelhouse a few hours earlier that the battle had been won was now being treated as a deceit, and any further proclamations of decisive victory over the *ratten* would never be believed. I could, however, claim a victory of a different sort: the fear of Roland entering the housing was far greater than the need for fresh air and, without any further argument, the doors to the accommodation had been closed for the night. The messroom was already benefiting from being a little cooler.

Dressed in my protective clothing of goggles, gloves, a pair of old shorts and wellie boots, I redistributed the few remaining blocks of rat poison and the bottoms of water bottles filled with the 'deadly' liquid that had been safely decanted from the plastic container. This time I used some of my own initiative and placed a network of poison traps not only in the towing winch area, but also around the windlass on the foredeck where Roland had last been seen. I could almost sense his beady and calculating eyes watching me from the darkened steel interior of the windlass bedplate as I painstakingly laid out his evening meal, supper and bedtime drink. The only accoutrements missing were the sounds of romantic music, the starched white napkins and the soft twinkling light from the aromatic table candles. I had really become quite determined in my efforts to finish with the little furry bastard once and for all: over the past few days he had caused me sufficient aggravation and strife to last a lifetime.

Nothing in the way of food or liquid seemed to have been touched overnight and I wondered again whether success could be claimed. I chose to remain silent and to await further developments. My afternoon walk was reduced to a shorter and less interesting route and involved a quick succession of laps around the aft deck only; to include the foredeck in my nautical rambling might have caused an unprovoked attack and I thought it far too restrictive to be wearing wellie boots for my exercise. With Egypt drawing closer and the air temperature steadily rising, I couldn't stick being out on deck for too long and quickly abandoned the heat and high humidity for the comforts of my much cooler cabin. It was only later, as we sat down to eat our evening meal, that I was informed of a very foul smell wafting out from the windlass bedplate. We quickly concluded that Roland had been unable to dive into the sea in his search for water and had, very inconsiderately, died on the spot knowing full well that the final process of decomposition would occur where he couldn't be reached. 'No bad smelling of dead rat' had obviously not applied to the Maltese poison.

I knew that decisive victory over the *ratten* could at last be claimed when the doors to the accommodation were again hooked back in the open position, and all the benefits of having a comfortable messroom were abandoned in the desperate quest for hot and humid fresh air. The battle of the open doors was one I knew I could never win.

The final morning before our arrival was spent in preparing the port papers for Egypt, a rag-tag collection of meaningless and repetitive forms that haven't been updated for many years and all listing demands for the same pointless and irrelevant information, but in differing formats. While there is no disputing that certain facts and figures are required so that canal and harbour dues can be accurately and fairly assessed, Egypt and the African continent as a whole take great delight in keeping the wheels of bureaucracy and the traditions of baksheesh forever turning.

In the afternoon Shwe and I both donned wellie boots and gloves and emptied out the nautical miscellany and rubbish that had been allowed to accumulate over the years around the towing winch. There was no way of explaining why we had left it so long, but the overwhelming desire to discover if there were any more rat bodies quietly rotting away before the appalling smell of decomposition asphyxiated us all had become pressing. Apart from creating an empty space, our time and efforts were wasted. Not a trace of any rat occupation could be found, no droppings, no nests and no festering bodies. Our unwanted guests had finally left us to our own devices.

The following morning saw our arrival off Port Said. A flurry of excited and chaotic communications on the VHF radio, in which details of the two tugs were eventually relayed to the Port Control, resulted in advice that we would be entering port immediately. Despite an insurance requirement that both the tugs remain together for the duration of the voyage, we had agreed that No. 1 tug should pass through the canal at the earliest opportunity and leave us to follow once the generator had been repaired. Pieter would wait for us at anchor outside port limits off Suez. We steamed in slowly towards the breakwater where the pilots boarded each tug in turn from the pilot launch. The noisy and futile demands from the launch crew for cartons of cigarettes as baksheesh for a service that is not only compulsory but already paid for in the harbour dues levied upon each and every ship entering the port or the Suez Canal were totally ignored. No. 1 tug proceeded ahead of us through the busy harbour to the small vessel waiting area near the entrance to the canal, while we headed towards the berth that had been arranged by the agent for the carrying out of our generator repairs.

It never ceases to amaze me that there aren't more collisions in the Port Said approach channel and inner harbour. Double-ended ferries, always seemingly overcrowded and laden to the gunwales with passengers and vehicles whether it is day or night, ply their hectic trade across the bustling waterway between the two cities of Port Said and Port Fouad. They appear to pay, at best, scant attention to the navigational rules of the road. Launches, harbour tugs and bumboats scuttle in all directions, apparently immune to the ever present dangers of colliding either with each other, or with the larger cargo ships and bulk carriers being piloted to the mooring buoys that lie in a regimented line in the middle of the channel. The scene is one of total and bewildering confusion, a nautical Piccadilly Circus without any of the benefits of lane control, roundabouts or traffic lights.

Port Said, or Bur Said as it is known in the Arabic-speaking world, lies beyond the water's edge, a hectic city that squeezes a heaving throng of humanity numbering nearly one and a half million inhabitants into a muddle of narrow and choked streets that are overlooked by a mixture of dowdy tenement blocks, some older and more traditional houses with grand balconies on all floors, and several domed mosques. A loud and thunderous cacophony of twenty-first-century noise erupts without break from within its midst, confirming to all those within earshot that life, and all the associated bedlam that accompanies the act of existence, continues unabated with every passing second of the day: the sound of silence will never be heard within Bur Said or its immediate surroundings.

We weaved our way through the waterborne turmoil and approached our berth, which lay just ahead of the permanently moored rusty hulk that is used as a floating grain terminal. A few minutes later we were safely berthed and awaiting our agent, port officials, watchmen, canal inspectors, traders, scrap dealers and the dozens of other professionals all desperately keen to give us the Egyptian welcome they thought we deserved. Our punishment for 'industrial action' was soon to begin.

A speedy repair

Peace was to reign for less than an hour, a well-deserved respite from being verbally harassed by the harbour pilot, who arrogantly believed it was his divine right to claim every cigarette on board as a reward for his assistance in safely negotiating our passage through the crowded and teeming Port Said harbour. He refused to accept that I wouldn't be contributing to his unhealthy nicotine addiction, and seemed surprised by my lack of response to both his disparaging remarks and unscrupulous demands. We parted not the best of friends. The sight of his angry and contorted features had already convinced me that he should join the growing band of Suez Canal Authority employees whom I have absolutely no desire to meet again. He may not have realised that he had become one of that less than civilised group who have succeeded in making the transiting of the Suez Canal every seafarer's worst possible nightmare: the attitude of the ignorant few has resulted in the perfectly amiable and proficient majority being unable to command one iota of respect from those sailing on the very ships that provide them with the work on which their livelihood depends.

Mohammed, our agent, was at the head of the long column of officials and non-officials who appeared together on the quayside to climb onto the gangway in a concerted and disorganised rush aimed only at being the first to grab the few available seats in our overcrowded and noisy mess. Profession, rank, age or infirmity seemed to play no part in who took the seating. I have had the delight of witnessing exactly the same routine so many times before when passing through the Suez Canal. After the briefest of handshakes and welcomes, Mohammed made his excuses and took the electrician, quite clearly an old friend or business acquaintance, down into the engine room to investigate the woes of our sickly generator. I was left alone to deal with the shopkeepers, port officials, ship's chandlers, bumboat men, unemployed baton-carrying watchmen, scrap dealers, and numerous other persons, all purporting to be my very old and long-lost friends despite my having absolutely no recollection of ever having met any of them before.

Some of the greetings from the officials were less than sincere and were solely a rather naïve and unsubtle introduction to the battered briefcases already lying open at their owners' feet in the optimistic belief that the traditional baksheesh would soon be deposited therein. They were destined to be unlucky. I had absolutely no intention of parting with our limited stocks of the fragrant weed and promoting what has become an open, tiresome and distasteful practice, bordering on unchecked and blatant corruption. Although a former smoker myself, my shipmates would never have forgiven me if I were willingly to hand over the boat's entire cache of precious cigarettes to some unknown Egyptian administrator in return for a trouble-free canal transit.

The non-officials, like the watchmen, scrap dealers and traders, joined the noisy throng in trying to attract my attention, in the hope that the tatty and often barely legible pieces of paper they presented extolling their unquestionable dishonesty and their varied incapabilities would result in a business deal, or a few hours of much-needed work. None of them had realised that such noteworthy characters as 'Winston Churchill', 'Margaret Thatcher', and 'Mickey Mouse' had signed some of their meticulously handwritten and often humorously and ambiguously worded endorsements. No deals or promises of work were given despite their persistence and inability to recognise a lost cause. The need for ship's security and the countless number of bad experiences from the past have all played their part in the complete lack of trust that most seafarers have developed for some of their Fagin-like Egyptian hosts. Even aboard our little *Oriental* tugboat we had taken the elementary precaution of locking away everything that could possibly be stolen, and ensuring that only one door into the accommodation remained open so that access into the housing could be controlled as required.

The entry formalities proceeded at a lethargic pace until it finally dawned on the officials and their assistants that their expectations of customary gifts were unlikely to be fulfilled. They magnanimously accepted defeat and eventually withdrew back to the quayside to await the docking of a more considerate and generous visitor, leaving me with Mohammed to await news from the electrician.

Mohammed and I first met many years ago. We had been reminiscing for only a few minutes when the unmistakable sounds of a diesel generator engine being coaxed reluctantly into life interrupted our casual conversation. The smiling local electrician, accompanied by an even happier Remy, swaggered confidently into the messroom a short while later. Unbelievably, the electrician had taken less than ninety minutes to confirm Remy's fault diagnosis, and in less time than it takes to blink, to fit the printed circuit board he had brought with him on the off-chance that his understanding of the problem, as described by the messages from Holland, had been correct. The all-important ship's stamp and my acknowledging signature were quickly appended to his outrageously extortionate invoice detailing his working and waiting time and the supply of the replacement board. I had not the slightest of regrets or hesitation in presenting him with the two cartons of cigarettes he quite openly demanded as a reward for his success: the apprehension we had all been feeling at the thought of being held up for a few days in Port Said had evaporated with the fitting of a small Bakelite panel and the turn of an electrician's screwdriver. Four hundred cigarettes was a small price to pay for the weight that had been lifted from everyone's shoulders. I knew there would be no recriminations from my shipmates for my uncharacteristic generosity.

After making one or two telephone calls, Mohammed was able to advise me that the authorities had granted permission for us to accompany our sister tug through the canal on the southbound convoy departing from the port before sunrise the next morning. As luck would have it, the generator was back online and running without either tug having lost a second of time. Despite the Singaporean owners being faced with yet another expensive bill, I felt reasonably confident that they would be sharing our happiness at incurring no further delays.

I managed to pass the good news to Pieter on the VHF radio. In many ways I felt sorry for him, for I knew that, in all probability, he was still being besieged by bumboat men and scrap dealers at the small vessels waiting area close to the entrance of the canal. I have been there many times before. The tugboats, oil rig supply boats and other small commercial craft standing by to join the southbound convoy all have to complete a traditional 'Mediterranean moor', with their sterns held by ropes at right angles to a quayside cluttered with scrap, and their bows anchored at the edge of the channel using one or two anchors. It is an area from which there is no respite from the passing traders, vagabonds and thieves in their sun-bleached bumboats. Despite maintaining a two-man deck watch, it is virtually impossible to prevent unwanted guests from climbing on board and attempting to purloin whatever takes their fancy. Padlocks and chains are essential security items when passing through the canal.

The Suez Canal Authority inspector, accompanied by his assistants, the canal electrician and the two mooring boatmen, boarded in the early evening after we had enjoyed the luxury of a couple of hours of almost total peace and quiet. I recognised the inspector from previous visits and knew him to be a principled and fair man with a respectful and polite nature. We spent a few minutes in the wheelhouse exchanging pleasantries and reminiscences while he examined the boat's trading and class certificates. He then had the painstaking task of filling in countless sheets of paper and mandatory forms before accompanying Marco and me outside to the foredeck, where he watched us lower and raise each anchor in turn to satisfy himself that the windlass was in good working order. Fortunately, the darkness and inferior lighting prevented him from seeing that both the anchor chains had twisted as they were being lowered down to the water's edge and that we were unable to stow them properly. Not that it was of any real consequence, for both of us were only interested in establishing that we could let go the anchors in the event of an emergency.

It was then the turn of the portable Suez Canal projector and the electrician, a pretentiously deceptive job description if ever there was one, for a person employed to adjust two weak and paltry beams of light shining from a small and ineffective searchlight. The inspector insisted upon seeing the light wired up and connected to the boat's electrical supply, a task that Remy ended up completing after observing the 'electrician' struggle with the relatively simple chore. Once the light was working, the split beam penetrated the darkness no further than the length of the tugboat and certainly not the 150 metres or so that represents half the width of the canal at its narrowest point. Originally supplied as a visual navigational aid for the pilots in simultaneously lighting up both the canal banks so that the ship's position within the channel could be ascertained, the compulsory hiring of the light and its operator has merely become an additional expense for the privilege of transiting the 100-mile-long waterway. The widening and deepening of the canal over the years has rendered the projectors less than useless for their intended purpose.

Happy that everything was in order, the inspector and his assistant bade their farewells. The one-kilogram pack of medium-roast ground coffee I had been politely requested to supply as a goodwill gesture between friends had been carefully wrapped in some inconspicuous sheets of a local newspaper before being placed inside the inspector's briefcase. I remembered him from a few trips before as being one of the few non-smoking canal officials I had ever met, and one of the least objectionable.

With the projector 'electrician' and the two mooring boatmen, who would accompany us for the duration of the transit, bedded down on the bench seat and one of the tables in the messroom, we retired for the night to await the boarding of the pilot in the early hours of the morning. Thankfully, our stay in Port Said had been far less traumatic than we could possibly have anticipated.

8

THE SUEZ CANAL

Sand, ships and stories to tell

Shwe wasn't to know that the pilot boarding times advised by the authorities on the VHF radio always err on the exceedingly optimistic. It was to be no exception in this instance, and some forty-five minutes after we had been called out on standby and started the main engine, the launch emerged from the confusing background of lights in the harbour and came alongside to allow the pilot to embark. He appeared to be a quiet and inoffensive man, tidily dressed in a white shirt and trousers and proudly sporting a naval hat complete with gold leaf on the peak and a cap badge bearing the insignia of the Suez Canal Authority. Speaking very clear and precise Oxford English, with only a trace of a Middle East accent, he asked some pertinent questions about our engine power and the speed we could hope to achieve during the canal transit. Obviously reassured by my answers, he settled down on the pilot's chair with a mug of coffee to read a magazine he extracted from the well-used briefcase that all canal employees clearly consider to be an essential travel accessory.

Not so many years ago that very same leather briefcase would have caused acute embarrassment and unhappiness among the crew of any deep-sea vessel. In bygone days the pilots would arrogantly insist that a crew member, and preferably an officer, should carry his briefcase up the ship's gangway from the launch and into the wheelhouse of the vessel he was about to pilot. The same would occur when the pilot disembarked, only then the briefcase would be that much heavier with the baksheesh that had been demanded during the transit and, it has to be said, willingly paid out. The unfortunate, but very predictable, loss of a few bulging briefcases, either mysteriously mislaid somewhere en route from the wheelhouse to main deck, or accidentally dropped into the water when being passed from gangway to launch, has virtually brought to an end this unacceptable and demeaning practice. I am told that the pilots nowadays carry their own briefcases.

After waiting a further twenty minutes, instructions were received from the canal authorities to let go our mooring ropes and to proceed on passage. As we eased our way into the channel to adopt what had become our regular position behind Pieter and No. 1 tug, our searchlight shone feebly into life, but, after four or five minutes of shouting angrily through the open wheelhouse window at the 'electrician' manning the split beam control handle, the pilot gave up the idea of focusing the light onto anything useful and retired to the back of the bridge and the solitude of the pilot's chair. A brief order to me instructing me to keep in the middle of the canal and a safe distance behind our sister tug ended any hopes I might have had of enjoying a few hours of scintillating conversation. Just before five o'clock in the morning we cleared Husein Basin at the southerly end of Port Said harbour and entered the canal. A day of much sand and navigating through the desert had just begun.

There is no denying that the Suez Canal, originally dug by over 30,000 forced workers between 1858 and 1869, is an incredible feat of labour and engineering. If Ferdinand de Lesseps had accepted the preliminary survey made at the end of the 18th century, which erroneously concluded that the Red Sea was about 10 metres higher than the Mediterranean, the canal might never have been excavated and the generations of seafarers that have sailed through its 163-kilometre length wouldn't have been faced with the trials and tribulations that have existed since its inauguration 140 years ago. Even though the British, with their colonies in India and the Far East, recognised the canal as being an important trade route, international opinion was doubtful of its continued success or value. One particular sceptic even claimed that 'it will never become an accessible way for large ships in any case'. The canal authorities expect that supertankers with an underwater depth equivalent to the height of a seven-storey building will, in the future, be able to transit the canal between the Red Sea and the Mediterranean.

The canal holds some very mixed memories for me, many of them from my younger and more impressionable days when I was a deck cadet serving out my apprenticeship with one of the old family-run shipping companies based in Liverpool. My first deep-sea voyage was aboard a cargo ship sailing from the Royal docks in London to Fremantle, Sydney and various other ports around the Australian coast, via the Mediterranean and the Suez Canal. A very important consignment of cargo was three animals: a Dalmatian bitch, a randy male poodle and a lovable but nondescript neutered terrier that were being taken out to Western Australia to join their emigrating owners. The dogs had been originally kennelled on the boat deck, but after several nights of continuous howling and barking that just happened to be well within earshot of the captain's accommodation, I and my five co-first-trippers were ordered to take them into the three small double-berth cabins that were our homes for the voyage. The specially constructed kennels and adjoining outside exercise area were abandoned, with the solemn warning that we would be held jointly responsible if so much as a whine from any of the animals was ever heard again. While the poodle and terrier quickly settled into the domesticated comforts of living in their new and homely quarters, the Dalmatian became obsessively protective of her two young cadet handlers and would show only snarling teeth and aggression to anyone else who approached her. The captain was to use this trait to his very real advantage during our stay in Port Said and the subsequent canal transit.

It was, and still is today but to a far lesser extent due to worldwide security precautions, a tradition and an accepted practice for many Egyptian shopkeepers to set up dozens of small stalls around the ship's internal alleyways, lounges and messrooms as soon as the vessel arrived in either Port Said or Suez. Anything and everything could be purchased at a price that was customarily established only after a prolonged but mandatory period of often quite humorous haggling and determined negotiation. Picture postcards, often in grainy sepia or black and white, that boasted the touristy delights of Cairo, the Pyramids or the Sphinx's inscrutable smile, shared pride of place with lurid photographs of bestiality with dogs or donkeys; highly polished onyx ashtrays stood alongside carvings of the boy king Tutankhamun; imitation 'leather' wallets and writing cases were displayed next to copy watches, pens and cut-glass jewellery, and so it went on.

I have horrific memories of buying a leather pouffe, or stuffed footstool, only to discover a short while later when one of the stitched seams split open, that the so-called leather was nothing more than cleverly brushed cardboard, and that the stuffing was comprised of foul-smelling and unwashed bloodied bandages obviously stolen from the local hospital's waste disposal bins. Needless to say, my attitude to Egyptian shopkeepers has been somewhat prejudiced ever since that awful and unforgettable day.

We were not to know, but our intrepid captain, who was on his last voyage before retirement, also shared an abhorrence for the shopkeepers and their intruding presence aboard his ship: perhaps he had been swindled on a previous occasion or, like myself, had suffered a truly bad experience during one of his earlier voyages. I can clearly remember to this day being called to his cabin behind the chartroom to be given the 'Order' book, which I was to take round the ship collecting the signatures of every officer, quartermaster and cadet as well as the Indian serangs. The 'Order' to be acknowledged was the advice that everyone should retire behind the locked doors of their cabins before twelve o'clock, for precisely at noon, which would be confirmed by the sounding of the fire bells, the seafarer's traditional time signal, the Dalmatian would be released from the cadets' cabin in which she was living and set free to roam the accommodation at will.

The noise from around the alleyways shortly after midday must have been music to the ears of our vindictive and smiling captain, who was spotted standing on the bridge-wing rubbing his hands with glee at the sight of the shopkeepers frantically abandoning ship, either by jumping straight into the harbour or by shinning down ropes and makeshift ladders into the bumboats waiting alongside. Indignant shouts, squeals and horrific cries of agony were often drowned out by the joyous barking of the dog as she went on the rampage. Thirty minutes later the Dalmatian returned quietly to her quarters, exhausted from the unexpected exercise, and with no more targets upon which to set her sights or teeth. Shreds of bloodied Egyptian linen and other pieces of torn cloth, clearly recognisable as having once belonged to trousers or jackets, hung proudly from her slavering jaws. We remained shopkeeper-free for the rest of the transit.

I can also remember from another voyage during my apprenticeship being awestruck by the skills of the well-known and long-established gilly-gilly man, Jock Macdonald. I know not from where the phrase 'gilly-gilly man' originates, or from where an Egyptian entertainer from Port Said gained the name 'Jock Macdonald', but, suffice it to say, he was probably one of the fastest and most dexterous of magicians I am ever likely to have the pleasure of witnessing. His incredible tricks involving the undetected removal of bunches of keys, fob watches or wallets from the pockets of his innocent and unsuspecting audience and the planting of day-old chicks in their place, left everyone completely bemused and dumbfounded, and checking for days afterwards that nothing else had been taken from their person without their knowledge, or that a day-old chick hadn't been left to die within their clothing.

Very little in the Arab career aspiration to become a shopkeeper has changed. The two boatmen who had arrived with the canal inspector the previous night awoke from their night of nautical camping in the messroom to set up shop on one of the tables. While their optimism couldn't be faulted, I suspected that their achievable sales from our small crew would be next to nothing. Their sales stock gave every appearance of being identical to that of their relatives some forty years ago. King Tutankhamun still reigned supreme in his onyx splendour, as did the dozens of cheap copy watches, imitation leather goods, sandals and flip-flops, and small stuffed animals that bore little or no resemblance to the one-hump camels their original designer had probably envisaged. Leather pouffes were noticeable by their absence.

The boatmen, complete with the inflated Zodiac stowed on the aft deck, are on board for the duration of the canal transit. In the event of any emergency, or where it becomes necessary to moor in one of the by-pass channels to allow the convoy proceeding in the opposite direction to pass, the boatmen will take our mooring lines ashore to the bollards positioned at frequent intervals along the canal banks. On larger vessels transiting the canal, the mooring boats are of rigid wooden construction and are suspended over the ship's side from the vessel's derricks or cranes, ready to be launched at a moment's notice should the need arise.

The first glimpse of morning twilight saw us converging with the Port Said by-pass that was excavated to permit deep draft vessels direct access to and from the Mediterranean: its construction effectively turned Port Fouad into an island, with man-made waterways on three sides and the sea on the remaining northern side. The canal is measured in kilometres, and two hours after sailing from Port Said we passed kilometre 25 and the El Tinah signal station. Dawn was just beginning to break, illuminating the station in a breathtaking collection of colours from the deep indigo of the night sky to the blues, greens and reds that lasted for only a few minutes before surrendering to the dazzling light of the sun as it made its dramatic and eye-catching ascent into the cloudless morning sky.

The signal stations have been built at approximately 10-kilometre intervals and are manned twenty-four hours a day with the purpose of visually advising the pilot of the precise time of passing the station and the speed that has been made since the previous station. The information is relayed by means of large numerical boards, similar to those seen at a cricket ground, which are clearly visible to each ship as it passes by. The name of the station is also displayed in large letters to reassure inexperienced navigators of their exact location, not that it is particularly difficult to get lost within the canal. Sometimes the pilot will step outside onto the bridge-wing as a station is passed to wave frantically at his colleague in an effort to renew old friendships, or merely to show he is still awake and not fast asleep in the pilot's chair or suffering from nicotine withdrawal symptoms. The absence of a bridge-wing prevented our pilot from making such an announcement, although he could have opened one of the windows had he wished to show his face.

During the transit the scenery lacks sophistication and can be monotonous at times. The Sinai Peninsula lies to the east of the canal and is nothing more than a vast expanse of sand dunes and desert. Close to the canal bank huge sand ramparts still exist from which both Israeli and Egyptian defensive positions were constructed during the Six Day and Yom Kippur wars. I was fortunate in being aboard a vessel making a northbound canal transit in mid-April 1975, shortly after the canal had been reopened at the end of hostilities. Then the sand ramparts existed on both sides of the canal for most of its excavated length, huge mounds of sand built far higher than the superstructures and masts of the passing ships, into which observation points and gun emplacements had been built. I can still recall seeing one such rampart, which had a blackened sand face that glistened with an almost glass-like crystalline appearance. An Israeli-held forward position, it had been under repeated Egyptian flame-thrower and napalm attack, the sand becoming so hot it had almost been turned to glass. It was not so long ago that the last pieces of destroyed military equipment that could be seen cluttering the desert in every direction were taken away and sold as scrap.

The Egyptian army still maintains a highly visible presence along the west bank of the canal. Small army camps can be seen at regular intervals, with their basic accommodation blocks dotted haphazardly around a dusty parade ground bordered by a boundary of evenly spaced white-painted rocks and centred by a white flagpole from which the Egyptian national flag proudly flies. Army trucks and jeeps are tidily parked in regimented lines close to the boundary fences marking the camp perimeters. Adjacent to the camps, the sand ramparts are still occasionally used as gun or tank emplacements, with the long barrels and the gun turrets of the tanks only partially concealed as they protrude over the peaks of the mounds. The service road that runs alongside the canal is frequently interrupted by vehicle barriers and checkpoints manned by slovenly and lethargic-looking young soldiers. On the canal itself, at one or two strategic points, lie dozens of independently powered floating bridge units that can be quickly and easily manoeuvred into position so that they can be linked together to form a pontoon bridge to enable the army to cross the canal. The sand dunes and canal banks on both the east and west sides have been cut away and tarmacked by the crossing points so as to make an easier access for the heavy military vehicles and armour.

The sweet-water canal, which is supplied from the Nile delta and was excavated before the digging of the main canal, has made the land on the west bank of the canal fertile and arable. Smallholdings and farms nestle within isolated clumps of palm trees, their plots laid out in neat and tidy patterns and watered by rows of irrigation ditches. Occasionally an elderly and stooped farmer, followed a few paces behind by his humble wife traditionally dressed in the black burkha, can be seen walking along the canal bank guiding his faithful donkey laden with panniers of rushes and straw. The scene is one that has remained unchanged for hundreds of years.

A short distance to the west of the canal runs the main road linking Port Said to Suez. For almost every hour of the day and night a continuous stream of trucks, buses and cars drive at breakneck speed in both directions, the two-lane highway often supporting an additional lane of traffic as the horn-blowing drivers hurtle headlong into overtaking manoeuvres that look almost suicidal to the uninitiated. Behind the road runs the railway line. Every so often a train can be seen lumbering past, the carriages virtually hidden from view by the hundreds of non-fare-paying passengers hanging on for grim death to the barred but glass-free windows, or squatting precariously in a vast immovable mass of perspiring humanity on the carriage roofs.

As we passed El Qantara Signal Station the huge and impressive Friendship, or Suez Canal, Bridge could be seen in the distance. Built with assistance from the Japanese government, it stretches in a parabolic arc 70 metres above the canal, supported by two huge concrete pillars set into each bank. Countless subsidiary pillars bear the road that disappears into the distance and the desert on either side. Every time I've passed underneath there has seemed to be little or no road traffic crossing overhead, giving the impression that it might just be one of those bridges that leads from somewhere to nowhere. After steaming through the El Ballah by-pass, an 8-kilometre section of twin canal that allows for convoys to pass one another safely, the El Ferdan Railway Bridge came into view. With a span of 1,100 feet, it is the longest swing span bridge in the world and one that appears equally impressive in both the open and closed positions.

Five hours after leaving Port Said, we were approaching Ismailia when the pilot advised that our transit speed had been too slow and that we would have to anchor in Lake Timsah. I knew from previous experiences that arguing the toss would achieve very little, despite our passage time being in excess of the fourteen kilometres per hour the authorities have deemed to be the minimum acceptable speed for making a transit: our position as convoy-tail-end-Charlie severely restricted our ability to increase speed, especially when overtaking is normally prohibited.

Ismailia is located at almost the geographical centre of the canal. Originally established in the 1860s as the construction campsite for excavating the canal, the administrative centre of the Suez Canal Authority has been built near to the waterfront at the edge of the lake. Close to its building lies the Suez Canal tug basin and the Ismailia Yacht Club, a white-painted colonial-type structure overlooking a heavily fendered quayside to which many yachts making their passage through the canal will tie up for a few days for their crews to relax and to play the tourist. I have had the privilege of securing to the very same quayside on two separate occasions, once on an oil industry workboat in which my crew and I were made honorary members of the Yacht Club, and the second time on the *Justine* when the canal pilot rudely abandoned us. On each occasion, and for no apparent reason other than that both my erstwhile commands were rust-streaked commercial vessels and clearly unsuited to be among such a distinguished yachting fraternity, I was asked within a very short space of time to remove them back out to the Lake Timsah anchorage where they should unarguably have been in the first place.

We anchored in the lake behind No. 1 tug just before our mid-morning coffee break. I disliked the idea of anchoring, for fear that we might encounter problems in weighing the anchor when it was time for us to depart. Nothing had changed since Las Palmas to convince me that the windlass was fully functional and capable of raising the anchor later. The pilot disembarked shortly after our arrival: I was sorry to see him go, for he had been a friendly and undemanding person, admittedly of few words, but when he had spoken, it had been with sincerity and politeness.

Our anchorage position was in full view of the distant beach complex at the northern side of the lake, and not far from the President's summer residence. Through the binoculars I could see some holidaymakers and day visitors already on the sand surrounded by white plastic tables, sunloungers and coloured parasols. It brought back memories of many years ago on the cargo ships, when we took great delight in surreptitiously increasing our speed, without the pilot's knowledge, shortly before making the turn on the canal bend that swings sharply away from the beach. The subsequent wash from our bows would hit the gradually sloping sand like a succession of tidal waves, roaring up the beach to create absolute pandemonium among the sunbathers, sunloungers, parasols and tables. Many a time we could look back to see a scene of total devastation, with picnic boxes, towels and all the other accessories that are taken for a relaxing day out by the side of the canal, floating at the water's edge and beyond. Childish, malicious, mischievous, call it what you may, but we saw it as a relatively innocent way of getting our own back for all the hassle and bother we had received from their fellow countrymen just a few hours earlier.

We remained at anchor in Lake Timsah for most of the day. The northbound convoy, numbering twenty-eight ships of varying types and tonnages, steamed past us in the main channel shortly after we had anchored. There is a low-lying sandbank being situated between the lake and the canal, and so we were only able to see the superstructures and masts of the passing vessels, their hulls remaining hidden from view by the man-made island created by dredging the waterway. It soon became evident that our pilot had been perfectly correct in telling us that we would be joining the second southbound convoy in the early evening, and not continuing our passage with the convoy with which we had sailed from Port Said. The authorities had clearly decided that the *Oriental* tugs were better suited to making the remainder of the canal transit at night-time, when no one else would be able to see us.

The pilot embarked shortly before sunset. I recognised him instantly, from two previous transits, as being one of the most obnoxious and rude officials with whom I have ever had the displeasure of sharing a wheelhouse. He showed no signs of having remembered me, and chose to ignore my slightly less than warm greeting. I couldn't help following his eyes as they fruitlessly searched the bridge in the fading light. I knew from memory that he was looking for the flag-locker and for a flag that could be spread out onto the deck to be used as a prayer mat. Without saying a word, or even acknowledging my presence, he reached for the folded newspaper that had been left on the pilot's chair, and spread open a couple of pages on the ribbed deck matting in front of him. With a curt instruction to heave up the anchor, he knelt upon his improvised prayer mat, kicked off his shoes, and began his evening prayers. Being somewhat undecided in my true beliefs, I have absolutely no qualms with religion of whatever faith or denomination, and am a firm believer that everyone in this world has the right to worship whomsoever or whatever they choose, but when it interferes with their work, or lacks a tolerance or awareness of other beliefs, I become a little less understanding. The fact that the pilot was on his knees praying in the wheelhouse made little difference to the power of the windlass in picking up our anchor, but I've been in the canal with the same person when prayer time coincided with an event requiring his undivided attention, and it wasn't forthcoming. When someone is involved in the professional world I believe that to be inexcusable.

My apprehension concerning the ability of the windlass to pick up the anchor wasn't entirely misplaced. The process was painfully slow and, had we not anchored in shallow water where the weight of chain had been reduced by the depth, I suspect we would still have been there to this day. Anchors and Lake Timsah bear a lasting grudge against me. It wasn't the first time I had experienced that fearful premonition of being permanently attached to the lake-bed off Ismailia for the rest of my seagoing days.

Darkness had descended by the time the anchor was stowed and everyone's prayers had been completed and answered. The lack of light prevented me from spotting if the pilot's white trousers bore the legend of the newspaper's headlines. We followed the stern light of No. 1 tug from the lake back into the main canal, passed the illuminated War Memorial, and then proceeded towards Suez and our ultimate destination of the Gulf of Suez and the Red Sea. Progress was faster than it had been in the morning, and just over an hour later we entered the western branch of the Deversoir by-pass canal that leads directly into the Great and Little Bitter Lakes.

Whenever passing through the Bitter Lakes I can't help recalling the group of fourteen ships of eight different nationalities that was sailing in the northbound convoy which became trapped in the Great Bitter Lake as fighting broke out between Israel and her Arab foes in the Six Day War of June 1967. I was very lucky in that I had been sailing in a ship in the penultimate southbound convoy prior to the closure of the canal. The 'Yellow Fleet', as the ships became known after they had become progressively covered in desert sand, were to spend eight years at anchor in the lake. Stories abound about the experiences of some of their crews, not that any of them were to spend anything like the eight years aboard. The 'Great Bitter Lake Association' was formed to provide support for all those trapped aboard their ships and to promote and cultivate friendship and joint undertakings. They were later to organise a yachting club and such prestigious events as the 'Bitter Lake Olympic Games' to complement the 1968 Olympics in Mexico City. Perhaps their most lasting and recognised contribution was the one they made to the world of philately, with the production of their very own 'local postage stamps', which were purely decorative labels without any postal validity. Nevertheless, they have become collectors' items much sought after by stamp enthusiasts throughout the world.

During my deep-sea career, one of my colleagues, who had also been sailing as a Master with the same company, had the distinction of being appointed the United Nations liaison officer between the Egyptians and those on board the trapped ships. He told me of one particular Christmas Eve night when the Egyptians, fearing an Israeli raid, instructed the anchored vessels to black out and extinguish all their lights. Unknown to the Egyptians, the crews had been busy making a large Christmas tree, which had been positioned in one of the vessels' lifeboats before being towed out, trailing a long electrical cable, into the middle of the lake. At the stroke of midnight, despite the entire fleet obeying the order to be in total darkness, the lights on the Christmas tree were switched on in a colourful and illuminating festive display that accompanied the multilingual carols being enthusiastically sung from the decks of the fourteen vessels. Amazingly, among all those trapped, the two German ships made it back to their home port of Hamburg under their own power in May 1975, to be greeted by 30,000 persons lining the quayside applauding their safe and long-awaited arrival.

Shortly before midnight we passed El Kabrit Signal Station, marking the imaginary boundary between the Great and Little Bitter Lakes. Fifty minutes later we had crossed the lake and re-entered the excavated section of the canal at El Gineifa. The pilot, like his predecessor in the morning, soon gave up shouting angrily at the 'electrician' controlling our searchlight, and left me to steer the boat in the middle of the waterway between the lights spaced at regular intervals along the canal banks.

When the town of Suez was still some distance away the pilot started making his incessant and shameless demands for cigarettes. These were ignored, as were the equally begging and vociferous claims for baksheesh from the electrician and the two boatmen who had entered the bridge en masse to get their attendance papers signed and stamped. A few minutes later they were obliged to board their respective launches empty-handed, leaving me with an elderly Suez pilot who, after adjusting his eyes to the darkness of the wheelhouse, informed me of the course I should steer before, also, demanding a carton of cigarettes as payment for imparting the information I had already gleaned from studying the chart. Five minutes later he had also disembarked empty-handed, leaving us alone to navigate the bend of the Eastern Channel and into the well-buoyed Newport Rock Channel leading out to the open sea.

Pieter on No. 1 tug was just as delighted as I was at clearing the canal. The company had kept to their promise, and had arranged for the ship's chandler in Suez to supply a second air-conditioning unit for the lower deck accommodation. It had been safely delivered while their pilot had been disembarking.

The transit had taken us twenty-three hours, but we had finally negotiated the Suez Canal and successfully dealt with everything it had offered. The enervating heat of the Gulf of Suez would be upon us at daylight.

9

Suez to Djibouti

The heat is on

Aleisurely, if not almost pleasurable, night-time cruise down the Newport Rock Channel saw our eagerly anticipated departure from the bustling and congested waters of Suez Bay. Being the last two vessels in the convoy, we enjoyed the luxury of being able to proceed down the middle of the waterway at our economic speed of eight knots, and without the need to watch our sterns anxiously for the larger and faster deep-sea ships coming up behind us. Although the international maritime 'Rules of the Road' require the overtaking vessel to keep clear of the vessel being overtaken, it can become a dangerous free-for-all when a convoy of ships is leaving the constraints of the Suez Canal. The function of being rule-abiding and sympathetic navigators, with the responsibility of overtaking slower vessels with caution and a wide berth, can sometimes be completely disregarded in the almost indecent haste to cover as many miles as possible in the least possible time. The jostling for the most advantageous position at the start of the traffic separation scheme is not unlike the start of a Formula One motor race, when every driver is hell-bent on reaching that first and most crucial of bends in pole position. It seems as if arriving at that first point at the head of the fleet will have a hugely commercial effect on the remainder of their all-important and carefully planned voyage, but, assuredly, every Master will deny that this is ever the case.

As we turned into the southbound lane that would route us down the western side of the Gulf of Suez, the well-known seafarer's landmark of Conry Rock light could be seen flashing on our port bow. I was more than happy, ecstatic might have been a better description, not to be seeing it on the opposite bow: had I done so, it would have meant we were inbound, with all the anxieties and tight-lipped frustrations of the canal transit ahead of us. A quick glance astern showed the lights of Suez receding into a hazy and unidentifiable obscurity, confirming that my almost childlike and euphoric celebrations were not the slightest bit misplaced. We were back at sea, to the south of Suez, and steaming further away from that incredible excavation through the desert on which Ferdinand de Lesseps was so rightly proud to have stamped his name almost 150 years ago. It is unfortunate that his crystal ball and theodolites had no way of predicting that his undoubted engineering capabilities could possibly create such extreme levels of stress and turmoil for the innocent and compliant victims of the international seafaring community several generations later.

Handing over the bridge watch to Marco, I went below to my cabin to grab a short but much-needed sleep before waking less than five hours later to relieve Shwe for my morning watch. The early sun, although still relatively low above the near horizon, was shining directly into the unshaded wheelhouse windows, making hand steering by compass virtually impossible against the background glare of blinding and eye-searing light. Aiming our bows at the wake of No. 1 tug was infinitely easier than squinting into the poorly silvered mirrors of the compass periscope in the hope of observing the point to steer on the faint and almost indistinguishable compass card. A couple of hours later the sun had risen high into the cloudless blue sky, and we were set to experience the hottest day of our voyage to date.

After our traditional coffee break in the wheelhouse, Marco and Shwe tried to re-stow the anchors. The anchor flukes, the two blades that swivel on the stock to dig into the seabed, had flipped over on both the anchors, preventing us from heaving them fully up into the hawse pipe, where they would normally snuggle tightly against the flared and strengthened sides of the tug's bows. I ruled out the accepted practice for dealing with the problem by stopping the boat and lowering the anchors about 30 metres into the water to allow the chain to unwind itself. My concerns that the windlass might be incapable of hoisting them back on board had been reinforced after watching its interminable struggle to lift the anchor from the bed of Lake Timsah the previous afternoon. After several futile attempts at trying to persuade the flukes to flip back over into their correct position by trailing the anchors at the water's edge, we gave it up as a bad job and stowed them as best we could, securing and tensioning the chains on deck with steel wire ropes and bottle-screws. With the relatively sharp arrow-head of the flukes jammed inwards and stabbing the shell plating of the bows, it was absolutely imperative to prevent the anchors moving or banging in bad weather, when the flukes could cause some serious damage to the hull, and possibly even to the watertight integrity of the boat itself.

The remaining part of my morning watch passed quickly. As the Gulf of Suez is quite narrow in places, our track took us within two or three miles of the western shore with its desolate mountain ranges of towering cliffs and precipitous slopes soaring majestically behind the narrow and dusty coastal strip. The landscape is breathtakingly beautiful in its own mystic way, devoid of colour apart from varying shades of sandy yellow, and lacking trees or vegetation except leafless scrub and the occasional clump of spiky date palms. The barren outline, stretching as far as the eye can see, provides a fascinating, almost awe-inspiring, sight set against the rich, deep blue of a cloudless sky and the backdrop of dry and arid peaks veined with craggy and shadowed rocky outcrops. The occasional collection of flat-roofed buildings, and the dozens of rounded silver and white painted oil storage tanks in the tank farms, mark the route of the road extending down the 200-mile length of the Gulf; I couldn't imagine residing in a more inhospitable or unwelcome place.

Egypt is virtually self-sufficient in oil. The first of the many oil rigs we would see in the next few hours loomed into view shortly before midday. The North Amer oil field consists of several rigs that lie well within the shipping lane, but which pose little threat to navigation. Although some of the rigs are no more than a single steel tubular leg rising vertically from the sea to support a small work platform, they are clearly visible by day and well-lit at night. In the background, and to the east of the northbound shipping lane, the huge production platforms of the October oil field could be seen with their flare stacks continuously burning off the unwanted gas, the flames and shadowy trails of grey smoke barely discernible against the glare of the midday sun. Seeing the wind-bent flares again brought back vivid memories of the *Justine* and *Martha* voyage when we had been passing the East Zeit oil field during my watch on our way north towards Suez. What Remy and I had at first thought to be the flames from a platform flare stack proved to be the flames from a funnel fire on board the *Martha* – a particularly memorable night of a particularly unforgettable voyage.

The heat during the day was far too uncomfortable to spend longer than a few minutes outside; I felt no guilt whatsoever in abandoning my leisurely stroll around the deck after lunch for the delights of a few hours of rest. I slept well, no doubt making up for the change in my sleep patterns during the previous couple of days. My pleasure in having an afternoon's sleep in the comfort of my air-conditioned cabin evaporated somewhat in the course of my regular VHF radio conversation with Pieter during our evening watch. He told me the atmosphere on No. 1 tug was unpleasant and extremely tense, and could be cut with a knife: his crew were voicing their loathing and exasperation for all individuals employed in the profession of ship's supply and chandlery. The second portable air-conditioning unit for their lower deck accommodation, which had been hastily delivered in Suez during the few minutes of demoniac chaos involving the exchange of pilots, the unloading of the inflatable Zodiac, and the disembarking of the canal boatmen and the electrician, didn't work. Although of the correct output, voltage and electrical frequency, the long-awaited appliance had, unfortunately, been supplied without its vital charge of freon gas, the essential cooling agent that creates the subtle difference between the machine operating as an expensive air-circulating fan and an air-conditioning unit providing cold and dehumidified air.

I could imagine, having stood in the hot and humid atmosphere outside for only a few minutes, what the conditions would be like in their airless and stuffy accommodation below the waterline. The single portable air-conditioning unit already in their possession, which admittedly had been inconsiderately purloined in Valletta without so much as a caring thought for Mieke, Marco, Shwe and Tin, would be hard-pressed to control the temperature in the alleyway, let alone in the four adjoining cabins. I felt genuine sympathy for Ton, Bas, Albert and Maung, although I could well have been accused by my own crew of being disloyal and deceitful for possessing such feelings. I also felt sorry for our office colleagues in Holland who had, after all, made every effort to honour their well-intentioned promise made in Valletta, but to no avail.

Undoubtedly, the unlucky ones and obvious losers were the four occupants of those unbearably sticky and suffocating cabins in the forepart of our sister tug; they would be suffering the most in the exhausting and unrelenting heat of the next few days.

Why always me?

During the evening watch we passed the Ashrafi Islands in the Gubal Strait and headed on towards Shaker Island, which lies at the western side of the relatively narrow strait marking the entrance to the Gulf of Suez. Over on the eastern side lay Ras Muhammad, the southernmost tip of the Sinai Peninsula, and the Strait of Tiran leading into the Gulf of Aqaba. We had safely entered the Red Sea by midnight, the long-awaited end of my monotonous four hours of hand steering, staring at the eye-watering twinkling incandescence of an off-white stern light. The only respite had been to mark hourly positions on the chart, and continuously to check our immediate surroundings for other shipping. Ahead of us lay the unpalatable prospect of five days' steaming through arguably one of the hottest parts of the world in the month of August. No one was particularly looking forward to it, least of all, I suspected, the occupants of the lower deck cabins aboard our sister boat, the *Oriental Tug No. 1*.

We passed El Akhawein, the Brothers, during Shwe's watch in the morning. Two coral outcrops located less than a mile apart, they emerge from the sea at the edge of a small coral reef to reach only a few metres high, barren and arid and with a prominent lighthouse, a white rounded 30-metre tower, built on to a square-shaped dwelling near the centre of the north island. In the days before satellite navigation it provided the all-important landmark for vessels proceeding towards the Gulf of Suez, with the light reported to have been seen at distances of over one hundred

Oriental Tug No. 2 *in choppy seas*

miles during times of abnormal atmospheric refraction. The islands are miles away from the nearest landmass and, with the heat and the loneliness, the discomfort of living in such lifeless isolation is truly beyond comprehension. To be incarcerated upon such a desolate and uninviting place, and to man and be responsible for tending such a lighthouse, could only have been, and might still be for all I know, either a merciless punishment for the most heinous and dastardly of crimes, or an act of unselfish and extreme dedication by single-minded and devoted keepers to the worldwide seafaring community as a whole. Having never stopped to ask and find out, I'm unsure where the truth lies.

Being in the open waters of the Red Sea, our watch-keeping and steering duties became less interesting and more tedious. Monotony set in, broken only by the sighting of overtaking ships as the previous day's southbound convoy finally caught up with us in their headlong rush for the Bab-el-Mandeb Straits and the Indian Ocean beyond. The heat became almost suffocating in its intensity, the conditions exacerbated by a north-westerly wind blowing directly from astern that nullified any cooling effect there might have been from the breeze created by our own speed. Marco rebuilt the swimming pool yet again, safe in the knowledge that on this occasion there would be no nasty surprises from unwanted four-legged grey furry guests emerging from their hiding places to escape up the main deck. With the ambient temperature approaching 50 degrees Celsius around midday, we waited until the cooler airs of the early evening before venturing out on deck for a few minutes of splashing around in the lukewarm seawater like young and exuberant children.

In addition to our normal watches, the owner's request for detailed repair lists for the planned dry-docking of both the boats in Singapore ensured that everyone was kept busily occupied for the first three days of our passage down the Red Sea. Although repairs had been carried out in both Abidjan and Las Palmas, they had been made with the safe progression of the voyage in mind rather than the longer-term and more testing requirements of full-time commercial employment.

Our catalogued lists became technical and comprehensive as measurements were taken for the replacement of corroded and rotten steelwork, details were noted for accommodation refurbishment, model types and serial numbers were recorded for equipment to be overhauled and tested, sizes and dimensions were listed of pipework to be renewed, of fuel and water tanks to be opened and inspected, of machinery to be stripped down and serviced, and so it went on, until it became almost a full-time secretarial task transcribing our rough and often frustratingly illegible notes into email format for satellite transmission to Holland and onward forwarding to Singapore. I sincerely hoped the owners would study our reports constructively and with an open mind, rather than introduce the too-frequently used red pen in a cost-cutting exercise that would benefit no one and prove that we had been wasting our time. While on board to assist, we were not their employees. Our sole responsibilities lay in delivering the two tugs safely and expeditiously, as per the negotiated and agreed terms and conditions of the delivery contract; I knew we would be a long time home before our erstwhile commands had been fully repaired and ready to work.

Three days after clearing Suez, the port of Jeddah lay on our port beam, but many miles distant, out of sight and beyond the horizon. Some fifty-five miles to the west of Mecca, the birthplace of the Prophet Muhammad and the holiest city of Islam, Jeddah is the port to which the Hadj ships used to sail, and still do so, but to a lesser extent now that air travel has become more popular and competitive. The Hadj ships, often cargo ships trading between Asia and Europe, would include in their homeward itinerary a port in one of the main Muslim countries in the world such as Pakistan, Indonesia, the Philippines, or East Africa. There they would embark their human cargo to take to Jeddah on their way to the Suez Canal and their final destinations in Europe. It became a profitable sideline transporting some of the thousands of Muslim pilgrims, who have a religious obligation to make a once-in-a-lifetime pilgrimage to the Kaaba in the centre of Mecca. Carrying pilgrims by sea eventually became a dedicated employment for ships that were either converted or specifically built for the trade, many of them having a capacity of over two thousand deck passengers and a small number of first-class passengers.

One of my colleagues from a marine safety company told me of an inspection of such a Hadj ship he had made many years ago in which the ship's officers played a sweepstake gambling on the number of living souls they would disembark either at Jeddah, or at the original home port. The pilgrims would be counted aboard as they embarked but, during the voyage, the captain would have to stop his ship at the same hour every evening to commit to the deep those who had passed away during the previous twenty-four hours and consequently wouldn't be making their long-awaited pilgrimage to the Kaaba. With many of the female pilgrims being pregnant and near to giving birth when they embarked, the babies born while sailing on passage would compensate for the deaths, but obviously never in quite the same proportion. From all accounts, the rather macabre sweepstake was often worth a considerable sum of money, especially if it had been carried over a number of times to the following voyages due to the correct number not having been drawn.

My friend also proudly showed me a photograph of himself posing in one of the Hadj ship's double-banked wooden lifeboats that had been safely stowed in its davits on the boat deck at the time of his safety inspection. Although the main part of his torso remained hidden behind the gunwales, his head and shoulders were clearly recognisable in the picture. A closer and more careful look revealed one of his legs protruding awkwardly through the bottom of the boat's rotten planking, which had completely given way as soon as he had climbed on board. Thankfully, modern ships' lifeboats are now made from strengthened rigid fibreglass to comply with the vastly improved safety standards that the international maritime community demands.

The barbecue we had planned for the early evening as a well-earned reward for conscientiously completing our dry dock repair lists had to be cancelled with the wind veering to the north-east and strengthening to force 5–6. While having the wind on our port beam gave us the much-appreciated benefit of slightly cooler air, the seas that sprang up with the wind effectively put paid to our evening festivity. Having glowing red-hot charcoal embers lying inside a paint drum that had been cut in half and mounted on a welded framework supported by four pieces of round steel bar as legs couldn't really be considered compatible with a constantly tilting and spray-soaked deck. The truly veritable feast of chicken drumsticks, kebabs and sirloin steaks escaped the indignity of being frazzled to a turn and were, instead, properly cooked on the galley stove and eaten in the confines of the sweltering messroom.

Being unable to have our evening meal in the slightly cooler environment outside was a huge disappointment to me. The continuing saga of the need for hot and humid 'fresh air' had rendered the messroom virtually uninhabitable and ended up with Mieke and I having a bitter argument as to why it should be necessary to open portholes and doors while an air-conditioning unit struggled to maintain a comfortable temperature. In my eyes, there was little or no pleasure to be had from eating my daily meals in the airless and stifling atmosphere of the messroom, with perspiration dripping profusely from every pore of my overheating body. It seemed to me to be such a wasteful abuse of the air-conditioning unit we had been given in Valletta not to be using it to its full potential, especially when our colleagues on No. 1 tug were struggling on with a small and totally ineffectual portable unit. The lack of support from Remy and Marco and their obvious reluctance to side with either point of view for whatever reason, was only too clear; despite the acute discomfort we were all feeling, their silence confirmed not only my fears that they had no desire to become involved, but also my initial apprehension that the portholes and doors would revert back to the open position even if I closed them whenever the opportunity occurred. I vowed there and then to be antisocial and enjoy my food alone in the cooler surroundings of my air-conditioned cabin. Little did I realise, but keeping the promise I had made to myself for longer than a day would turn out to be far more difficult than I had originally envisaged.

Pieter and I agreed we that would make our arrival at Djibouti shortly after daybreak, with the intention of taking on fuel, water and stores during the day and sailing before nightfall. With twenty-four hours of the passage remaining, we passed Hanish Al Kubra island, followed a few miles further on by the Haycock islands, three small islets of barren rock carrying the names of Northeast Haycock, Middle Haycock and Southwest Haycock. Middle Haycock is described in the pilot book as being 'cone-shaped and remarkable' – its hidden attractions remaining 'remarkably' obscure and, as far as I'm aware, yet to be discovered. At noon we were only a few miles away from joining the traffic separation scheme that would lead us into the Bab-el-Mandeb Straits and out into the cooler airs of the Indian Ocean.

My afternoon nap came to an abrupt end with my waking lathered in sweat and feeling as if I had been incarcerated in an overheated sauna for far longer than the recommended time for continued good health and weight-loss. My initial fears were confirmed as soon as I staggered weakly from my bunk to inspect the battered and long-suffering air-conditioning unit: it was silent and appeared completely lifeless. Having carried out a perfunctory examination of the plug and cable connections,

I called upon Remy to confirm my diagnosis that not only had an untimely death occurred, but also that surgery would have little or no chance of success in restoring life to the worn-out and heavily corroded parts. The small electrical meter with its dials and flickering needle told Remy everything he needed to know. The compressor unit had failed, and the cold breath of life that had come to be so vital for my well-being had been permanently extinguished. My vow that I would eat all my meals in the comfort and solitude of a cool and air-conditioned cabin had been cruelly broken before it had even started: not a solitary morsel had passed my lips since that impulsive promise made to myself a few hours earlier.

I had now joined, albeit unwillingly, the environmentally friendly club whose multiracial membership survives in the harsh and unforgiving climate and temperatures of the real world rather than in the one artificially controlled by man and his machines; as I opened my forward-facing porthole in the hope of catching just a trace of precious breeze, I knew I wouldn't enjoy being a member one little bit. Like the millions of other members, I was now experiencing life as Mother Nature intended, the only difference being that I was entombed in a man-made steel shell that showed nothing but indifference to the heat of the midday sun.

I joined Shwe in the wheelhouse for our transit through the Bab-el-Mandeb Straits, the narrow channel that forms the mouth of the Red Sea. While he steered I could plot our position on the chart and admire the not so distant scenery of what was once known as Perim Island, but which has now reverted to its more established local name, Mayyun Island. During the relatively short time I've been at sea, the island has changed hands at least twice, as colonial powers with different political ambitions and motives have occupied Yemen in the mistaken belief that they might influence the Yemeni people and their government into a new way of thinking. The island lies in a crucial position in the middle of the busy channel between Africa and Arabia, and effectively divides the waterway into two straits with the narrower of the two being reserved exclusively for local dhows and small craft. Blessed with a large bay in the southern part that acts as a natural harbour, Mayyun Island is of huge strategic and military importance in controlling access to and from the Red Sea.

Once clear of the straits we turned to the south and followed No. 1 tug into the Golfe de Tadjoura, where we reduced our speed so that we could time our arrival off Djibouti for daylight the next morning. Passing close to the west of Îles Moucha at sunrise, we proceeded towards the pilot station, where we received instructions on the VHF radio to moor one behind the other on the end of the main cargo ship quayside. There was obviously an administrative misunderstanding about the length of pier available and the combined length of our two tugs. As Pieter was in the lead, we watched him manoeuvre alongside and then edge forward close up to the stern of the vessel lying ahead of him. His efforts were wasted as there was quite clearly insufficient space remaining for us to moor to the quay. Marco, who was gaining some practice in tug handling, did the only thing possible and gently placed us alongside our sister. We had arrived in Djibouti, and yet another leg of our long voyage to the Far East had been safely completed.

10

DJIBOUTI

The day of the flies

Despite my many years of serving on vessels sailing from Europe to the Indian subcontinent and beyond, I had never before visited Djibouti, the port and capital carrying the same name as the Republic. Strategically located at the entrance to the Red Sea, it became a French military base in the late 1880s, when the colony of French Somaliland was established to challenge the British dominance across the water in the port of Aden, in what is now the Republic of Yemen.

The British occupied Aden in 1839 and, after the completion of the Suez Canal thirty years later, it was to become a vitally important refuelling port for vessels trading to India and beyond. Calling at Aden for provisions, fuel and water en route to Ceylon and Burma was a tradition that was maintained for many years by the deep-sea shipping company for which I worked. I assume their selection of Aden in preference to Djibouti was based on important commercial factors such as the price and availability of fuel oil, rather than on patriotic motives to please the 'old-boy' network that obviously existed with the ex-pats and their long-established colonial enterprises. Aden was always a popular stopover for the crews on our ships. In the 1960s it was a duty-free port where we could buy cameras, radios, cut lengths of material for gentlemen's suits, and a variety of other luxury goods that were all sold on in the black market for a vast profit in Colombo and Rangoon. It was the only way we could finance a lifestyle of luxury that was way beyond our means as low-paid apprentices with aspirations and egos far beyond our tender years.

With the withdrawal of the British from South Yemen in 1967, the newly formed People's Republic established close ties with the Soviet Union. Aden started losing its replenishment business to Djibouti as supplies of fuel oil and provisions became more expensive and difficult to obtain. Operated by the ever-expanding and efficiently managed Dubai Ports Authority, Djibouti has gained in popularity over the years. The port not only handles more than half of Ethiopia's foreign trade, but also has a relatively thriving trade in petroleum products.

From what I could see while sitting on deck waiting for the port officials to arrive, there were many improvements in the port infrastructure still to be made. I could only guess as to what the day would bring. We had already received a message from Holland the previous afternoon advising us that neither the ship's chandlers nor the ship agents had acknowledged any of the office's messages placing orders or seeking information. I hoped it was only a temporary blip in communications and that the services we had requested would materialise without too many difficulties. I had half expected that as it had been the French colony of French Somaliland some twenty-five years ago, the Republic of Djibouti might have retained some of the habits and colonial efficiency of which the French are justifiably proud.

We didn't have too long to wait before the agent appeared, accompanied by two uniformed gentlemen, whose shabby-looking attire had clearly seen better days. The Port Health Officer fastidiously checked our vaccination certificates and the boat's de-ratting exemption certificate to confirm to himself that we weren't carrying any particularly nasty communicable European diseases to the Horn of Africa, while the police officer, who seemed to be acting for the immigration department, examined our passports and carefully compared the names and the numbers against the crew lists. Eventually satisfied that we were disease-free and unlikely to jump ship to lose ourselves among the 400,000 or so Issas and Afars who make up the population of this tiny nation, the two boats were entered inwards. After a few brief words with the agent the officers bade their polite farewells and disembarked to leave us to our own devices. At least the entry formalities had been conducted in a calm and civilised manner, unlike some of their African and Arab neighbours.

The agent knew nothing of any messages sent from Holland, and appeared to possess little or no knowledge of any arrangements that had been made with either the bunker company or the ship's chandlers. Frustration set in: the sole reason for our visit to Djibouti was to replenish our fuel, food and water for the ongoing passage to Singapore, but our agent seemed to know nothing about it. He looked to be a quiet and shy person with a disinterested and almost bored attitude. We were told, in a very indifferent and non-committal way, that the fuel oil was normally supplied either early in the morning or late in the evening after the sun had gone down, but very rarely during the heat of the day. The provisions order was a subject of which he denied all knowledge, although he did reluctantly promise to contact the ship's chandler and pass on our request that the stores be delivered as soon as possible. Both Pieter and I were assured that everything, including the supply of fresh water from the port authority, would be forthcoming in the fullness of time. Impatience was certainly never going to win the day in Djibouti. We watched him climb back ashore, unconvinced that any of our three basic requirements were likely to be fulfilled within the optimistic timetable we had set ourselves of sailing before nightfall.

Appearances can sometimes be deceptive: the agent was as good as his word, and within the hour a freshwater hose had appeared on the quayside and was being connected to our sister tug. While we waited for our turn to be supplied, Marco, Shwe and I busied ourselves with trying again to re-stow the anchors. Lowering and raising them both to and from the harbour bottom was eventually successful in untwisting the chains, and soon they were both brought home into the hawse pipes where they could sit securely and snugly against the bow plating. The work, although not of a particularly strenuous nature, had totally exhausted us, both physically and mentally.

The suffocating and searing heat from the mid-morning summer sun proved to be mercilessly debilitating, and had completely sapped our limited energy.

To add to our abject misery, swarm upon swarm of flies descended upon the filthy dock area to scavenge upon the foul-smelling and rotting rubbish lying heaped on the quayside. With unerring accuracy, they selected the *Oriental* tugs and their unfortunate crews as their secondary target. They were to make our lives even more unbearable than the gruelling heat. Circling in their thousands, they landed on any part of our bodies where they could feast on the salty sweat. It mattered little how many times we waved our arms, or how violent were the swatting motions we made with our hands. Any movement we made seemed to have no deterring effect, except to increase the flow of bodily perspiration, which, in turn, attracted yet more flies. It was a vicious and unpleasant circle from which there was no escape. They continued to hover and land, determined to indulge upon whatever they could find. Television pictures of refugee camps in African famines came to mind, horrific pictures that show emaciated children lying helplessly against their mother's milkless breasts, unable to keep the hundreds of flies from feeding on the mucus weeping from their unblinking eyes. I could now begin to understand the hopelessness the refugees must feel when faced with those unrelenting insects.

Although bearing no comparison to the misery of the starving African children, the flies were a horrendous experience, unlike anything I had ever undergone in my seagoing career. The only benefit to be gained from the winged invasion was the closing of the main deck alleyway doors and the battening down of the portholes in the messroom and galley; it would have been far too cynical of me to suggest that the flies, rather than the need for an air-conditioned environment, might have instigated their hasty closure. Despite our best efforts, many of the flies found their way into the accommodation. If only our very own Larry the lizard, or maybe chameleon, had lived a few weeks longer, the supply of flies from Djibouti might well have ensured his survival for many years hence.

The stifling heat and the lack of any breeze ensured that taking even a few minutes' rest during the day was completely out of the question. With the housing becoming similar to a fully heated oven, but without fan assistance, the main air-conditioning unit struggled to maintain a temperature only marginally cooler than that outside, and the predatory and hungry flies prevented us from venturing out on deck for a moment longer than was absolutely necessary. My cabin, like the lower deck crew cabins on our sister tug, had become virtually uninhabitable. I sincerely hoped the conditions would improve once we had left Djibouti and entered the Indian Ocean with its cooler and more friendly climate.

The road tankers containing our fuel supplies appeared on the quayside in the late afternoon, and two hours later Remy and Tin had braved the conditions to top up our tanks with sufficient fuel to reach Singapore safely. With only the provisions still to come, we were two-thirds of the way towards being able to resume our voyage.

The ship's chandler eventually arrived quite late into the evening, and at the same time as the road tankers returned with the fuel for No. 1 tug. Working under the deck lights and the dingy background illumination from the port facilities, we spent a chaotic and sweaty couple of hours sorting out the stores and passing our order across No. 1 tug, onto our deck and into the storeroom. At least we could be thankful that the flies had disappeared for the night, and that the sun had dipped below the horizon to give us a few hours of much-needed respite from the dazzling glare and the heat.

Despite our original plan of sailing in daylight, both Pieter and I thought it a good idea that, having replenished our fuel, food and water, we should leave without further delay, rather than waiting until morning. Neither of us could face another day, or even just a few hours, similar to the ones we had just experienced. Our proposal to sail as soon as possible was not well received by some of my crew. The angry voices of dissent from Mieke and Marco, demanding that we stay the night because they had been unable to rest during the day, sounded as if I was in for yet another Malta-style industrial dispute, only this time I would be unable to telephone the office for support or advice. I found it extremely difficult to understand why they should wish to remain in such an inhospitable and uninviting place, although to some extent I could sympathise with their tiredness. The bad-tempered protest was to last for less than ten minutes before being emphatically silenced by the appearance of a loud-voiced and over-zealous port official, who demanded to know the reasons behind our not sailing. He showed not the slightest inclination to listen to any compromise proposals that we might remain alongside for a few hours until everyone was rested, insisting that an inbound vessel scheduled to arrive within the hour required the berth we were occupying. Being honest with myself, I was rather appreciative of the official's timely support, and agreed to our immediate departure. I couldn't quite visualise how a ship would be able to berth alongside the pier we were vacating, but that was not my problem. The official was not to be easily deflected from seeing that his instructions were obeyed, waiting impatiently on the poorly lit quayside to watch us slip our moorings and ease our way out into the buoyed departure channel directing us away from the port.

Having been secured on the outboard side of No. 1 tug, we led our two-boat pro-cession into 'Passe Est', the passage to the south of Îles Moucha that points the way, very conveniently, towards the deeper water of the Indian Ocean. No. 1 tug overtook us once we were out of the channel to adopt her usual role as our guiding light. We were back to our mindless hand steering and playing 'follow my leader'.

The lights of Djibouti, with its unrelenting flies and insufferable daytime heat, slipped slowly away into the distance, never to be forgotten and, hopefully, never to be revisited: ahead of us, the monsoons of the Indian Ocean and the final nineteen-day passage steaming to Singapore.

11

THE INDIAN OCEAN

Pirates, beware!

At noon on the day after sailing from Djibouti we were forty-five miles to the south of Aden, making over eight knots, as we headed for a position to the north of the island of Socotra, where we would turn south-east into the Indian Ocean. We were steaming into bandit country, one of the areas of the world gaining in notoriety for its cowardly piracy attacks on international shipping. Our coffee break earlier in the morning had been a subdued and quiet affair, everyone aware of the pencilled position marked on the chart by a previous user indicating the location of a 'pirate attack': it lay unavoidably ahead of us, close to our course line, a set of coordinates recording the place where an unfortunate innocent victim had been singled out for attack. Helpless resignation summed up our mood: a feeling of despondency and alarm that is experienced by almost every seafarer when the ship in which he is sailing has to traverse such an area in order to reach her destination. It becomes pot luck, similar to crossing a busy road without the benefit of pedestrian crossings, whether or not your ship will pass safely through the danger zone without being attacked. It is a sobering fact that around the world there is an average of one piracy attack a day, and one associated crew fatality every week; to have over fifty seafarers a year murdered in cold blood simply because the vessels in which they were sailing just happened to be in the wrong place at the wrong time is an appalling and shameful statistic.

The attacks are not that frequent when put into the perspective of the total number of ships at sea; for that reason alone, the news of such attacks often appears only as an article printed in a maritime publication, rather than in the world headlines where they rightly belong. By the very nature of their business, merchant ships are unarmed and defenceless, unlike the modern-day pirate. No longer is he a one-eyed swashbuckling buccaneer, sporting an unkempt beard and armed with a cutlass in one hand, and with a squawking parrot perched upon his shoulder: nowadays he carries machetes, side-arms, machine-guns, and sometimes rocket or grenade launchers. The attack will be pressed home from several high-speed boats carrying many of his heavily armed compatriots. Often the boats will pose as innocent fishermen in the hope that their victim can be lured more easily into their ambush. They will board their target using grappling hooks and ropes, and will be intent upon stealing money and high-value items that can easily be carried off and sold on in the areas from which they operate, often poor and neglected coastal communities without access to either luxury or material goods. The more adventurous and sophisticated pirates, especially those in the South China Seas, are hijacking small ships while underway, murdering or setting their crews adrift, and giving the ship a new and phantom identity. If a cargo is carried, then that too will be unloaded and sold.

There is a growing belief by some authorities that organised crime has become involved, and that many of the perpetrators are professionally trained. Sometimes they will take senior crew members hostage, and hold them to ransom for often quite considerable sums of money. I have been told that, in such an event, shipowners and operators are immediately distanced from the delicate negotiations because of their personal relationships with their employees, and that the hard bargaining for the safe return of the hostages is left solely in the capable hands of the insurance company mediators, who have been trained and are experienced in such matters.

Despite our doom and gloom, and knowing our route was taking us through a particularly dangerous area, I was determined, even if only for morale purposes, that we should be positive in making every effort to protect ourselves in the event of a pirate attack. Mieke, for the very obvious reason of being a woman, was particularly worried about the possible dangers of being captured, while the others showed varying degrees of concern. We all recognised the unpalatable fact that our *Oriental* tugboats, like every small craft, were extremely vulnerable to being boarded. With our main decks lying no more than a metre above the sea, and with a maximum speed of a little less than fourteen knots in a following wind, we had little or no chance of out-manoeuvring a determined attack, and even less chance of repelling armed boarders.

We decided to test the three large water monitors on the monkey island above the wheelhouse, one of them positioned at the top of the mast and controlled

Testing the water monitors – a line of defence against pirate attack

by electric motors and a joystick in the wheelhouse, and the other two manually operated and directed by someone standing behind them. Remy and Tin were surprisingly successful in persuading the diesel engine that independently drove the large seawater pump supplying the monitors to start, even though it had not been test-run for many months, if not years. The high-powered jets of water emitting from two of the nozzles were just as impressive as the jet escaping from the corroded and holed pipe on the starboard monitor. With Marco managing to stop the leak by closing an isolating valve, we became an important step closer to having our very own pirate-boarding deterrent. Small boats can very quickly become flooded if caught in a high-volume water-jet from a firefighting monitor, and pirates, like most people, dislike getting wet. Our second line of defence was to prepare our fire hoses, coupling them in readiness onto the hydrants with the adjustable brass nozzles set in the jet position and lashed to the bulwarks, so that additional jets of water were aimed down each side of the boat.

We agreed to adopt the 'citadel' approach whereby, on the sounding of the alarms, we would all retire to one secure place. The engine room was chosen as our 'citadel' because it could only be entered through a steel door and a hatch that could be secured from the inside. By controlling the engine room we could maintain, or shut down, both power and services as we saw fit. Like all the best plans it had its good points and bad points: I chose not to mention that it would be very simple for someone on the outside to lock us into the engine room and prevent our escape, a fact I didn't like to dwell upon for too long in case my fears of being trapped indefinitely got the better of me. We carried two or three cases of drinking water, cartons of fruit juice, buckets, toilet paper, and our emergency hand-held VHF radios down below and stowed them in a safe place. There was very little else we could do except to reorganise our bridge and lookout duties so that we had three persons awake, and on call, during the hours of darkness. The six of us would, effectively, become two watch-keeping teams.

Ton, No. 1's chief officer, called us up on the VHF radio after lunch, with the very acceptable offer to share a large dorado fish they had caught earlier in the day. Albert, or Appie as he prefers to be known, had already gutted and cleaned the fish, and cut it into individual steaks. I left Marco to make the bow-to-stern manoeuvre that allowed for the parcel to be safely passed from one boat to the other. Mieke's suggestion that the steaks be barbecued in the early evening before we adopted the first of our anti-piracy watches was instantly welcomed. The wonderful aroma of cooking over charcoal and the subsequent delicious meal of freshly caught fish that had never seen the inside of a refrigerator or freezer were the perfect antidote to the apprehension we were all experiencing.

Our anti-piracy watches were to last only the one night. Marco and I changed to working six hours on and six hours off in the wheelhouse, accompanied by Mieke and Shwe, who split the long hours of darkness between them. We passed the position on the chart that marked a previous pirate attack without seeing a thing. By sunrise the wind had increased to a force 6 from the south-east, bringing with it sea conditions that would have made it impossible for anyone to climb on board had they wanted. Our preparations may have turned out not to be needed, but they were certainly not uneccessary.

With the weather conditions remaining much the same throughout the day, we passed seventy miles to the north of Socotra the following night, and headed out into the safety of the Indian Ocean. Our anti-piracy measures could be relaxed for the time being until we neared Aceh and the Malacca Straits, the next area on our route prone to attack.

A loss of air

The wind and the seas increased during the night to a full-blown south-south-westerly gale on the starboard beam. Sleep became a hopeless dream as the boat rolled violently from side to side in the beam seas, a movement made all the worse for Remy and me with our cabins being located high in the accommodation block. With the boat's centre of gravity being low in the engine room, we were lying almost at the extremity of a long and swinging pendulum, hanging some 30 degrees from the vertical on one side before being swung back in a fast-moving and sickening ride to the same angle on the other. Attempting to stand up when being swung through a 60 degree arc in just a few seconds defeats the human brain and its mechanism for balancing. Free movement, without resorting to the use of handrails and any other fixed objects close to hand, becomes not only foolhardy and risky, but also incredibly difficult. Amusement park and fairground rides, despite their modern technology and computers, can never hope to simulate the motion of a harbour tugboat caught out at sea in a force 8 gale.

The rolling brought with it all the noises of a severe upheaval within the housing: furniture drawers sliding out to tip their once neatly stowed contents onto the cabin decks in a confusion of clothing and personal effects; wardrobe doors, released from the folded paper wedge that has improvised for the broken latch for many years, swinging free to bang noisily open and closed; laundry buckets, lavatory brushes, air-fresheners, and all the other domestic items that have stood in their designated places for several weeks suddenly discovering that they too can have a life of their very own. The commotion and chaos of liberation slowly ended as the escapees were rounded up and secured in new and more suitable homes.

The waves were gaining in height by the hour, angry waves with white rolling crests that were caught in the wind to become airborne spray and spume. With every lurching roll, seawater cascaded over the bulwarks and poured across the main deck in a raging torrent to crash against the drums of lubricating oil we had taken in Djibouti, and the raised hatch leading down into the deck store. Nothing on deck that hadn't been secured was safe. Rope lashings became severely tested as stores and accessories being held in place made every effort to break free from their hurriedly prepared restraints.Our treasured swimming pool, although less than half full, col-lapsed and emptied in a twisted heap of broken pallets and torn plastic sheeting as the tidal wave of shallow water inside gained in momentum and height with the tilt-ing of the boat until nothing could prevent its escape onto the partially submerged deck. Short of turning both the tugs into the seas and heaving to, there was little to be done, other than to watch the deck anxiously from behind the safety of the wheelhouse windows to confirm that nothing of importance was breaking free or being damaged.

Remy was an exceedingly unhappy man when he ventured into the relative comforts of the engine room for his morning watch. It had taken nearly eight weeks for the damp conditions I had suffered on the passage from Abidjan to Las Palmas to be replicated. Not that I wished him any ill, far from it, but now I felt that my lonely opinion that had been so vigorously opposed at the time was about to be vindicated. Seawater was entering his cabin through his air-conditioning unit. Not, as yet, in huge quantities, but progressively increasing as the weather deteriorated. By early evening his cabin was awash, and a bad-tempered Remy had taken up residence in the dryer and more comfortable environment of the messroom.

I decided to say nothing, knowing that to commiserate with his discomfort would only exacerbate the situation. I guessed that he now completely appreciated my original viewpoint in the discussion over the air-conditioning units before I was outvoted by three to one. In the cold light of day, I still felt that to have restored our cabins to their original watertight condition with the refitting of the portholes in Las Palmas would have been the most sensible solution, but perhaps I was being biased by having no air-conditioning unit to sacrifice. I had nothing to lose and we weren't to know the weather would turn so nasty. Although no mention of the subject was made with Pieter during our daily chat on the VHF radio, I thought it highly likely that Willem would be suffering from a similar ingress of water into his cabin as Remy. It was extremely unfortunate that the opportunities for rectifying the problem had long since passed.

Swimming pool damaged by bad weather

The gale-force winds showed no signs of abating during the day, that night, and into the following morning. Sleeping, whether attempted in the cabins or messroom, remained nigh on impossible. There was to be not the slightest respite from the heavy rolling, and from all the associated bangs, crashes and discomforts of being helplessly thrown around. The sheets of wind-driven spray continued to curl their inexorable way up the starboard side of the superstructure before uncannily finding the square opening that had been so crudely cut to receive Remy's air-conditioning unit: the seawater poured in! A collective effort was made to mop out his flooded cabin every so often, before the level became sufficiently high to cross his threshold and run down the stairs into the rest of the accommodation.

No one, least of all I, was prepared for the devastating news that Remy brought with him when he made his late entry into the wheelhouse for what was already a pretty miserable and uncomfortable coffee time spent hanging on for grim death. The main air-compressor motor had been on fire and was now burnt out. He had managed to start the engine on No. 2 generator, which provided the power take-off for the emergency air compressor, but the pressure in the air-storage cylinders was still slowly leaking away. A disaster was in the making. We had, apparently, about thirty minutes of steaming before the air-driven control systems exhausted the remaining air in the storage cylinders and shut down the main engine. Remy, accompanied by Tin, abandoned the wheelhouse almost immediately to return to the engine room, leaving me with Marco, Shwe and Mieke to ponder our plight.

'No. 1 tug, No. 2 tug calling, come in Pieter.'

There was a moment's delay before my call on the VHF radio was answered. 'Yes, Dave, No. 2 tug replying.'

'Pieter, we have a big problem on board, maybe you will have to tow us or at least keep our bows into the wind. Our main air compressor has been on fire and Remy has told me that we have only enough air to keep the main engine running for about another thirty minutes.'

'Okay Dave, maybe we should turn into the wind now and I will ask Ton to prepare a towing line. He is very experienced in towing, I am not.'

Ton took charge of the preparations for towing. With both boats steering head into the wind and seas and almost hove-to, Marco and Shwe were able to venture safely outside and open the rope-store hatch on the aft deck. Within a few minutes the 200-metre mooring rope we had purchased in Las Palmas to satisfy the Suez Canal regulations was being pulled out onto deck. They were doing the same on No. 1 tug, although Ton had already voiced his opinion that the combined 400-metre-long polypropylene tow-rope wouldn't last too long before it chafed and parted in the appalling weather conditions. We had neither towing wires, bridles nor pennants to do the job properly. Little did we know it, but our efforts were wasted.

Remy staggered back into the wheelhouse some fifteen minutes later, sweating profusely, but clearly in a slightly more cheerful mood. The main engine air-control system from the bridge, which we knew to have several quite large but inaccessible leaks, had been isolated and shut down, and the pressure within the air-cylinders was holding steady. We had won a temporary reprieve, some valuable time in which to consider our position more rationally. I knew I had an important choice to make: either to continue the voyage towards Singapore in the hope that the situation wouldn't deteriorate further, or to seek the nearest port of refuge where, hopefully, repairs could be made.

I sought Remy's opinion, initially as an engineer, but then as a colleague and friend. He advised me, in a calm and factual manner, that the emergency air compressor appeared not to have been run for many a long day, and that its general condition reflected that of a poorly maintained machine of some twenty-eight years of age. He reminded me of the importance of air, and that without it, the main engine could not be started. He cautioned me not to place too much reliance on the generator engine providing the power for the air compressor: should that fail, for whatever reason, the vital production of compressed air would immediately cease.

I thanked Remy for his highly valued opinions and advice, and watched him leave the wheelhouse to return to the engine room. I pondered for a short while to consider all my options, at the same time trying to concentrate upon steering a course that kept us heading into the gale-force wind and the 4-metre waves. A quick study of the chart showed that Salalah, in Oman, was less than two days' steaming away. I conferred with Pieter on the VHF radio before making my decision.

The polypropylene rope that had been retrieved from our aft-deck rope locker was hurriedly lashed down on deck. We turned the boats round and pointed our bows towards the Arabian coast. Within a few minutes we had returned to the heavy rolling we had been experiencing before, only this time the wind and the waves were on the opposite side. I dreaded to think what was happening in my cabin down below, now that the boot was on the other foot, so to speak.

Nautical camping

I had every right to feel apprehensive about what might be occurring one deck below the wheelhouse: my fears were totally justified when I entered my cabin after my watch. Now that we were heading towards Oman, the wind and the seas were on the port side, and they had lost none of their accuracy in finding the openings where portholes had once existed. The change in our course had benefited Remy, but at my expense. My vinyl-covered settee was already soaking wet, and seawater was starting to collect at the aft end of my cabin, where it was quietly sloshing from side to side with the motion of the boat. I knew it wouldn't be too long before it would be deep enough to bale out, providing the bucket agreed to remain in one place for longer than a few seconds. I conveniently forgot the weeks of comfort I had enjoyed with the air conditioning, and cursed the day in Buchanan when someone had taken their cutting tools to the side of the housing. Both Remy and I, and no doubt Pieter and Willem, were now paying the price for that over-zealous attack on the steelwork.

I enjoyed the lunch that Mieke had valiantly managed to prepare and turned in for the afternoon, wedging myself against the Formica bulkhead at the side of the bunk by placing my cabin life jacket under the outboard edge of the mattress.

Determined to ignore the elements, I somehow managed to fall asleep. My success was tempered a couple of hours later when, only half awake, I climbed off the bunk and stepped into a lake. Vinyl floor tiles from my cabin deck had become unstuck and were being casually swept from one side of the cabin to the other in the swirling water that was synchronising with the heavy rolling. The surging waves had become higher than the bottoms of the two drawers under my bunk, soaking the clothes that were stowed inside. My baggage grip looked as if it had been floating around for most of the afternoon before becoming jammed at the far end of the settee. The scene was one of total havoc; until the weather showed signs of moderating, there was nothing to be done but abandon the cabin and join Remy in setting up home in the messroom.

I can't say I was hugely impressed by my night of nautical camping. Remy's snoring sounded particularly loud and full-throated without the benefit of a flimsy bulkhead to separate our two mattresses. Midway through Shwe's watch, just before sunrise, I was called to the wheelhouse. The main engine seawater-cooling pipe had sprung another leak and we would have to proceed at a slower speed. Any nagging doubts I might have had earlier about the wisdom of turning round and heading towards Salalah for repairs were rapidly evaporating: it was already looking as if it might have been one of my better decisions.

The south-westerly gale was to continue for most of the day before easing in the late afternoon. At long last I had the opportunity to bale out my cabin without additional water entering through the air-conditioning unit to nullify my strenuous efforts. With the majority of our possessions being damp or soaked through, both Remy and I opted for another night in the messroom. I had hoped to sleep a little better than on the first night, but it wasn't to be: Remy's snoring was no less sonorous the second time around.

As we approached the Omani coast the weather conditions changed quite dramatically. The wind and the sea, which had mercifully continued to abate so that our rolling was no longer a problem, became calm and rippled. Within a few minutes we had entered what appeared to be a low-lying cloud, a white shroud of mist that hung like an enveloping blanket over the two boats to effectively prevent us from seeing much further than a few hundred metres. The loss of visibility was totally unexpected and had come at an inconvenient time. We were navigating by a chart that Marco had drawn up by expanding the scale from a small-scale chart and by plotting the latitude and longitude of important features such as buoys, lights and the breakwater tips from information he had gleaned from the pilot book and the Admiralty List of Lights. While his pencilled efforts may have appeared a little Heath Robinson to the uninitiated, I was extremely confident of their accuracy, and equally sure we could use his chart to find our way safely into the port. It was most certainly better than having no chart at all. The inconvenience of being unable to see where we were going was extremely ill-timed, but merely added an extra dimension and an additional challenge to the traditional skills of dead-reckoning navigation.

If I had needed any further convincing that proceeding to Salalah for repairs had been the right decision, then No. 1 generator provided the final and ultimate confirmation. With the safety of the port virtually within our grasp it chose this moment, when we had only a couple of miles to go, to give up the ghost altogether, the positive electrons and negative protons no longer combining together to give us electricity. Our single surviving machine was left to struggle on, providing us with both much-needed air and electrical current. The repair lists, and Remy's considerable anxiety, were lengthening by the minute.

We were instructed by the Port Control to wait outside the port by the fairway buoy, which emerged from the haze almost exactly where we had expected. Marco's hydrographic expertise had passed the ultimate test with distinction. Almost two hours later, after watching a continuous stream of container vessels entering and leaving the port, we were given permission to proceed inwards. Leading the way so that we could moor first, we steamed past the container berths with their huge 'War of the Worlds' type gantries that dwarfed the ships lying beneath their extended arms, and on towards the quayside on the opposite side of the port.

A few minutes later, No. 1 tug had secured to our outboard side, and the engines had been shut down. Our repairs could begin.

12

SALALAH

Patch and mend

By mid-afternoon the agent and the port officials had made their visitation and the boats were cleared inwards. Bureaucracy had been kept to a minimum, but at the cost of dispensing the last few cartons of cigarettes I had been keeping for such an occasion. It mattered no longer: I had already ensured that the smokers on board had been given more than sufficient stocks to see them through to the end of the voyage. The agent, a friendly and forthright man of Indian descent, seemed quite unperturbed and calm when discussing the repair list, confidently assuring me that the local services within the immediate port area would be more than adequate in satisfying all our repair requirements. With the port located only fifteen kilometres to the southwest of the city, further assistance could be called upon should the need arise.

I hadn't realised until after conversing with the agent that the city of Salalah possessed such an interesting and historic heritage. Known as the 'perfume capital of Arabia' because of the abundance of frankincense trees within the surrounding area, it is the second largest city in the Sultanate of Oman and the birthplace of the Sultan, Qaboos bin Said. The Sultan traditionally lived in Salalah, but, after ascending the throne in 1970, he broke with ancient custom and moved to Muscat, the capital city. Dating back to pre-biblical times, Salalah boasts the ruins of a palace thought to have belonged to the Queen of Sheba, and is reputed in Islamic tradition to be the resting place of the prophet Job and also of Nabi Imran, the father of the Virgin Mary. I only hoped its modern resources would live up to its legendary and fascinating past.

A representative from a local electrical contracting company boarded in the early hours of the evening to carry out some preliminary fault-finding investigations on the generator that had so inconsiderately failed earlier in the

Removing the window box air conditioning unit from the Chief Engineer's cabin, Salalah

morning, and to prepare the main air-compressor motor for landing ashore the following day. We had already been advised that the motor repair would take at least three days due to the time required for baking the motor insulation after the rewind. I had a gloomy premonition that the air-compressor motor would be the least of our worries.

Remy and I set to with mops and buckets to attack the chaos within our cabins. We had discussed our misfortunes shortly before arriving off the port, and had agreed that a firm of steelwork contractors should be employed to weld steel plates over the holes that had been cut to install our air-conditioning units in Liberia. Permanently sealing the sides of the housing appeared to be the only sensible and practical solution to preventing seawater from causing further devastation and damage to our cabins and belongings. We both knew that, unless the problem was resolved, our accommodation would be flooded again as soon as we exchanged the welcome shelter of the port for the wind and the waves of the south-westerly monsoon. While nautical camping in the messroom had provided us both with long-lasting memories, it was an experience that neither of us had any desire to repeat in the immediate future.

Although both their cabins had suffered from a similar flooding to ours, I was slightly taken aback when Pieter and Willem chose not to repeat the work on No. 1 tug. Perhaps they thought that with only three weeks or thereabouts of the voyage remaining, the benefits of remaining dry would be outweighed by the permanent loss of their air conditioning once we encountered the warmer weather. It was to be their decision: a personal choice that mattered not to Remy and me.

Our first evening in Salalah was spent sitting together outside on a still and unmoving deck, enjoying the cool and balmy temperature that came with the sunset. The bad weather of the last few days had taken its toll, and it wasn't too long before everyone on both the boats had retired to their bunks for a proper night's rest. Despite the shambles in my cabin from the flooding, the fact that I was climbing up onto my stable mattress rather than gingerly lowering myself down onto a tilting messroom deck meant an awful lot to me. It provided all the confirmation I needed that my days of sea-scouting were an adventure of the past.

We were up bright and early, the benefits of everyone having had a full night's sleep clear for all to see. There was a new spring to our step as we tidied and cleaned the boat after the ravages of the bad weather. Shortly after enjoying one of Mieke's very special cooked breakfasts with all the trimmings, we welcomed two Indian electricians aboard to repair the generator. They found the problem quickly.

The diode plate, a large Perspex washer some 30 centimetres in diameter, had become distorted and had broken its connecting wires to the rotor, one of the integral and main components of the generator. I had no recollection of having seen a diode plate before, but even to my inexperienced eyes this diode plate looked particularly poorly. Its clear plastic-like surface bore many large cracks that had been ingeniously knitted together by thin pieces of aluminium sheeting bolted onto the plastic wherever there was space for a bolt to be fitted. It was a stunning and artistic

Generator diode plate. Repairs in Salalah

example of make-do-and-mend oriental engineering that had a deeply embarrassed Tin blushing to the core of his suntanned Burmese complexion.

The indisputable fact that the generator had successfully provided electricity for many hundreds of hours after his makeshift repairs in Buchanan was the ultimate proof of his incredible resourcefulness, inventive skills and sheer determination. The fault, if it could be described as such, lay in his aluminium patches being positioned unevenly; the lack of symmetry caused an imbalance to the plate when it was rotated at high revolutions, resulting in ever-increasing oscillations that eventually became sufficiently pronounced to break the wire connections to the rotor. With the absence of suitable materials and the very basic shipboard workshop and tools at his disposal, Tin would never have been able to balance the plate in any case. It was a great pity his employers would neither see nor recognise the fortitude and ingenuity he and his other engineering colleague had displayed during their long stay in Liberia.

The Indian electricians showed little concern for the damage they had found. We discussed the possibility of locating spare parts, but this was never going to be an issue: they would take the diode plate to their workshops where it would be used as a template for the manufacture of a replacement. Broad smiling faces, and the repeated nodding of heads in the customary Indian style of conducting business, provided all the reassurances I needed that their plans for copying the vital part would undoubtedly be the quickest and most propitious solution to carrying out the repair. The diode plate was taken ashore along with the burnt-out air-compressor motor. Extracting the heavy motor from the engine room and lifting it from the main deck onto the quayside that was now nearly two metres above us, due to the tidal range in the port, proved hugely awkward and dangerous. We all agreed it would have to be craned back on board upon its return from the workshops.

The sight of two Indian welders and a rickety and flimsy aluminium ladder leant precariously against the side of the superstructure finally convinced me that the days of seawater entering my cabin were, at long last, numbered. The heavily rusted and broken-down air-conditioning unit was ceremoniously lifted from the externally fitted support brackets and lowered none too gently to the deck below. My view from inside the cabin was instantly replaced by a rectangular frame of cloudy skies and the forever smiling, happy face of one of the welders perched on the ladder outside. He had the distinction of possessing the most heavily betel-juice-stained teeth I think I've ever seen in my many years of visiting the Indian and Arabian subcontinents.

In almost chaotic scenes reminiscent of a Laurel and Hardy plot, but where the leading roles bore no similarity whatsoever to those marvellous characters in the films, it took the two Indians the best part of the afternoon and into the early hours of the evening to cut the seam welds holding the unit's two support brackets and its protective cover to the outside of the accommodation, and to dress the pitted surface with an electric grinder in preparation for the fitting of the steel plate. The approach of nightfall saw the hasty abandonment of the job, leaving me to tape up the crudely cut hole with a black plastic garbage bag to keep out the insects and any other undesirable intruders intent upon entering my gutted abode. The barbecue on the main deck with everyone from No. 1 tug was thoroughly enjoyable. I managed to have a long conversation with Albert, or 'Appie', who proved to have had such an interesting life that I found it surprising no one had previously told me of his chequered career and his many exploits. He had not only sailed the world many times over, experiencing adventures and hardships that could fill many a page, but had also fought with the Israelis against their neighbouring Arab nations in the Six Day War; being of Jewish blood, he had considered it his duty to enlist in the army reserves despite having lived in Holland for the whole of his life. Like most war veterans, he declined to go into great detail about the conflict, but clearly some of the sights he had seen and the fighting in which he had been engaged had left memories that would stay with him for the remaining years of his life. All too soon the food had been eaten and the glowing charcoal embers allowed to cool. We retired to our beds, appreciative of yet another full night of undisturbed sleep to help us back to normality.

The Indian steelwork contractors returned in the morning. With a fire-blanket draped around the opening to protect the cabin interior from the sparks, the large steel plate that now covered the hole where the air-conditioning unit had once been fitted was welded in place. By mid-afternoon my side had been completed, and the work on Remy's side could commence. The patch looked neither tidy nor pretty, but if the seawater was kept at bay, its appearance mattered not in the slightest.

Yachties and goats

The welders continued the next day with removing the air-conditioning unit from Remy's cabin and blanking the hole in the side of the housing. I set to in my cabin cleaning up the mess of the past few days and slapping two or three coats of white paint on the inside face of the newly welded steel plate in a futile attempt to make the cabin decor just a little more appealing and homely. My well-intentioned efforts at home improvement were a complete aesthetic disaster and only succeeded in drawing attention to the very rudimentary repair. By appearing whiter than white against a picture frame of dingy chipped Formica that lined the rest of the cabin interior, the shiny rectangular piece of steel became an example of one of those obscure and totally meaningless displays so often praised as the epitome of modern abstract art. Not only that, the sickly sweet chemical smell that some paints possess was to linger on our accommodation deck for quite a few days. To rub salt into the wound, I was severely barracked by my shipmates for my lack of artistic imagination, and bluntly advised that I should stick to navigation, where I appeared to have just a little more understanding.

Later in the morning I went for a walk along the length of the quayside and past a warehouse that, from where we were moored, effectively blocked our view of what lay beyond. To my surprise, there appeared to be an inner harbour providing a safe and sheltered anchorage for half a dozen yachts, and a wharf to which a couple of local dhows were secured. The area was heaving with activity, with several high-sided open trucks waiting to join two or three similar vehicles that were in the process of reversing across the quay so as to be close to the sides, but at right angles, to the dhows. The deafening clamour from the open decks of the dhows sounded upsetting and quite pathetic, a harrowing caterwauling from hundreds of scrawny goats bleating loudly as if in a desperate attempt to make their sorry plight known.

As I watched from a safe distance, the first three lorries successfully manoeuvred and lowered their tailgates. The sides of the makeshift wooden pens on the decks of the dhows were opened and the goats, frightened by the Arab crewmen shouting and waving their arms, were herded towards the sides of the dhows and the waiting trucks. A frantic leap saw the first of the terrified animals skid, limbs askew, into the back of the open vehicles, only to have those jumping behind them land heavily on their backs in a hideous and pitiful confusion of spread-eagled legs and crushed bodies.

One petrified nanny completely missed her way and managed to land on the quayside. Free from the madding crowd, she stood alone, completely confused and disorientated for just a few seconds, before running along the jetty and leaping straight from the edge into the harbour some two to three metres below. I willed her to swim away strongly and to make her escape, but it wasn't to be. A crewman dived into the water from one of the dhows and, with a few strong strokes, caught up with the poor shaking animal and dragged her back to the jetty. A rope was lowered to the swimmers and moments later, the struggling goat was being lifted none too gently back onto the quayside, from where she was casually thrown, kicking and bleating pathetically, into the back of one of the waiting trucks. There wasn't an ounce of doubt in my mind that the distressed animals had sensed that death, in the strict ritualistic Muslim traditions of halal, lay only a short and fateful journey away.

I watched for a few minutes longer before sensing from the angry stares of the truck drivers and other people on the quay that I had overstayed my welcome. As I turned to make my way back towards the two tugs I saw a small inflatable dinghy being paddled from one of the yachts towards the jetty. A few minutes later I was talking to an engaging Dutch couple who were making one of those trips of a lifetime by sailing around the world. I judged them to be in their late forties, bronzed and carefree, and obviously relishing every minute of their nautical and sightseeing adventure. We strolled back to the boats together, where they were invited aboard No.

1 tug for lunch. I felt sure that being able to converse in their own language with some new faces in the largest port in Oman was not only an unexpected pleasure, but also one that made their afternoon, as it did for us, an enjoyable and memorable occasion.

In the early evening the Indian electricians returned to the tug proudly carrying the new diode plate that had been fabricated for the generator. It certainly bore no resemblance to the aluminium-strengthened piece of plastic that had left the boat just forty-eight hours earlier: I was convinced that even the generator manufacturer would have been hard-pressed to differentiate between one of their own carefully produced spare parts and the locally made copy. Three hours later, the diode plate had been successfully reconnected to the rotor and the generator started. It ran for only a few minutes before disaster struck. One of the rotor bearings failed and became red hot before welding itself onto the drive shaft with a horrible mechanical squeal and little whispers of grey curling smoke.

Seeing that it was nearing midnight, the electricians wisely called it a day and agreed to return in the morning. They had already advised Remy that a replacement bearing would have to be despatched from Muscat, and that we could expect to be waiting for anything up to thirty-six hours before it would be fitted. Escaping the clutches of Salalah appeared to be far more difficult than any of us could possibly have envisaged. Had my decision to seek refuge been entirely wise after all, I wondered, as a mood of despondency set in.

An unfriendly fan

After spending four long and disheartening days under repair in Salalah I thought that, with the exception of our accommodation now being watertight for the first time in the voyage, we had very little to show for our time in port. I felt nothing but sympathy towards our shipmates on No. 1 tug, who had done their very best to be supportive and understanding in our efforts to get the work finished and resume our passage to Singapore. As they had no repairs of their own to complete, they were merely keeping us company in compliance with the insurance requirement that the boats remain together for the duration of the contract. I had no doubt that being moored alongside one another more than satisfied the insurer's clause 'till death do us part'. At least her engineers, Willem and Bas, were trying to keep busy by attending to the many planned maintenance jobs that they would otherwise have had to carry out while their boat was at sea.

Aboard our No. 2 tug we were becoming more depressed by the hour with the apparent lack of any real progress. I had to make a conscious and very determined effort to keep smiling and to be outwardly cheerful, and not to appear either bad-tempered or frustrated with the shore technicians. They were, after all, doing their level best to help us; it was just unfortunate that they had little to show but further problems for their endeavours. To add to my melancholia, I could also sense, from the slightly impatient tone of the messages from our office in Holland, that our managers were having an uncomfortable time in convincing the owners in Singapore that our delays were being kept to the minimum.

A small mobile crane inching its way down the quayside, accompanied by a pickup truck carrying the air-compressor motor, stirred us from our lethargy. With its exhaust belching black smoke, its cab without any windows, and its body heavily stained with oil from countless small leaks, the crane gave every appearance of being ready for the scrapyard. After shunting itself into a position close to the edge of the quayside it managed to lift the motor from the back of the truck and lower it slowly, but far from smoothly, onto the main deck. As the jib was hoisted to be relocated into the stowed position, one of the main hydraulic hoses gave a little kick followed by a quiet, but extremely disconcerting, plopping-cum-whooshing noise. A jet of hot hydraulic oil under pressure squirted unerringly, and with great accuracy, straight onto the main deck. The Indian crane driver seemed totally unperturbed, choosing calmly to ignore our shouts and waves of warning as he concentrated on stowing the jib. Once it had safely landed on its pad, he isolated the crane controls to stop the leak, and jumped down to survey the mess. Burst hydraulic hoses were obviously a regular occurrence with his tired and poorly maintained machine. He smiled, nodded his head sideways a couple of times in the traditional Indian fashion, and jumped back into his glassless cab to retreat down the quayside at a far greater speed than that of his arrival. We were still soaking up the oil with sawdust and rags an hour later when Remy returned on deck to advise me, in a very unhappy and disillusioned voice, that all was not well in the engine room. Progress seemed to be an ever-elusive word.

The air-compressor motor had been reconnected and switched on for a test run. Within seconds smoke was seen to be coming from inside the motor housing and it was immediately switched off. The electricians spent the remainder of the day investigating the problem before locating a fault in the main switchboard. Unlike our electrical cycle difficulties in Las Palmas and Valletta, this was, apparently, a problem of phases. I could recall from my college days many years ago that electrical current not only comes in cycles, volts, watts, amperes and no doubt many other meaningless names I had no interest in remembering, but also in phases. A single-phase electrical supply, as Remy so patiently told me in my second electrical lesson of the voyage, is adequate for domestic use, but for industrial, or heavy-duty purposes, a three-phase supply is required. Despite my concentration and his perfectly coherent and unambiguous explanation, I eventually had to concede that my understanding of all things electrical basically remained non-existent. He ended his technical lesson a few words later by advising me that a two-phase supply was only useful in creating smoke, which was probably why the motor had burnt out in the first place.

Later in the day Marco and Shwe emptied out the rope locker located under the main deck, a job that had been waiting for a suitable opportunity to be done since our boarding in Abidjan. Buried beneath years of accumulated rubbish, all of which had to be lifted up and manhandled through a narrow hatchway onto the main deck, they found a selection of towing accessories that would be more than sufficient for either boat to assist the other in the event of an emergency. Had we known of its existence, our concerns about being powerless in the Indian Ocean would never have arisen.

Ton was delighted with our find, and spent the rest of the afternoon arranging a towing wire on No. 1 tug, while Marco carefully laid out and rigged a towing bridle complete with shackles in the forepart of our boat. I made no comment during the lengthy preparations, but managed to voice my grave concerns a little later. I questioned the assumption that our sister tug would be doing the towing: to my mind it indicated a worrying lack of confidence in the ability of my command to complete the voyage to Singapore under her own power, although secretly I had to admit to myself that sometimes I was becoming just as despondent and perturbed as my colleagues. The sight of a burnt-out contactor from the main switchboard being taken ashore as I spoke did nothing to support my tenuous opinion. Somewhat disenchanted, I retired to my bunk shortly afterwards in the hope that a new day would bring us some progress, and a promise of when we could sail.

Patience is indeed a virtue. After a couple of very long hours following the electricians' return in the morning, the distinctive rumble of No. 1 generator engine running confirmed that the new bearing on the rotor had been fitted. The Omani diode plate was performing as intended, and the generator was, unbelievably, producing electricity in all the right voltages and phases, and to all the right places. With the various pipework repairs also having been completed, we were now back to fixing the air compressor, the very cause of our diversion to Salalah just one week earlier.

Perseverance and success are inextricably linked: after finding that the fault still remained on the switchboard following the installation of the new contactors, the problem was eventually traced to a defective circuit breaker. Shortly before midnight, and with a replacement supplied and fitted, Remy at long last announced he was satisfied. The provisional arrangements for sailing in the morning, which I had made in one of those rash and unexplained moments of optimism, could be confirmed. An email was hurriedly sent to Holland advising the office of the long-awaited completion of all the repairs and of our planned departure in a few hours' time. No one could ever have anticipated that an electric motor burning out at sea could cause two tugboats a 400-mile diversion and six days spent alongside in port.

My last night in Salalah was frustratingly restless. Knowing that we would be sailing into monsoon weather with its wind and waves should have provided every incentive for sleeping well and for enjoying the comforts of a stable and unmoving bunk and a quiet and vibration-free cabin, but it wasn't to be. I wasn't alone in having a sleepless night. Everyone was up bright and early, breakfast eaten, and the final preparations made for departure long before it was fully daylight. We were ready to leave. Peering out from the bridge windows I could see from the shimmering exhaust smoke rising from the funnels on our sister tug that Willem had started No. 1's engine and that Ton, Maung and Albert were patiently standing by on deck ready to let go their ropes. The silence was eerie as we waited for Remy to start our engine.

His sudden appearance in the wheelhouse came as a complete and unpleasant surprise. My stomach knotted as he told me, in a despondent and miserable voice, that one of the main supply fans for the engine room ventilation wouldn't start, and that he thought its motor had burnt out. All the emotions of dejection, disbelief and dismay struck me simultaneously, leaving me totally crestfallen and dumbfounded. We stared at each other, at a complete loss for words, but with our thoughts racing as to the implications of this latest setback. Leaving Remy to tell our colleagues on No. 1 tug, I cancelled our departure plans with the port authority and called the agent to ask the electricians to attend the boat yet again. The email to Holland was contrite and apologetic, but the situation was really no one's fault; I just wished it had happened on Pieter's boat so that he could have shouldered some of the frustration, low spirits and self-pity we all were feeling.

The electrician confirmed Remy's diagnosis that the fan motor had burnt out. Shwe and Tin spent the whole of the morning chiselling off the rusted bolts that held the louvred ventilation grille vertically in place over the intake trunking in which the fan was supported. Its location in the funnel housing at the side of the towing winch severely restricted access, and made the task of lifting the fan from the trunking all the more difficult. The situation was exacerbated by the mild steel circular fan casing being almost totally corroded and in danger of completely disintegrating with all the manhandling. It was early in the afternoon before we had managed to lift the remains ashore, and into the back of a vehicle. Despite now having the task of fabricating a completely new casing, the electrician promised to have the motor rewound and the fan unit back on board by the following evening. I was beginning to appreciate how fortunate we were in having a local business community that thrived on old-fashioned skills, and a willingness to offer their customers a service that was second to none.

The electrician was every bit as good as his word and shortly before sunset the following evening, the rewound fan motor, sitting proudly inside its brand-new freshly painted steel casing, had been installed and was being test-run. The ventilation grille was bolted back in position, the main engines were started and the ropes let go.

With No. 1 tug leading the way we steamed slowly in convoy through the floodlit harbour, out past the breakwater, and into the welcome darkness of the Indian Ocean beyond. Never had the sound of the sea and the feel of the waves been so keenly awaited.

13

ALL OVER AGAIN

Cochin or Colombo?

The immense relief of departing from the port after eight days alongside was almost indescribable, despite our rolling around once again as soon as we drew abeam of the fairway buoy and set our course into the Indian Ocean and towards the southern coast of Sri Lanka. We had all found the lengthy stay in Oman to be tedious and frustrating, a feeling brought about by our inability either to influence or assist in the repairs. The contractors and electricians in Salalah had all been extremely attentive and helpful. No one could deny that they had performed minor miracles in restoring some of the old and worn-out equipment to a semblance of working order but, at the end of the day, we were seafarers and more than happy to be making good our escape back to sea and embarking upon the final passage of our long-overdue voyage. Not that Salalah had been an inhospitable place, far from it, but adding another week onto an itinerary that had already been extended by three to four weeks with our stays in Las Palmas and Valletta had stretched the domestic calendar for some of us almost to breaking point. Holidays that had been booked many months earlier were in danger of having to be rearranged, and other social events that had been planned with friends and family were in danger of either being postponed or completely cancelled. Even Mieke's slightly optimistic hope of coordinating her time of arrival with that of her husband's in Singapore had been finally dashed. His telephone call the night before we sailed from Salalah was to tell her that his crew-training contract in Papua New Guinea had finished exactly on schedule, and that he was now residing at home in Holland patiently awaiting her homecoming. Provided we had an unexpected run of good luck and a trouble-free passage, I calculated that Erik would be sitting alone on his settee for at least another two weeks. I hoped his patience and understanding would prevail.

We slipped back into our watch-keeping routine as if it had never been broken. Although we were rolling quite heavily in the beam seas of the south-west monsoons, it was having only a minor impact on our living conditions. We knew what to expect from our previous attempt at crossing the Indian Ocean, and had learnt from our mistakes. This time, anything and everything that gave the slightest hint of being able to move had been properly lashed down or safely stowed away. With the wind and the waves once again on Remy's side of the accommodation, he seemed quite delighted to be residing in a dry and habitable cabin. The loss of his air conditioning had yet to be felt, with the weather being neither too hot nor humid. We guessed that Willem's cabin on our sister tug would now be ankle-deep in seawater, but the subject was never mentioned by Pieter during our regular VHF conversations, and I didn't raise the question for fear of sounding as if we might be gloating over our colleague's probable discomfort. He had, after all, been given every opportunity to carry out the same welding work to his cabin as we had with ours, and had chosen to do nothing. Both Remy and I were living dry, and to us, that was all that mattered.

Remy's capacity for imparting bad news had not diminished during our unscheduled stopover in Oman. He appeared in the wheelhouse not long after I had handed over the bridge watch to Marco, and as I was preparing the noon message for transmission to Holland. His downcast and miserable face bore all the hallmarks of dismay, resignation, sorrow and hopelessness associated with yet another mechanical failure. His monotone voice sounded tired and impassive, as if recognising that the final skirmish in the decisive battle had already been as good as lost, and that defeat and the subsequent surrender lay only minutes away. The main air compressor had failed again. He thought it likely that the motor that had been rewound only a few days earlier had burnt out a second time. Our predicament didn't end there: the engine room alarm system that should have been monitoring both the high and low pressures in the air-storage cylinders had failed, allowing the pressure within the system to fall away unnoticed. With the cylinders virtually empty, we had insufficient compressed air to start the generator engine that provided the power take-off for the emergency air compressor.

For once I was speechless, totally and utterly lost for words. We had been at sea for only thirty-eight hours and here we were, back in exactly the same situation as we had been eleven days earlier and, as the crow flies, not so many miles from where it had all started. Remy had already isolated the control air-systems so as to contain whatever air we had remaining. As I studied the chart, in the forlorn hope that the hydrographer might have left a hidden solution to our problem in his mosaic of ocean soundings, I speculated whether Ton and Marco might have been more than a little psychic a few days earlier when laying out the towing equipment. The ability of my aged and tired command to reach her destination under her own power and without a little help from her friend had suddenly appeared in doubt. The lengthy preparations the two chief officers had made for our being towed had become, in just a few seconds, not only an excellent idea, but an example of conscientious effort and effective forward planning that deserved my eternal gratitude. I only wished that the idea had been mine in the first place.

I took over the steering to allow Marco to leave the bridge and accompany Remy back to the engine room. Their short conversation in Dutch had left me with no clue about what they had been discussing. Some thirty minutes later they reappeared, both lathered in sweat, but clearly much happier than they had been when leaving. Their news was almost too good to be true. They had somehow managed, through brute force and sheer strength, to crank over the generator engine manually with a starting handle sufficiently fast for it to kick in and fire. The emergency air compressor was running, and already a slight positive pressure was showing on the air-cylinder pressure gauges. While Remy shared my obvious relief, he was quick to remind me of the advice he had given me before Salalah, that neither the emergency air compressor nor generator engine should be relied upon for running indefinitely, and that compressed air remained a vital commodity for starting the main engine. I not only appreciated his opinions, but also the temporary reprieve that had been won. Some precious time had been gained to ponder our situation and to determine the most sensible course of action.

To go forward or to go back seemed to be the stark choice I had inherited. I knew from my brief conversation with Pieter that he would be supportive of whatever decision I made. While the commercial option was only too clear, the safety of my crew and the boat had to be paramount in my mind. With the weather showing signs of a most welcome and forecast moderation, and with the towing preparations already fortuitously made, I came to the realistic conclusion that the failure of the main engine would place no one in any particular danger. I also realised that, if the emergency air compressor and the suspect generator engine were to continue working normally and as long as our consumption of compressed air was strictly controlled and kept to an absolute minimum, then we could live with most of our problems. The main engine would only stop if there was an unpredictable mechanical failure, and no doubt sod's law, and not us, would dictate when that would occur.

The advantages of continuing in the direction we were steaming were beginning to outweigh those of turning back. A study of the Indian Ocean chart and pilot books showed that both Cochin and Colombo were ports that required only a minimal deviation from our planned route; a final choice as to which port we headed towards could be deferred for two or three days. I pencilled some distance arcs on the chart and arrived at a position to which we could steam where either port could be nominated at a later date without adding too many miles to our already extended voyage. We would head for the position I had plotted, but at a maximum speed that would be governed by the fuel consumption commensurate with the limited reserves we held in our tanks. I didn't want to be seen to be lingering once the decision had been made.

Pieter and Willem gave further credence to my plan in the evening with their willingness to donate from No. 1's main air compressor the identical electric motor to the one that had burnt out. The diesel-powered machine that had been supplied from Holland and installed on our sister tug during our stay in Las Palmas had been operating quite successfully and in preference to the original electrically powered compressor. They reasoned that it was infinitely more desirable for each boat to have one good air compressor rather than one tug to have two, and the other only a half. I couldn't have agreed more with their logic, despite my unsubstantiated suspicions that they wished only to convince me that turning back to Salalah was not entirely in the best interests of all those participating in the joint venture. It also raised the question as to why none of us had thought of the same solution to a similar problem nearly two weeks earlier, although the terrible weather we had experienced at the time would have made the exchange impossible.

Both Remy and I were genuinely grateful for the offer, and an agreement was made with Pieter that we would attempt the transfer as soon as the weather and sea conditions permitted. We knew from our experience in handling the heavy motor in perfectly still conditions in Salalah that passing it across the bulwarks from one boat to the other wouldn't be quite as simple as our shipmates thought, especially in a seaway when the boats would be rolling and pitching against one another.

The weather continued to ease as we made a good speed towards the middle of the Indian Ocean and the point of no return. Despite Remy's initial and well-founded fears, the emergency air compressor was managing to cope quite adequately with the task it had been given. We passed the halfway mark between the Arabian and Indian continents, unable to contemplate a manoeuvre alongside our sister tug to transfer the motor because of the long and deceptively high swell. There was a collective sigh of relief in the wheelhouse at coffee time when I announced that the unpopular step of returning to Salalah had finally dropped out of the equation and that we would be continuing on our south-easterly course towards either Cochin or Colombo.

As we neared the Lakshadweep Islands, formerly known as the Laccadive Islands, or the 'Laxative' islands as I recall them being nicknamed many years ago in my apprenticeship days, Cochin became the second place to be ruled out as a port of refuge. We entered the Nine Degree Channel and altered our course a few degrees to the south to pass Kalpeni Island, a small low-lying atoll densely covered with coco-nut palms. At one end, we could make out the white lighthouse, a rounded stone tower decorated, for some obscure reason, with black-painted bands that gave it an appearance similar to that of a traditional funnel of a tree-covered passenger liner.

Remy's ability to shock knew no limits. While taking the air on deck after lunch he sidled up to me as I leant on the bulwarks to tell me, in a far happier voice than I had heard him speak for a couple of days, that he had discovered a fault in the supply cable to the motor of the air compressor. He had cobbled up some repairs, and the motor was back online with the compressor producing compressed air as if there was no tomorrow. I didn't know whether to laugh or to cry. The mental anguish of the past two or three days was instantly lifted: my joyous shout was probably heard on No. 1 tug over half a mile away, but I cared not the slightest. As luck would have it, we had made the right decision in pressing on with the voyage rather than returning to Oman. Had we done so, our delicate little problem might well have been identified and easily resolved by an electrician within a couple of hours. Acute embarrassment would have inevitably followed the host of searching and impossibly awkward questions that I knew would have been asked, and to which only less than honest excuses could have been given as replies.

I was very happy that the delays we would have incurred by stopping off at Colombo had been avoided, despite an inner desire to revisit Sri Lanka and to see all the old haunts I could recall from my carefree days as a young deck apprentice: Singapore and our flights back home lay only nine days' steaming away.

Dad's Army recalled

The worldwide fleet messages being received every two or three days from the International Maritime Bureau's piracy reporting centre in Kuala Lumpur made grim and terrible reading. The Indonesian pirates in the Aceh area off the north coast of the island of Sumatra were on the rampage, seemingly able to attack and board any ship of whatever nationality or tonnage with total impunity.

The international community appears indecisive and strangely muted when it comes to piracy. Not a single country seems willing to stand up and be counted. Politicians pontificate and promise action, but no one becomes sufficiently motivated to make a positive move in military terms towards protecting the lives of innocent merchant seamen and the ships in which they sail. If it were passenger aircraft under the threat of attack, then the worldwide reaction, and response, would surely be very different. For us very ordinary seamen, we're the forgotten people, out of sight and out of mind. Innocent seafarers, undoubtedly, lack the impact and interest for making dramatic news when compared with airlines and their multitudes of equally innocent international fare-paying passengers.

Reading the bureau's reports, it appeared that the size or type of vessel made little difference to the pirates' target selection, the only criteria being the ease with which their victims could be boarded, and the anticipated proceeds that would result from their piracy action. Our small and slow-moving tugboats were unbelievably easy prey for the heavily armed and ruthless gunmen. We possessed none of the deep-sea ship defences of speed, a large crew, or a high vertical ship's side that makes boarding from small boats just that little bit more difficult. Two low-pressure fire hoses and a couple of leaking fire monitors provided our pitiful and inadequate protection against uninvited boarders stepping onto the deck from high-speed boats no bigger than those to be seen messing around off our beaches on a sunny Sunday afternoon.

Pieter and I had had many discussions on the subject of piracy and how best we could defend ourselves in the event of an attack. We both knew, in our heart of hearts, that, once we had been spotted and singled out for boarding, there was very little we could do except to submit peacefully and acquiescently to whatever demands were made of us. With the eleven male members of the two crews such submission and surrender, although emotionally difficult to deal with, would probably result in no harm coming to us, but with Mieke the situation and consequences might well prove more complex and awkward. We both agreed that our best line of defence lay in not being sighted in the first place, and that was where our difference of opinion lay. I quite passionately believed, and still do, that the convoy practice of the Second World War of proceeding at night in totally blacked-out conditions should be adopted, whereas Pieter favoured the official and recommended procedure of utilising the maximum amount of overside lighting and strategically placed deck lights whenever possible.

The experts' viewpoints, no doubt collated, debated and promulgated from the luxurious comforts of well-appointed offices and hotel suites, suggest that an increase in illumination shows an alertness to the possibility of an attack, and provides those on board with the means of sighting the attackers. To my somewhat cynical mind, I take the opposite view and consider that the lights are only good for revealing one's position, and that being immersed in a pool of tungsten-style illumination invariably makes it more difficult for those on the inside to spot those on the outside beyond the glare and arcs of lighting. The discussion, and difference of opinion, became quite heated between the two boats, and between individuals on each of the boats.

As we neared the south-western coast of India, we carried out an anti-piracy exercise to try and amicably resolve our differences one way or another. I persuaded both Mieke and Remy, who had been keeping me company in the wheelhouse for an hour or two during my evening watch, to leave the bridge for just a few minutes while all the lights on No. 1 tug were completely extinguished. After altering course so that Pieter's boat was no longer directly ahead of us, I invited my shipmates back into the wheelhouse. Despite it being a clear and moonlit night, they were unable to locate No. 1 tug even by scanning the horizon with binoculars. When Pieter switched his lights back on, our sister tug was clear to see in all her glory, less than a mile away and just forward of our port beam. Although my point had been emphatically illustrated, the argument had not yet been won.

The following day, Pieter and I agreed that we should ask the bureau in Kuala Lumpur for their advice on navigating through the Sombrero Channel and the use of lighting, and that we would abide by their recommendations. We thought that, by steaming through the channel between the islands of Katchall and Little Nicobar, we would remain sufficiently far away from the piracy capital of Banda Aceh in the north-west of Sumatra to reduce significantly the risk of being attacked. The reply from the centre advised that there had been no record of pirate activity in the Sombrero Channel, and confirmed their suggestion that extra lighting should be used during the hours of darkness whenever practicable. I conceded defeat and asked Remy to sort out some additional lights before we arrived off the Malacca Straits. A celebratory party, in the name of a ship security exercise, was held on No. 1 Tug, with the crew donning their anti-piracy protective clothing with which they hoped not only to frighten, but also to repel all boarders. Judging from their intimidating appearances, their Dad's Army tactics, and their fearsome array of home-made weapons, I felt sure that their piracy defence plan would be resoundingly effective.

We passed Cape Comorin at the southern tip of India and headed towards a position off Galle on the south coast of Sri Lanka. I took to walking the decks again in the hope of losing some weight in the last few days of the voyage, but the heat and humidity made the exercise uncomfortably sweaty and not the least bit enjoyable. The wind being westerly and right on our stern, we were suffering from the Red Sea syndrome of having little or no air passing around the decks. Both Remy's and my cabins became hot and muggy; with no breeze to be had from our forward motion through the seas, there was precious little benefit in opening our portholes in the front of the housing. The boot was now firmly on the other foot. Although Pieter and Willem chose to say nothing, as we had done when we thought they might have been flooded, it was easy to visualise them relaxing in the comfort of their air-conditioned cabins now that the tropical weather conditions were becoming more sultry with every day's progress.

Galle looked no different through the binoculars from when I had last seen the town and small fishing port many moons ago. Neither did the fishing boats we had to alter course to avoid, with their hollowed-out log hulls and single wooden outriggers that combine to support a long bamboo mast with a lateen sail. The ageless design has successfully stood the test of time for countless generations of fishermen, who have known nothing else other than scraping a living from the sea that lies just a few sandy yards from their beach-home doorsteps. The coastline of Sri Lanka slowly receded into the distance as we headed in an easterly direction across the next leg of the Indian Ocean towards the Nicobar Islands, the Sombrero Channel, and the entrance to the Malacca Straits.

With the wind remaining behind us, we made good speed towards the islands, and four days later we were steaming through the Sombrero Channel on our way towards the coast of Thailand and Malaysia. The time passed quickly, despite our mood being one of apprehension and anxious foreboding. We knew we had taken every possible precaution against a pirate attack, as had our colleagues on No. 1 tug with their array of protective clothing and terrifying armoury of knives, axes and heavy shackles on the end of ropes. Our policy of making the engine room a 'citadel' to which we should all retreat in the event of being boarded had been reinstated, and our fire hoses and fire monitors tested and made ready. Marco had also spent some considerable effort in securing a steel mesh grating across the outside of the wooden wheelhouse door to give, if necessary, the bridge watch-keepers a few precious seconds of extra time to make good their escape downstairs and towards the safety of the engine room.

We doubled up the lookout watches in the wheelhouse, positioned the two boats abeam of each other just a few hundred metres apart so that we were steaming on parallel courses, and switched on our overside lighting as darkness fell. Not a single ship was seen during that first night, which confirmed that not only had we all been blinded by the bright lights, but also that our plan of avoiding the main shipping routes had proved more successful than we had anticipated.

Our course was taking us closer to the Malaysian coast and safety. Thirty-six hours later we were in the middle of the straits, out of the immediate danger area, and entering the traffic separation lane that would lead us to our final destination of Singapore. We agreed that the extra deck lighting was no longer necessary and reverted to sailing at night with only our mandatory navigation lights. Aboard our sister tug Dad's Army stood down; knives were returned to the galley, axes to their fire stations, and a degree of normality to everyone's lives. Changi airport and a long-awaited flight home lay not far away.

Strait to the end

We passed to the south of Blenheim Shoal and entered the traffic separation scheme that keeps the south-east-bound ships to the south of the channel and away from those on the Malaysian side bound for the Andaman Sea, the Indian Ocean, and beyond. With the one-way shipping converging into a traffic lane no more than three miles wide, we were soon surrounded by a wide variety of vessels all heading towards Singapore and the South China Sea. It was immensely reassuring to see the huge but nonetheless sleek and speeding container vessels, the heavily laden and cumbersome tankers, and the slab-sided ungainly-looking car-carriers speeding past us as if there was no tomorrow. Being singled out for some unwanted piracy attention was far less likely with so many other vessels in the immediate vicinity. Collision avoidance and maintaining a safe navigational watch could once again claim our whole and undivided attention, without the need to be continuously peering over our shoulders on the lookout for gun-toting pirates attempting to climb aboard to do their very worst. Not that we could relax entirely, far from it, for the Malacca Straits has been a notorious area for piracy attacks in previous years, but the Malaysian, Indonesian and Singaporean navies have been stepping up patrols in the area, achieving some success in reducing the frequency of incidents. I knew I was not the only one among my crew to be wishing we had already completed the passage through the Straits and had safely arrived in the sanctuary of Singaporean waters.

With our hotel bookings and flight details having been received the previous evening, the only attacks from which we all appeared to be suffering were thankfully those of the 'channels', a long-recognised and inescapable nautical affliction that has probably existed for many centuries, but under the guise of other names. A generally accepted diagnosis describes the 'channels' as an infectious mood of euphoria that occurs within seconds of a lovesick seafarer being advised of his home-going travel arrangements. It will almost always result in caution being thrown to the wind and possessions, whether his own or those of his shipmates, being thrown into whatever receptacle is closest to hand. Irrational and unpredictable behaviour is acknowledged as being a worrying side-effect of this very peculiar and untreatable malaise.

Marco had already started packing some of our nautical publications, used charts and other company equipment in readiness for transportation to Holland, confirming that our thirteen-week marathon delivery contract was finally drawing to its long-awaited and overdue conclusion. I will be the first to admit to succumbing to a 'channels' attack in the afternoon, and to spending a happy couple of hours sorting out my personal belongings and determining what could be binned and what could be salvaged for my next voyage away. It seemed difficult to believe that I would shortly be abandoning a cabin that had become my home for almost a quarter of a year, an insignificant time when compared with Shwe's incredible three years on board.

In the early evening we were abeam of Melaka, formerly known as Malacca, the capital city of the Malaysian state of the same name, which was an important port and busy trading post in its heyday of the sailing ship era. With just over one hundred miles to steam to our destination, we received an unexpected message from Holland advising us that the owners had yet to finalise an agreement with a shipyard for the planned dry-docking and repairs. While the setbacks and delays of the previous few weeks had obviously frustrated the booking of a dry dock and suitable repair facilities, I thought it a little bizarre and inefficient that alternative contingency plans hadn't been made for our planned arrival.

The message also informed us that provisional arrangements were being made with the agents and port authorities for us to proceed to a suitable anchorage from where we could safely disembark. We were further instructed that, in the event of the owner's representatives being unable to visit the two tugs after our arrival, we were to hand over their care to Shwe, Maung and Tin, our Myanmar shipmates. Incredibly, there had been absolutely no communications from their employers concerning their repatriation to Myanmar for some long-overdue leave.

Horrendous tropical rain showers and dramatic streaks of forked lightning that arced their way down through the night skies to illuminate the distant horizon meant that what I had hoped would be a peaceful last evening watch on the bridge was spent struggling to see the stern light of our colleagues just a short distance ahead. With our radar malfunctioning to the extent that its performance was less than remotely useful, the monsoon-like weather did its very best to make my last few hours of navigation extremely tense and difficult. Remy and Mieke remained in the wheelhouse for most of my watch, acting as helmsmen while I was navigator, and as extra navigators while I was helmsman. The system worked well and shortly before midnight, when Marco was due to take over the watch, the tropical storms had moved away and dissipated, to leave a dark, clear, and starlit sky. It was as if our guardian angel had at long last recognised that, in less than eight hours' time, we would be finally arriving at our destination.

As I descended the stairs to my cabin after handing over the bridge watch to Marco, I found myself quietly singing the words to that most memorable John Denver song, 'Leaving on a jet plane'. The 'channels' and its mystifying behavioural patterns had unaccountably struck again.

14

DONE AND DUSTED

A visit to the Sultan

'**A**ll my bags are packed I'm ready to go —'.

I was still singing the words, only a little more loudly, when I ascended the staircase back into the wheelhouse just after 5.30 in the morning. Sleep had been abandoned to an overactive brain that had left me mentally drained and more wide-awake than when I had climbed onto my bunk shortly after midnight. The opportunity of spending what I sincerely hoped would be my last few precious hours of darkness aboard the *Oriental Tug No. 2*, moulding myself once again to the unforgiving boulders within my West African mattress, had been irretrievably lost to the frequent 'channel' attacks to which I had unhappily succumbed. Instead of grabbing some much-needed sleep, I gave up restlessly tossing and turning, and spent most of the night sitting at my desk reading a book and confirming that the various reports and documentation required by the office at the end of the voyage had been correctly completed. Even those relatively straightforward and simple tasks had been constantly interrupted and deflected by those few famous song words that, for some strange and inexplicable reason, kept on repeating themselves as if they were refusing to leave my befuddled brain until the message behind them had been successfully concluded.

Entering the wheelhouse to see the myriad of lights surrounding the glowing loom of the brightly illuminated city confirmed that our trials and tribulations had almost ended. Faithfully following the guiding stern light of No. 1 tug a short distance ahead of us, we arrived at the end of the traffic separation lane as the pale yellow and orange streaks of morning twilight announced the approaching dawn. The horizon slowly became more visible as the night sky gradually surrendered to the onset of yet another, what surely would be, hot and humid day. Altering our course 90 degrees to port, we entered the crossing area which would permit us to head towards the Western Boarding Ground A, to which we had been instructed by the Port Control to proceed. With No. 1 tug still in the lead, we slowed down to allow a seemingly endless procession of west-bound ships to pass ahead of us, and then, belching black and billowing clouds of polluting exhaust smoke from our twin funnels, we increased our speed to the maximum to cross the shipping lane quickly before the next vessels heading west reached our position. With over 50,000 ships passing through the straits every year, it was hardly surprising that we had to wait our turn before crossing the 'road'.

A pilot boarded No. 1 tug shortly after we arrived at the boarding point, and with strict instructions to follow a short distance behind, we set off in our familiar two-boat procession towards the West Jurong anchorage. The pilot selected a suitable spot to anchor No. 1 tug and then guided me by VHF radio to a position 100 metres off her port side where we also dropped our anchor. Within a few minutes the pilot had disembarked into the pilot cutter, leaving us to our own devices. I emailed a short message to our agents confirming our anchoring time and requesting information as to their intentions for the day. No response was forthcoming, total silence being their unwelcoming acknowledgment of our safe arrival.

The two immigration officers who boarded thirty minutes later to clear the two boats inwards had no information for us, and were unaware of whether, or when, we would be landed ashore. After a quick perusal of our documentation and passports, they too abandoned us to sit it out to await further developments. I tried telephoning the agent's office, but the number I had been given was either unavailable or had been incorrectly written down. Frustration set in after several more failed attempts. We had never envisaged being totally ignored after successfully completing a voyage that had, at times, tested our resolve and determination to the limits. I found it difficult to understand why the owners hadn't had a representative awaiting our arrival to inspect the boats for themselves and to confirm their general condition and the repairs required. I hadn't experienced such a situation before: it was as if we hadn't been expected to arrive safely – a somewhat neurotic and chilling notion, and one I quickly dispelled in a brief moment of logical thought as being one of those totally ludicrous ideas that could only have originated from being over-tired.

We remained at anchor throughout the day, our agent ignoring every attempt we made to contact him. Initially, the idle time was put to good use by ensuring that every item, whether company or personal, had been properly packed and clearly labelled. We checked and double-checked before calling it a day, resigning ourselves rather reluctantly to the unacceptable reality that we might well be spending considerably longer in Singapore than had been the original intention. The bridge became our communal resting and meeting place, not only out of necessity for maintaining anchor watches, but also for the benefit of having everyone present to hear, or to see for themselves, any message that might be passed on from the agents. The weather during the day became typically monsoon, heavy dark clouds frequently encroaching upon the blue skies to unload torrential rain showers that obliterated everything from sight as they passed overhead. The atmosphere became incredibly humid and steamy, and one that made my staying in the air-conditioned wheelhouse infinitely preferable to attempting to grab a couple of hours' rest in my cabin that had, like Remy's, become extremely uncomfortable in the tropical heat.

The pilot boat appeared unannounced in the late afternoon and in the middle of one such torrential rain shower. After ensuring that the pilot had safely clambered onto the main deck under the shelter of a huge multi-coloured umbrella that would have done justice to a six-person table in a garden jamboree, the boat sped off the short distance to deliver another similarly rain-protected pilot to No. 1 tug. Shwe escorted our pilot to the wheelhouse, where he could obviously sense from our questioning expressions that we were unaware of the plans that had been made in our absence and without our participation or knowledge. We were, he advised, going to proceed to a small shipyard in Jurong, situated up a narrow creek for which we had no chart and, therefore, little or no idea of its precise location.

While Remy and Tin started the main engine and prepared for getting under-way, Marco, Mieke and Shwe braved the elements and went outside onto the fore-deck to start weighing the anchor. Within seconds the three of them were soaked through to the skin and shivering with cold despite the warmth of the summer rain and the humidity of the late afternoon. The first 30 metres or so of slack anchor chain were hoisted aboard relatively easily, albeit slowly, before the windlass ground to a complete halt as the combined weight of the chain and anchor stretching vertically to the seabed below proved far too much for the worn-out hydraulic machinery. My unproven concerns in Las Palmas about the power of the windlass had returned to haunt me. Signalling Marco to engage the brake, I tried moving the boat ahead and astern with the engine in the hope of achieving some slack in the chain, but to no avail; we were going nowhere until either the anchor was raised, or the chain slipped at a joining shackle to be recovered later at considerable expense.

Pieter and I agreed that No. 1 tug should proceed towards the shipyard on her own, leaving us to follow once we had exhausted every possibility for lifting our anchor. The pilot consulted with the port authority before suggesting that we could attempt to steam slowly towards the Sultan Shoal, a sandbank that gently slopes to just above the surface and upon which a lighthouse has been built. Seeing my look of obvious apprehension, he assured me that there were no telephone cables or other underwater obstructions that could foul the anchor as we physically dragged it along the shoaling seabed into the more shallow water. We set off very gingerly, trailing the chain and the anchor down the boat's side as we aimed for the lighthouse less than a mile ahead of us. The act of intentionally heading towards a clearly identified and prominent danger seemed rather perverse and against everything I had been taught in my months at nautical college, and my many years of safely sailing the seas.

We continued steaming at a snail's pace until every detail in the construction of the white-painted lighthouse could be seen quite distinctly through the open wheelhouse window. My nervous system was on the verge of being severely tested, when the pilot, evidently sharing my anxiety and sphincter tightening, judged we could proceed no further before running aground. Stopping the engine, we tried weighing the anchor again. The windlass turned slowly but surely, and to the sounds of loud cheers of relief from the foredeck, the links of gleaming sand-cleaned chain were hesitantly hoisted aboard before disappearing down the spurling pipe and back into the chain locker from where they had been released less than eight hours earlier. A few minutes later, the loud clunking noise of steel landing against steel confirmed that the anchor had been brought home and was safely stowed.

We set off at full speed in hot pursuit of our colleagues, who had disappeared out of sight towards the West Jurong Fairway and a nameless creek lying hidden somewhere in the back of beyond.

An inglorious end

Vibrating heavily from running at full speed, we raced towards the West Jurong Fairway, where we caught a glimpse of our sister tug some distance ahead of us turning to port and leaving the main channel. The two pilots were constantly conversing with one another in Malay on the VHF radio, their voices occasionally becoming raised and agitated as if there was some concern as to where we might be heading. Our pilot frequently studied his tide tables, but when I sought confirmation that the creek into which we would shortly be entering had a sufficient depth of water for our draft, he merely grinned with one of those inscrutable and non-committal oriental smiles and assured me there would be no problem. His performance and undoubted competence off the Sultan Shoal had already given me some confidence in his ability, so I didn't pursue the point. In any case, having no Admiralty chart for the creek and only an approximate idea of where we were going, I was unable to check for myself. The abbreviation 'T.M.O. & P.A.' (To Master's Orders and Pilot's Advice) had already been written into our ship's log-book shortly after the pilot had boarded. Irrespective of log-book entries and their unambiguous meanings, I had the unfortunate choice of either accepting his advice and local knowledge, or abandoning our docking and returning to the anchorage. With Pieter ahead of us acting both as pathfinder and guide, I took the easy way out and chose to go on.

We passed the Long Shoal and Tembuan buoys and followed No. 1 tug into the channel adjacent to Jurong shipyard. Within a short distance the main shipyards were behind us and, with our speed reduced to a manageable slow ahead, we entered the narrow creek that would lead us to our destination. Sampans and a variety of other small craft lay moored to the muddy banks and crowded together in untidy rows in shallow basins leading off the main waterway. Many of the decrepit-looking sampans were quite clearly floating homes, with the domestic accoutrements of pots and pans, bicycles and lines of well-worn and tatty clothes strewn untidily across their rattan-covered sleeping quarters. Large families, encompassing three or possibly even four generations, crowded together on their haunches at the sterns of their craft to silently watch our two rust-streaked and equally tired-looking tugboats inching their way slowly past them. Even the scantily clad but happily smiling children stopped their playing to peer at us inquisitively with those innocent stares of fascination that only come with youthful curiosity and incomprehension.

No. 1 tug was approximately 150 metres ahead of us when her forward progress came to a slow and gradual halt. Spiralling clouds of black exhaust smoke started belching from her funnels, and agitated water could be seen violently frothing at her stern. We had already stopped our engine by the time Ton was warning us on the VHF radio that they had run aground with less than 50 metres to go to their designated berth at the small repair yard ahead of us. Pieter's voice could be heard in the background shouting loudly at his pilot as Ton was telling us of their unfortunate predicament. It became all too clear why the pilots had been impatient at the time it had taken for us to raise our anchor. The tide was still ebbing, and, with every minute we delayed, the depth of water was decreasing and with it the likelihood of our suffering a similar fate to our colleagues. Looking at the banks of the creek, I was quietly confident that the boats would come to no harm in the soft and glutinous mud, but there was always the possibility of landing on some man-made debris that could, quite conceivably, cause impact damage to the hull. The other very real and far more serious worry lay in our cooling water intakes for the main engine and generators: if these became choked with mud, it would be virtually impossible to continue running our machinery without overheating. The consequences of losing all our power in such a place were far too problematic to even begin to contemplate.

I was informed that a dockyard boat was being sent to assist us in berthing alongside another craft, where there would be sufficient water for us to remain afloat. This time I sensibly chose to ignore my pilot's advice. Having drifted to a halt rather fortuitously adjacent to a small dock area lined with sampans and their uninterested occupants, I manoeuvred astern into some clear and unobstructed water at its centre. With rolling clouds of foul and evil-smelling black mud bubbling to the surface of the dock in the propeller wash, we made a protracted and somewhat difficult six-point turn in the cluttered space before managing to point our bows back in the direction of the main deep-water channel. Glancing astern, I could see a couple of small line boats attaching ropes to our sister's bow and stern in preparation for pulling them off their temporary resting place and helping them to berth at wherever we were meant to be going.

The entrance to the creek was safely reached before I reluctantly agreed to the pilot directing us alongside an oil-support barge where we could moor to await further developments. There was an ulterior motive behind his suggestion: a few minutes after securing our ropes and stopping the main engine, he disembarked into the pilot cutter, clearly embarrassed and upset by the unfortunate turn of events. Prior to his departure, I was politely informed that our berthing would now be the responsibility of the shipyard. Our pilot had thrown in the towel and had, unilaterally, decided he no longer wished to be an active participant in our docking plans.

Pieter, an ex-Rotterdam pilot himself, was still extremely angry with the pilots when I spoke to him an hour later on the radio. He advised me that the two dockyard boats had eventually succeeded in pulling No. 1 tug off the mud, and had helped with her berthing alongside the end of a large pontoon. The very same two boats were, he told me, on their way out to tow us to another berth on the same pontoon. Knowing that the tide had turned and would shortly be flooding, and with Pieter's assurance that there was sufficient water alongside the pontoon at low tide, it would have been inappropriate for me to refuse to return down the creek. Fifteen minutes later, the mooring boats had secured their lines, and with our engine idling ready to give assistance if required, we set off for our second attempt at reaching our destination.

With darkness fast approaching, we were pushed alongside the pontoon and, a few minutes after making our mooring lines fast, Remy stopped the main engine for the last time in what had been an epic voyage. We had finally arrived in Singapore.

The agent's runner boarded about an hour later. Being a junior member of staff, he knew absolutely nothing of our attempts to contact the office during the day, and had merely been despatched to advise us that two minibuses would collect us later in the evening to take us to one of the city hotels. Having spent the best part of ten minutes clambering in and out of barges and climbing across the cluttered main deck of a coaster in order to get from the quayside to the seaward side of the pontoon, he condescended, after a great deal of none-too-friendly persuasion, to arrange a boat in the morning to take our baggage and the heavy cases of company equipment ashore. A waterborne route to a landing point in the city would be so much easier than trying to manhandle everything across what was undoubtedly an extremely dangerous man-made obstacle course in almost total darkness.

The ongoing plans for the two boats were briefly discussed. A chief engineer would be joining Captain Maung on No. 1 tug the following morning and, after a preliminary inspection by the shipyard to sight the repairs that had been agreed with the owners, the two boats would be despatched, apparently without crews, back to the anchorage to await the yard's readiness to commence the work. The problem of lifting the anchor on No. 2 tug was never addressed. The agent had absolutely no idea how long the boats would be at anchor or, and far more to the point, when Shwe, Tin and Maung would be relieved to fly back home to their families and loved ones.

Along with my Dutch shipmates I felt so very helpless and desperately sorry for our Myanmar friends. To my mind, keeping them aboard for even further unspecified time was almost tantamount to giving them a prison sentence for a crime of which they were entirely innocent. Captain Shwe had been away from his family for nigh on three years, and while it could never be denied that he had sailed with us for the delivery voyage on a voluntary, but paid basis, I was sure, from having talked to him, that he had expected, as part of the deal, to be given a flight ticket home to Rangoon upon our arrival in Singapore. I was equally convinced that both Maung and Tin had the same expectations. The difference in attitudes towards their employees between our respective Far Eastern and European companies was only too clear to see: the expression 'cheap labour' was one I found almost impossible to ignore. For our Myanmar shipmates to be treated with such disdain left a bitter taste in my mouth; the fact that none of us could do anything about it was an even greater and more difficult pill to swallow. They had never once complained about any work they had been given, or the sometimes atrocious living conditions with which they had to contend. Always conscientious, respectful, friendly and quietly spoken, they had provided us all with the ultimate evidence of how different nationalities, creeds and cultures can live and work together without the need for aggression, ill-conceived rules and divisive regulation.

The two tugboats were handed over, as per our instructions from Holland, to Captains Shwe and Maung shortly before our minibuses arrived at the shipyard gates. With very heavy hearts, and with tears unashamedly welling from everyone's eyes, we bade our farewells before climbing over the bulwarks onto the pontoon and a perilous ascent in the darkness to the quayside in the distance, and a hotel in the city.

It had been precisely ninety-one days since the taxi had collected me early in the morning from my home in rural North Wales to take me across the mountains to Manchester airport. Thirteen weeks and almost ten thousand miles later, our voyage had come to its inglorious end. The *Oriental* tugs had been safely delivered.

'All my bags are packed I'm ready to go —'

POSTSCRIPT

Believe it or not

Guus Kouwenhoven was born in Rotterdam on 15 September 1942. After military service he embarked on a buying and selling career, dealing in anything from tax-free cars for NATO personnel to bulk supplies of rice from South East Asia. In the 1970s, he was mixing in high circles, not only in some of the Amsterdam nightspots, but in diplomatic circles in places as far apart as Beirut and Los Angeles. He was sentenced to two years' jail in Los Angeles for dealing in stolen paintings, but after serving only seventeen days of his sentence, he was deported from the United States.

In the late 1980s, during the presidency of the late Samuel Doe, Kouwenhoven appeared on the Liberian scene, running a business importing luxury cars. He later became involved in the hotel and gambling business with his stewardship of the infamous Hotel Africa in Monrovia. The hotel became the central meeting point for businessmen, government ministers and officials, with its fifty-two villas and three hundred rooms and the dozens of young prostitutes encouraged to ply their trade in the hotel bar. Guus Kouwenhoven was to become the central figure with whom important persons with any power or connections in Liberia would conduct their business.

With interests in a Malaysian timber company, he succeeded in acquiring five logging concessions in south-east Liberia. In early 1999 an agreement was reached between the Liberian government, himself, and a company registering itself as the Oriental Timber Corporation (OTC) for OTC to manage the port of Buchanan and to upgrade the dirt road connecting the port to Greenville and the surrounding logging areas. The government was controlled by Charles Ghankay Taylor, one of Africa's most prominent warlords, who was elected President of Liberia in August 1997 and who remained in power until August 2003, when he resigned after a United Nations justice tribunal charged him with war crimes and issued a warrant for his arrest. He fled to Nigeria, where he was arrested in 2006.

OTC was, apparently, owned by Global Star (Asia) Holdings Ltd, a member company of the Global Stars Group based in Hong Kong. During OTC's negotiations in 1999 the company was referred to as the Liberian-Malaysian Timber Company. There have been suggestions that the two companies might have been one and the same.

Around the time of the negotiations Guus Kouwenhoven reportedly became the chairman of OTC and managing director of the Royal Timber Company, and was also appointed to the board of the Liberian Forestry Development Agency, a government body with the role of monitoring timber extraction and preventing destruction of the hardwood forests.

As part of the improvement plan, two sister tugboats, the *Moin* and the *Eden*, were delivered to Buchanan in mid-1999, the *Moin* from Lisbon, and the *Eden* from Avonmouth. The owner of the tugboats at that time was believed to be a Singaporean company, Ocean Supply Pte Ltd, with a Captain Mok, whom the author met in Avonmouth, acting as a superintendent on their behalf. It is assumed that the two tugboats were purchased to assist in the docking and undocking of vessels using the port. At some time during their four-year stay in Buchanan, the tugs were respectively renamed *Oriental Tug No. 1* and *Oriental Tug No. 2* and flagged under the Liberian registry. When the boats commenced their voyage from Abidjan to Singapore in July 2003 it appears that the owners of No. 2 tug were Oriental Tug No. 2 Corporation. There is reason to believe that the agents, Sky Success Shipping Ltd of Hong Kong, were acting on their behalf, although the author has seen communications concerning No. 2 tug dated May 2003 addressed to Global Star (Asia) SM Ltd for the attention of a Captain Mok. It seems highly unlikely that two captains possessing the same name would have been involved in the venture. Perhaps the owners of the tugboats in 1999 and 2003 were subsidiaries of Global Star (Asia) SM Ltd, the same company apparently involved with OTC, the Oriental Timber Corporation.

From 1999 to 2003 OTC was allegedly felling and exporting around 90,000 cubic metres of Liberia's tropical hardwoods per month through its managed port of Buchanan to countries as far apart as France and China, much of it to be used for the manufacture of plywood. Had the same rate of extraction been allowed to continue, it has been estimated that the forest concession in south-east Liberia would have been entirely destroyed within as little as six years. When complaints were made that the logging was proceeding in flagrant violation of all Liberia's regulations and laws, President Charles Taylor went on record as saying that government officials were 'not to harass investors'. Taylor is reported to have called Kouwenhoven his 'pepper-bush', a local reference to someone being very close and protected.

The lobby group Global Witness alleged that weapons were being smuggled into Liberia through the port of Buchanan at the same time as OTC was exporting its timber. These Chinese and Serbian weapons were used not only by militias loyal to Taylor to kill thousands of civilians during the civil war between 1999 and 2003, but were also being transported down the upgraded road to the RUF, the Revolutionary United Front, a rebel organisation intent upon destabilising Sierra Leone.

Guus van Kouwenhoven was jailed for eight years in the Netherlands after being convicted, in June 2006, of selling weapons to President Taylor's government between 2001 and 2003 in violation of a United Nations embargo. In his judgment, Judge Roel van Rossum said that Kouwenhoven had 'contributed significantly to violations of international peace and to the destabilisation and danger in the region around Liberia'. The ruling also said that he had imported weapons through the port of Buchanan using OTC in cooperation with Taylor, despite knowing about the UN embargo, and that he had acted only with regard to his own financial interests.

And the tugboats *Moin* and *Eden*, or the *Oriental Tug No.1* and *Oriental Tug No. 2*, as they were later to become named? With their innocent and unsuspecting crews that were to work on them in the OTC-managed port of Buchanan between 1999 and 2003, they became a very small, but vitally important and intricate part of a huge and allegedly illegal global undertaking. The two tugboats were used for assisting approximately two ships a month to berth alongside one of the derelict quaysides. The visiting ships were either owned or chartered by the Oriental Timber Corporation, which probably also owned the two tugboats through distantly related companies.

The environmental damage and ongoing financial impact of the timber concessions granted by ex-President Charles Taylor to OTC through his intermediary, Guus Kouwenhoven, would be unimaginable to this impoverished and desperately poor country. The political consequences and the destabilising effect of the illegal arms dealing would be disastrous for the whole West African region. The extent of the corruption and the involvement of organised crime are only now coming to light many years later, but have yet to be proven. International opinion suggests that the government of Liberia at that time had become a vast criminal enterprise exchanging timber for guns and ammunition, which would be used in supporting armed rebel groups in the region in their attempts to take control of their respective governments and countries.

In March 2008 a Dutch appeal court acquitted Guus van Kouwenhoven of smuggling arms to former Liberian President Charles Taylor in exchange for logging rights. The appeal court overturned the weapons conviction, saying the prosecution witnesses, who had linked him to arms dealing, were unreliable.

The trial of Charles Taylor, the first African leader to be prosecuted for war crimes, finally began in January 2008 at a special tribunal in The Hague. After three-and-a-half years the trial ended on March 11th 2011 when both the Prosecution and Defence presented their concluding arguments. Judgment is not expected before the end of 2011.

On August 5th 2010, supermodel Naomi Campbell testified before the court about allegations that she had received a gift of blood diamonds from Charles Taylor in 1997, when they both attended a dinner in South Africa hosted by Nelson Mandela. The court later heard evidence from Issa Hassan Sesay, the former leader of the RUF. Charles Taylor is accused of receiving blood diamonds from the RUF, the Revolutionary United Front.

In May 2008 I met up again with Pieter, the captain of the *Oriental Tug No. 1* for the voyage from Abidjan to Singapore. He told me of some of the stories he had heard from Captain Maung, who had commanded the boat during the latter stages of her employment in Buchanan. With the timber concessions close to the border with Sierra Leone being halted by the second Liberian civil war and the overthrow of President Taylor, the Oriental Timber Corporation had considered evacuating their Chinese employees from Liberia aboard the two tugboats. Although some Chinese persons apparently visited the boats in Buchanan, the plan to use them as a means of escape was never implemented thanks to the employees' success in leaving Liberia by another route, presumably by either crossing a land border into a neighbouring country, or by flying. While he is obviously influenced by Captain Maung's unsubstantiated stories, Pieter speculates that diamonds, illegally smuggled from Sierra Leone, could have been concealed on board the two tugs by the visiting Chinese personnel prior to the boats' departure from Buchanan. If this was the case, it is to the great regret of both of us that we have to continue working for our living.

Pieter supports his theory with the undeniable fact that we were never to meet a single owner's representative during the entire thirteen-week voyage, including our arrival in Singapore where the two boats had to be handed over to the Myanmars because no owner's agent was available. It seemed as if no one wished to show his face. The owners spent extortionate sums of money during the voyage in ensuring the two boats arrived in Singapore whatever the cost, a financial commitment that many would consider as exceedingly imprudent when taking into account the age of the two boats and their scrap or second-hand value. Furthermore, the final destination in Singapore, the muddy creek, appeared to be one of those incongruous 'back-street' type of places less than suitable for carrying out the repairs we had considered necessary to render the boats capable of carrying out future commercial operations.

None of the above could ever be classed as a basis for suggesting the owner's complicity in anything illegal, and is supposition only. The truth is unlikely ever to be known, and the likelihood of meeting our Myanmar shipmates again in an attempt to glean any further information about what really occurred in the port of Buchanan is exceedingly remote.

Despite Pieter's credible conjecture, there was an unconfirmed rumour that the *Oriental* tugs were later employed for towing fish farms in the Far East.